WHERE IS GOD?

WHERE IS GOD?

Earthquake, Terrorism, Barbarity, and Hope

Jon Sobrino

Translated by Margaret Wilde

ORBIS BOOKS

Maryknoll, New York 10545

Founded in 1970, Orbis Books endeavors to publish works that enlighten the mind, nourish the spirit, and challenge the conscience. The publishing arm of the Maryknoll Fathers and Brothers, Orbis seeks to explore the global dimensions of the Christian faith and mission, to invite dialogue with diverse cultures and religious traditions, and to serve the cause of reconciliation and peace. The books published reflect the views of their authors and do not represent the official position of the Maryknoll Society. To learn more about Maryknoll and Orbis Books, please visit our website at www.maryknoll.org.

English translation copyright © 2004 by Orbis Books

Originally published as *Terremoto, Terrorismo, Barbarie y Utopía: El Salvador, Nueva York, Afghanistán*, copyright © 2002 by Editorial Trotta, S.A., 2002, Ferraz, 55. 28008 Madrid, Spain.

Published by Orbis Books, Maryknoll, NY 10545-0308.

Manufactured in the United States of America

Library of Congress Cataloging-in-Publication Data

Sobrino, Jon.
[Terremoto, terrorismo, barbarie y utopía. English]
Where is God? : earthquake, terrorism, barbarity, and hope / Jon Sobrino ; translated by Margaret Wilde.
    p. cm.
    Includes index.
    ISBN 1-57075-566-3
    1. Equality—Religious aspects—Catholic Church.   2. Earthquakes—El Salvador—Religious aspects—Catholic Church.   I. Title.
    BX1795.J87S6613 2004
    261.8'09'0511—dc22
                                                                    2004008361

CONTENTS

PROLOGUE TO THE ENGLISH EDITION

THE EMPIRE AND GOD

After the *earthquakes* of January and February 2001 in El Salvador, I wrote a small book about their significance for the believers' praxis and faith. But two things happened just when the book was ready for publication: first the September 11 *attack* on the World Trade Center in New York, and then the October 7 *bombing* of Afghanistan. So I added a chapter and revised the introduction to the book. Something similar happened when the English translation was complete: Orbis Books asked me to add a brief prologue, with a word about Iraq.

This book is the result. Its purpose is to contribute—as much as one can—to slowing down the dehumanization that is overtaking our world, and to encourage a humanizing hope and praxis. I want to emphasize this, because it is our greatest need. Ignacio Ellacuría spoke solemnly of it in Barcelona in November 1989, ten days before he was assassinated: "Only utopianism and hope will enable us to believe, and give us strength to try—together with all the world's poor and oppressed people—to reverse history, to subvert it, and to move it in a different direction."[1]

Yes, that's what he said. With Iraq, Afghanistan, Africa and Haiti dying either slowly or violently on the one hand, and with the affluent world causing the slow or violent death of the poor on the other, it is not enough to change policies and coalitions; we have to try to "reverse history," to move it in the opposite direction. Science and technology alone cannot do this; we have to "believe and have courage." It is not enough to proceed rationally; we must proceed with "utopianism and hope." Above all, it is "the hope of all the world's poor and oppressed" that can reverse history. So it is not enough—although it is also necessary—to make changes here and there in the direction the West is currently following; there must be radical changes, or at least important and meaningful ones.

---

[1]"El desafío de las mayorías populares," *ECA* 493-494 (1989), p. 1078.

One seldom hears words like these in our postmodern times, not even from a brilliant intellectual and a martyr, but they are still appropriate for "these days of Iraq." They are words of challenge and invitation. This preface will focus on two fundamental aspects of this challenge and invitation. We shall name them boldly: *the empire* and *God*. The empire leads to dehumanization; God leads to humanization.

THE EMPIRE

We begin with a preliminary note. This prologue will not analyze the religious militance of some Islamic groups, or the fanaticism which leads to self-immolation and murder. That is discussed in chapter 7 and will not be repeated here. Here we shall focus on what is happening and being done in the West. Our gravest concern is the empire. It manifests a specific evil that goes beyond human evil, whether in the East or the West, in the Jewish, Christian, Muslim, or any other religion.

Until recently the word *empire* seemed out of date, but the reality has returned. The prostration of the planet as a whole can no longer be described in simple terms of injustice and capitalism. Iraq has made clear that there is an empire, and today's empire is the United States. It imposes its will on the whole planet, with immense power. Its mystique is its triumph over all others, with cruel selfishness and in every sphere of reality: an economy with no thought for the *oikos*; an arms industry with no thought for life; international trade under iniquitous rules with no thought for fairness; the destruction of nature with no thought for Mother Earth; manipulated and false information with no thought for the truth; a cruel war with no thought for the living and the dead; contempt for international law and human rights in Guantánamo—and most shamelessly in Abu Ghraib, with the mounting flood of obscene photographs showing that shame is steadily disappearing in the West.

The scandal of Abu Ghraib has been monumental, unprecedented, and is still growing as I write these lines. On Sunday, May 9, 2004, a two-word headline was spread across the whole front page of *L'Osservatore Romano*: "Horror and shame." The article said:

> The Iraq conflict, already marked by grief and destruction, is now taking on even more tragic connotations with the revelation of the inhumane torture inflicted on the Iraqi detainees. . . . The abuse and mistreatment of prisoners is a radical consummation of the denial of human dignity and fundamental values. . . . This brutal offense against the neighbor is the tragic antithesis of the basic

principles of civilization and democracy. . . . This troubling scenario leaves the world questioning, stupefied, filled with horror and shame. . . . The people of the United States in particular feel deeply betrayed in their humanity and their history, by the knowledge that torture—an offense to human personhood—has been perpetrated under their flag, dishonoring it.

And archbishop Giovanni Lajolo, the Vatican secretary for U.S. relations, said that "the scandal is even more serious when we consider that these acts were committed by Christians."

Then there is the brazen insistence on denying or pretending not to know what was going on in Afghanistan, and in Iraq before and during the war. Months earlier the International Committee of the Red Cross had reported on abuses in the prisons in Iraq, to several officials of the U.S. and other coalition governments. Amnesty International, Human Rights Watch, and Human Rights First had done the same. But President Bush, when he could no longer claim in his speeches to have proof that Iraq possessed weapons of mass destruction, still triumphantly proclaimed that at least in the prisons, the invasion had put an end to the horrors of Saddam Hussein's time.

Thus the empire imposes its will directly on the peoples it is attacking, and indirectly on its coalition allies. But what is more serious in the long run—for it goes far beyond Iraq and today's wars—the empire may succeed in imposing on all humanity its own version of their reality, their dignity, their happiness. In this way it poisons the air our spirit breathes, and condemns the spirit to death. Most fundamentally it imposes the primacy of the *individual* and of *success* as superior ways of being human, and the selfish and irresponsible *enjoyment of life* as an indisputable value. All this without any consideration of resources, so that a celebrity athlete, singer, or movie actor in the United States can be paid the equivalent of a high percentage of the national budget of a country in Subsaharan Africa. We mention this disproportion because it is seldom noticed.

In short, the empire assumes the "culture of Dives and Lazarus" as the normal way of life. Brotherhood, compassion, and service to the weak may not be as vigorously scorned as in Nietzsche's writings, but in practice they are treated as cultural byproducts, tolerated but not promoted. It is not "politically correct" to insist on them. The *equality* of the French Revolution, and even more the *brotherhood* of the gospel, have become obsolete. In Afghanistan and Iraq the Afghans and Iraqis count for little, and in Africa the Africans do not count at all. The empire pollutes the atmosphere. That atmosphere, in short, suffocates, asphyxiates, and poisons the spirit.

This is all very alarming, but the empire employs biblical concepts to announce that the world it is creating has become good news, *euaggelion*. It proclaims the coming of the end of history, the *eschaton*, and the global village, the kingdom of God, the *basileia tou Theou*. Human beings today should consider themselves lucky to live in this world, whose defense and extension are the divine mission of the empire.

This may seem exaggerated, but in my opinion it is the message the United States has been communicating for years, all the more forcefully and brazenly in these years of Afghanistan, of Iraq, and of the neglected, silenced African nations. We turn now to some of the ways the empire controls human beings even beyond what we have been analyzing.

The empire considers itself lord and master of *time*, in all its density and quality. The calendar is not given equally to everyone as a way of marking their journey through history. 9/11 is a historical benchmark, but 10/7 (October 7, 2001) and 3/30 (March 30, 2003)—when the bombings of Afghanistan and Iraq began—are not. Those dates don't even exist. There is a 3/30 for the train attacks in Madrid, but—I say this without irony and with immense compassion for the victims—that happened within the imperial orbit.

The lesson is clear: there have been many 9/11s—like the one in 1973, the day of the murder of Chilean president Salvador Allende and the massacre in the Moneda Palace, with the backing of the United States—but they don't exist because they were never entered on the imperial calendar.

Let me give another example, close to El Salvador and to the United States. One 12/11 (December 11, 1981) about a thousand people were murdered in El Mozote, El Salvador, in three groups: the men closed into a church, the women in a house, and some 170 children (median age 6 years) in another house nearby—close enough for the women to hear and recognize their children's screams as they were being murdered, according to Rufina, the only survivor. They were all murdered by members of the Atlacatl Battalion, the same U.S.-trained battalion that murdered the Jesuits, Julia Elba and Celina, on November 16, 1989. The world, even the Western democratic world, did not react. U.S. embassy officials said they had no reports of deaths in El Mozote, and when the bodies could no longer be hidden, they said there must have been some confrontation with the guerrillas. The victims were not acknowledged or given a dignified burial, and of course there were no demonstrations against the terrorism of the Atlacatl Battalion, which was strictly state terrorism. That was out of the question. Salvadoran and international television, whose business it was—we might naïvely believe—to "show," showed nothing at all. To come out in the streets in protest, as people might do in New York or Madrid, would have meant risking one's life.[2]

One more example, a recent one: there was a 4/11 (April 11, 2004) in Fallujah, Iraq. Members of Christians for Peace reported after returning from Fallujah that Sunday: "Snipers from the U.S. Army are shooting everything that moves." Some 518 Iraqis died under U.S. fire that day, among them at least 157 women and 146 children, including a hundred under 12 and 46 under 5 years old.

Conclusion: the empire decides where and when time is something real, what dates should be recognized as benchmarks in human history. It says: "Time is real when we say it is." And the reason for this is ultimately metaphysical: "Reality is us."

Just as the empire controls the essence of *time*, in one way or another it also controls *space*. The empire has decided that we are now living in a good space, at least better than a few decades ago. The enthusiasm that followed the fall of the Berlin Wall led to that view of the planet's space. The *pax americana* has arrived, descended from the *pax romana* and not from the biblical *shalom*; the United States has become its promoter in the whole world. The United States very naturally also promotes and controls the process of globalization, and spreads the fallacy that the world is a blessed space because of its perfect roundness—without mentioning the holes, the chasms, the sharp corners and stridencies. There is room in it for everyone, although the empire is very careful to explain the difference between the global spaces to be occupied by citizens of Boston and Paris, Kigali and Calcutta.

Finally, the empire imposes its definition of happiness: "the good life." This is absolutely unquestionable, although Iraq has left this view of the good life somewhat shaken. There is a rising level of fear in the empire, and we shall close this part of the introduction by analyzing that fear.

In January 1989, on the occasion of the 500th anniversary, Ignacio

---

[2]Things have changed; the massacre was acknowledged, and the dead were buried, years later. Their family members remember and celebrate them every year. And a simple monument was built with the following inscription: "They are not dead. They are with us, with you, and with all humanity." The monument is dated El Mozote, December 11, 1991. But the change was due to the solidarity of many human groups, not to the action of the empire.

Ellacuría said that "in Latin America we are a continent of hope, facing other continents that do not have hope but only fear."[3] Can the United States really be fearful? Of what?

For years a large number of immigrants have been filtering illegally into the United States and Europe. A certain number are needed and it is good that they come, but if more arrive, it produces fear. They are a nuisance; they undermine the monopoly of language, customs, religion, etc. Nightmares get mixed in with the American and European dream. September 11 was the beginning of a new chapter of fear in the affluent world. The very perceptive can see that "progress," "prosperity," what Ellacuría called the "civilization of wealth," is not leading humanity to a safe harbor but to a precipice, as J. Moltmann puts it. That is obvious and I shall not dwell on it, but rather on what I consider the deepest fear—which is not contextual, like the fear of immigrants or terrorists, but structural.

Certainly the countries of the North have attained a high level of "the good life," although within them there are pockets of "bad life." They would give anything in this world to avoid losing or reducing that level. It is like a divinity, untouchable. It seems "normal" to the citizens of these countries, so much so that their "manifest destiny"—invoked by the United States when it annexed half of Mexico in the 19th century—becomes an essential element of their self-concept. Thus in the metropolitan powers and their client countries, the manifest destiny of the empire is "the good life." No need to ask about the price that the poor of this world have paid and must still pay for that life; destiny cannot be avoided. Nonetheless, the fear of losing "the good life" is growing. Here are some examples.

The great nations of the G-8 represent 12% of the world's population, and possess 60% of its wealth. They control everything, but when they met June 1-3, 2003, in Evian, they sought protection against demonstrators. Some 30,000 troops were mobilized to protect them, nearly one for every three demonstrators. The basic fear is not that violent acts might cause damage, but that a world order different from the present one might take shape; that "a different world is possible" in which everyone can eat, even if it means the affluent countries have to eat less. To put today's good life at risk, to reduce it significantly, is too much to ask. The fear is that this might happen.

The fear is expressed differently in the context of fissures opening up in the North. On the Iraq war, for example, to some degree the United States has gone one way and France and Germany the other,

---

[3]"Quinto centenario de América Latina. ¿Descubrimiento o encubrimiento?", *RLT* 21 (1990), p. 282.

and the disagreements have continued. But these fissures have not reached the point of rupture or confrontation. The differences have been overcome, not by ideals or ideologies, but by fear. "Rebellious" Europe is afraid its companies will lose their share of the profitable reconstruction projects, that its internal divisions will keep it from becoming a first-order world power.

We must add that this fear prevails not only among the leaders, rulers and politicians, but also among the citizens (with some exceptions). For example, there were innumerable protests against the Iraq war out of indignation over its cruelty, and out of irritation with the lies of Bush, Blair, and Aznar. Normal citizens felt provoked and called to action. Many positive things were evident in these demonstrations: an instinct toward justice, a good measure of compassion, and an aesthetic dimension in the protest, all of which is good and hopeful. But a friend in Spain has remarked that the results of the May 25, 2003, elections were far from reflecting the size of the protests and the results of the polls. The polls showed 90% of the Spanish people were against the Iraq war, but the election results showed far less rejection of the Partido Popular government.[4] Friends in the United States made a similar observation, to warn us against naïve optimism over the groups struggling against the war.

We can deduce that the North, in general, does not want to risk changing the current economic situation. We don't know how much the average citizen would be willing to risk for the survival of the poor majorities. But by all indications, they are afraid of losing the good life.

"What's wrong with wanting a good life?" people may ask, taking it for granted as their manifest destiny. We have already hinted at the answer: the precipice of dehumanization. In our world, structurally speaking, "the good life" is only possible at the cost of a "bad life" and death for the poor. No matter how we sugarcoat the language and the concept; no matter how necessary it is to support a culture of peace, dialogue, and cooperation; no matter how we celebrate the rhetoric of solidarity among all peoples in world cultural forums and Olympic games . . . in objective reality the world is fundamentally antagonistic. With all the wisdom of his eighty well-lived years, José Comblin

---

[4]The March 2004 elections showed a higher level of rejection, under the influence of other factors: the tragic consequences of participation in the war, the barbarity of March 11, the government's stubborn refusal to be held accountable for that event, and the lies, or distortion, or delay in identifying the perpetrators of the Madrid attacks.

says: "humanity truly is divided between oppressors and oppressed." And it will go on being that way, as long as the good life of the affluent countries remains untouchable.

Many of these things are not caused by Iraq, nor are they reflected only in Iraq. They were present in the chronic injustice of capitalism and of Soviet-style socialism. But they have intensified, so that now we must speak of empire. Iraq has made it unconcealable. Iraq has also made it utterly clear that the empire is leading us down the path of dehumanization.

GOD

In the last chapter of this book, the reader will find some reflections on God and on the question of theodicy, an obvious question in situations like this: where is God in a natural or historical catastrophe? Here I want to add some reflections on God in the context of the Iraq war.

a) There are no longer theocracies in the North, but the empire is moving toward something like it. In the United States, the empire is conceived in religious categories. Like a divinity, it possesses ultimacy and exclusivity. The accumulation of power is an expression of God's blessing, and a way of ensuring God's presence in the world. Also like a divinity, the empire offers salvation. It is beyond discussion, and no one can stand in the way of its triumph. It demands an orthodoxy and a style of worship, and above all, like Moloch, it must have victims to live on. And what does this empire have to say about the world's poor? Their turn will come; they will receive the crumbs handed out by the empire, if they are submissive to it.

This happens with every kind of empire, whether it is a religious or secular society, but George Bush has brought his own nuances into the theocratic dimension. His personal conversion has put a religious stamp on the empire, incidentally reflecting some old heresies. Let us look briefly at an analysis by Juan B. Stam, a North American theologian and biblical scholar living in Costa Rica.

The first "heresy" is Manichaeanism, which divides all reality in two parts: Absolute Good and Absolute Evil. The United States is a nation begotten by immaculate conception, which has attained total holiness, as in Wesleyan theology. The country's enemies, in contrast, have fallen into the total depravity attributed to human beings in Calvinist doctrine: these people's evil behavior cannot be explained, let alone justified. U.S. society was apparently never afflicted by original sin; that is why, in Bush's patriotic spirituality, there is no place for repentance or even for critical self-examination, let alone for conversion to God.

The second "heresy" is pseudo-messianism. Bush has said he is convinced that he was called by God to run for the presidency, and he seems to have no inhibitions about identifying God with his own agenda. His God looks like a good North American Republican, very patriotic, faithful to U.S. foreign policy. This is not a God who judges and questions, but one who legitimizes strategies for war and domination.

This religious ideology is accompanied by prayer, to the surprise of secular Europeans. Prayer has played an unprecedented part in the Bush presidency, and in the propaganda of the conservative evangelicals who support him. Bush is often photographed at prayer before and during a war.

Christians see this imperialism with religious connotations as an aberration, of course, but worse yet in the concrete reality of our world, it poses serious problems for the proclamation of the God of Jesus. As José Comblin has noted, the problem is not new, but it is accentuated in the context of today's U.S. imperialism. In Asia and Africa, with a few worthy exceptions, "Christian" has always been a synonym for "Western." Today more than a billion human beings, the Muslim peoples, see Bush as the expression of Christianity and the West. This is a problem for *Christian mission*, understood not as proselytism but as dialogue and fellowship; this partly explains the recent protests from the Vatican. How will people believe the two things are separate when the empire, Bush and his group, are shown praying to the God of Jesus and ignoring the Christians who oppose his policy, including John Paul II? As long as this empire prevails, despite positive steps toward Muslim-Christian dialogue, it will be hard to proclaim the good news of Jesus among Muslims.

b) The second reflection cuts in the opposite direction. After September 11 there was a wave of reflections on the dangerous or clearly harmful role of monotheistic religions: the "god" of any one of them can demand warfare in defense of the faith itself, and promote suicidal militancy leading to self-immolation and the death of believers in other religions. September 11 revived the memory of other religious wars, the crusades, the conspiracy of cross and sword in the discovery-concealment of America, etc. By generalization, the blame for this history was extended to all religions and their ideas of God. José Saramago, Nobel laureate in literature and a renowned advocate of justice and human rights, expressed this attitude clearly in an historic article about "the God factor." He does not condemn the reality of God—in whom he does not believe—but a "name," an "idea," a "factor" in personal and social psychology that pervades history and religion. "For the sake of God and in God's name everything is justified, especially the worst, the most horrendous and cruel." There is an undeniable grain of truth, as well as exaggeration, in what he says.

But something different happened, at least in Latin America, when the Iraq war began. Well-known thinkers and writers, defenders of justice, democracy, and human rights, were speaking of God in a different way. They seemed to be finding something good, real or ideal but in any case worthy of respect, in that term. They were invoking that God as a strong argument to condemn the war and its perpetrators, Bush, Blair and Aznar—and especially to defend the Iraqi victims.

Says Eduardo Galeano: "The president of the planet has announced his next crime in the name of God and democracy. This is slander against God, and also against democracy. 'Not in my name,' God roars." Says Theotonio dos Santos: "God seems to be protesting along with the millions who are taking to the streets around the world to say in full voice: 'you shall not take my Holy Name in vain.' " Says Ernesto Sábato: "In every language 'peace' is a supreme and holy word; it expresses God's wish for humanity." And Adolfo Pérez Esquivel recalls that during the Argentine dictatorship a prisoner wrote on the wall of his cell: "God does not kill."

In reality the debate over the dangers of monotheism is displacing another, more fundamental question: whether or not God is a God of the victims, regardless of the faith that God requires. Thus God may be a "factor" that we have created in our image and likeness, to favor our own interests. In that sense God may be a negative "factor" promoting fanaticism, exclusion, violence, and war. But God may also be a positive "factor," defending the victims. That, at least on a small scale, is the lesson of the crisis in Iraq.

The great majorities who condemn the war—believers and nonbelievers—do not blame it on the God of Jesus; rather they perceive God as the defender of victims and the promoter of solidarity. This changing perception of the God "factor" has not evolved out of conceptual arguments, nor even from a more balanced reading of history, but from the testimony of those who invoke God as a reality rather than a "factor." They seem to be saying that when truth and compassion accompany the invocation of a real God, "there must be something good" in that "factor." And if God is invoked unconditionally—sometimes to the point of total obedience—then there may even be something "ultimate" in that factor. The scriptures repeatedly warn believers: "The name of God is blasphemed among the Gentiles because of you" (Romans 2:24). That is not happening here; rather God's name, the God "factor," is gaining some respect. This is important from the viewpoint of Christian faith. It does not eliminate the question of God's existence and ability to avoid evil. But at least God—as reality or factor—is associated with "life," with "good news," rather than with surrender and death. The "kingdom of God" is not an "empire."

c) Imperial evil and its shamelessness, aggravated by its theocratic dimension, are alarming. It is necessary to unmask and struggle against the empire, but since it comes in a religious guise, this must also be done in the name of God. To do this requires honesty toward reality. It requires theologal honesty, if I may use that word; honesty toward the ultimate.

This honesty is not at all evident, even in progressive thinking. We need to rediscover what we used to mean—but sometimes expressed very badly—by "original sin": we human beings have not overcome our sinful inclinations, even when good things happen. The fall of the Berlin wall, the advances of the internet and biogenetics do not in any way guarantee the elimination of imperial control and oppression. We need to unmask the naïve assumption that now there can be good empires.

But since the empire is nothing but an idol, it has to be confronted *with the true God*. For Christians, that means the God of Jesus. Sometimes this needs to be made explicit; it is not always clear, even in some Christian contexts. The words of Monsignor Romero are appropriate here:

> People do not know themselves unless they have encountered God. That is why there are so many me-worshipers, so many arrogant people, so many self-centered worshipers of false gods. They have not encountered the true God, so they have not seen God's true greatness. (Homily of February 10, 1980)

"God alone is God." Not Caesar, not the empire. Confusion on this point, whether religious or secular, carries grave consequences.

d) As we have seen, it is also necessary to combat the empire's misappropriation of fundamental realities. With regard to *space*, Europeans are now saying it is important to make their region "more European" and work for its security. (Some are already asking if the security of the Olympic games in Athens will be assigned to NATO.) From God's standpoint, Europe has a more important task to fulfill on its own and everyone else's behalf: not to think only of the threat to European security but of the vulnerability of the world's poor to hunger and injustice, and above all to think in terms of solidarity with victims throughout the world. What we need is not a united North or a united Europe, with its eurocentric tendencies, but "a more open Europe, more African, more Asian, more Latin American." We need an international network of all victims, with their suffering, and for all people of solidarity, with their commitment.

With regard to *time*: the calendar must be returned to the peoples, especially to the victims of war and imperial policies. That means restoring their existence. We must keep alive the memory of all the planet's x/11s, without imperial favoritism. The memory of Auschwitz has been kept alive, but not Hiroshima or even the gulags. The terrible suffering of Rwanda, ten years later, still means nothing to the empire.

With respect to triumphalistic globalization, we must preserve the historic memory of what human beings have done with their progress. Sagely reviewing centuries of Western progress, J. Moltmann writes: "The killing fields of history that we have seen here, do not allow us . . . any ideology of progress, or any pleasure in globalization. . . . When the achievements of science and technology can be used for the annihilation of humanity (and if they can be, some day they surely will be), it is hard to get excited over the internet or genetic technology."[5]

e) Finally, with regard to the air breathed by the spirit, we have to go back to Jesus of Nazareth and ask: How does he go on humanizing this imperial world? Most fundamentally he challenges us to give priority to mercy; without it, nothing else has any meaning. His honesty toward reality, his will to truth, his judgment on the situation of the oppressed majorities and the oppressive minorities, his call to be the voice of the voiceless against those who have too much voice. His reaction to that reality: defending the weak, denouncing and unmasking the oppressors. His faithfulness in upholding honor and justice to the very end, in the face of internal crises and external persecutions. His freedom to bless and curse, to go to the synagogue on the Sabbath but also to place human beings ahead of the Sabbath; in short, his freedom to let nothing stop him from doing good. His vision of an end to the misfortunes of the poor and happiness (therefore, blessedness) for his followers. His embrace of sinners and the marginalized, his sitting at the table and celebrating with them, his joy over God's self-revelation to them. His signs—only modest signs of the kingdom—and his utopian horizon that took in the whole society, the world, and history. And finally, his trust in a good God, close by, whom he called Father, while at the same time he remained attentive to the Father who is God, the unmanageable mystery.[6]

These are marks of the anti-imperial spirit. They hold up to us the *ecce homo*, "behold the man," and invite us to go beyond the imperial arrogance of *civis romanus sum*, "I am a citizen of the empire."

---

[5]"Progreso y precipicio. Recuerdos del futuro del mundo moderno," *RLT* 54 (2000), p. 245.

[6]Cf. my analysis in *La fe en Jesucristo. Ensayo desde las víctimas* (San Salvador, 1999), pp. 395ff.

THE EMPIRE'S CLAY FEET AND THE POWER
OF THE CROSS

The Book of Daniel tells the familiar story about a huge statue, of extraordinary brilliance and frightening appearance. Its head was made of gold, its chest and arms of silver, its middle and thighs of bronze, and its feet of iron and clay. It made an imposing figure. But suddenly a stone broke off from the mountain and hit the feet of the statue, pulverizing them. Soon all was pulverized, and the wind carried the pieces off without a trace (Daniel 2:31-36).

Obviously the struggle against the empire must be waged in different ways, on every front. But we must also leave room for the little stones, apparently lifeless, a nuisance, useless. In the Christian faith, the logic of the "little stones" is essential to the struggle against the empire.

The heart of anti-imperial theory is that *liberation comes from the victims* of the empire. To undermine and eradicate the empire of course requires the appropriate use of power, but in the long run, power in itself is not enough to bring about a humane and humanizing liberation. For this reason, in the Christian biblical tradition, salvation arises from the weak and the small, from the powerless: a barren old woman, a small people, a marginal Jew; even more a suffering servant, chosen by God to bring salvation. "Only a difficult act of faith enables the singer of the servant song to discover what in the eyes of history seems to be just the opposite," Ellacuría used to say.[7]

When we think of liberation from the empire today, we have to draw on this same *powerful logic of the powerless*. It does happen. Let me cite the example of three Jesuit brothers from the third world, renowned intellectuals, two of them martyrs, who have advocated this logic. In Asia, A. Pieris says that the poor—not because they are poor but because they are powerless, rejected—are chosen for a mission: "they are called to be mediators of salvation to the rich; the weak are called to liberate the strong."[8] In Africa, E. Mveng shows the same insight in an intraecclesial context: "The African Church, because it is African, has a mission to the universal Church. . . . By its poverty and humility it must remind all its sister churches what is essential in the beatitudes, and proclaim the good news of liberation to the churches that have

---

[7]"El pueblo crucificado," *RLT* 18 (1989), p. 326.

[8]A. Pieris, "Cristo más allá del dogma. Hacer cristología en el contexto de las religiones de los pobres" (I), *RLT* 52 (2001), p. 16.

succumbed to the temptation of power, wealth, and domination."[9] In El Salvador, Ellacuría said: "All this martyrial blood, shed in El Salvador and throughout Latin America, has not led to discouragement and despair; on the contrary, it infuses a new spirit of struggle and new hope in our people."[10]

This specifically Christian dynamic must accompany and guide the struggle against the empire. And the logic has important corollaries, such as the following: The kingdom of God will come as a civilization of poverty, in opposition to the civilization of wealth. The highest authority on the planet is the *authority of those who suffer,* from which there is no appeal. It is time to go beyond the current uncritical praise for dialogue and tolerance, to make room for dialectic and the denunciation of oppression and control. And a very important corollary: We must struggle to take back control of words and their definition, so that future directions for the human family will not be set by the language of empire (of power, triumph, superiority, contempt) but by the language of God (of compassion, unguarded truth, brotherhood, utopia).

A CLOSING WORD

Many people in the United States are concerned over what their government is doing, and over the reactions of their fellow citizens, their institutions, even their churches. What concerns them is not only or mainly the political, military, and economic breakdown that the Iraq war may cause, but the human breakdown that threatens to pervade their nation, the Western world, and the whole planet. But there are also signs of hope.[11] Many have become aware of the truth and of the third world victims, in different ways.

On May 4, 2004, some 50 U.S. ex-diplomats spoke out against President Bush's Middle East policy, echoing the criticism of their British counterparts, including ambassadors to Baghdad and Tel Aviv: they saw a need to influence that "ill-fated" policy or cease to support it. U.S. citizens are also intensifying their criticism of their government's shameless support for Israeli prime minister Ariel Sharon's policy of targeted assassinations, the wall now being built in the West Bank, and his plan for unilateral withdrawal from the Gaza Strip without regard for the rights of three million Palestinians. They are trying to avoid a political fiasco, and I wish them success.

---

[9]Engelbert Mveng, "Iglesia y solidaridad con los pobres de Africa: empobrecimiento antropológico," in *Identidad africana y cristiana* (Estella 1999), pp. 273f.

[10]I. Ellacuría, "Quinto centenario de América Latina," pp. 281f.

[11]Cf. Luis de Sebastián, *Razones para la esperanza* (Barcelona, 2003).

Some are also trying to avoid the fiasco of dehumanization. Here are a few examples. Phyllis and Orlando Rodríguez, whose young son Greg died in the Twin Towers attack, responded with these now-famous words: "Our government is preparing for violent revenge. . . . That is not the way. It will not avenge the death of our son. Don't do this in the name of our son." In the same spirit, other victims' family members have organized a group called "Peaceful Tomorrows."

As I write, Camilo Mejía is in a military prison at Fort Stewart, Georgia, for disobeying orders. He had joined the army as a way of establishing social roots in the United States, which is not easy for a Nicaraguan immigrant. He was offered the opportunity to enlist for three years and study at the university. He was one of the 39,000 people chosen for the invasion groups that the marines call front-line soldiers in Iraq. His conduct on the battle front was exemplary, so he cannot be accused of cowardice. But he became a deserter:

"I deserted because it is very clear that this war is being fought for oil. They never found weapons of mass destruction or terrorist connections in Iraq. Now they are inventing other reasons, like a struggle for democracy and freedom in Iraq. Now while the workers have no social protection, and poverty is exploding in every corner of Iraq, the multinational corporations are taking over the oil. This is a dirty war fought for money and paid for with the blood of soldiers like me, with the suffering of our families, and with the lives of thousands of Iraqis. I never signed a contract to become a mercenary."

Where is God? is the title question of this book. Let us begin by saying where God is not: in the empire. Then where is he? In Greg's parents, in Peaceful Tomorrows, in Camilo. Mysteriously, he is also in all the victims that the empire produces—and that we all produce. God is not very helpful in understanding the horrors of Afghanistan, Iraq, and Africa. But the victims in those places help us not to be confused about God. He is not the God of the empire. The most courageous believers will tell us: he is the God of the victims. He is the God of Jesus, who was also a victim of the empire.

Jon Sobrino
San Salvador, May 12, 2004

INTRODUCTION

FORGETTING AND MANIPULATING TRAGEDIES

After earthquakes struck El Salvador on January 13 and February 13, 2001, a Spanish publishing house invited me to write a small book of reflections on what the earthquake tells us about human beings and about God. The book was almost finished when it was interrupted, first on September 11 by the terrorist attacks on the Twin Towers in New York and the Pentagon in Washington, and then by the barbarity that began October 7 with the bombing of Afghanistan. Returning to the book, I felt a need to add at least a brief chapter on New York and Afghanistan.

Two things moved me to do so.

First, after New York and Afghanistan, the earthquake in El Salvador seemed to lose relevance, at least in the First World. Forgetfulness had already set in with the passing time—eight months; even more with the amnesia inherent in our Western civilization, with respect to tragedies suffered by the poor in the Third World. Who still remembers such tragedies as the war in the Democratic Republic of the Congo, with two million dead in two years, or the floods in Mozambique in 2001, or the drought that began in August 2001 in several Central American countries? That drought has affected a million and a half human beings; 100,000 children are threatened by hunger, and some have already died. On September 9 the drought made the front page of *El País*, but two days later it was no longer considered newsworthy. Surely there would be little interest in a book about a tragic earthquake in a small Third World country like El Salvador.

The second reason is more important. Apart from the relevance or irrelevance of the earthquake, I felt a need to reflect on the terrorism of the towers and the barbarity in Afghanistan, because they have become the inevitable benchmarks of our time. But to reflect with understanding, not to distort them, as has been happening.

The terrorism of the towers, with its high toll of victims and its anguished survivors, must be condemned outright as the aberration it is. That is affirmed even by people who strongly criticize the U.S. reaction, including a group of Brazilian and Mexican bishops[1] and Noam Chomsky.[2] It is shocking for the way it was done. Airplanes were hijacked and crashed in full daylight into important buildings by suicidal religious fanatics rather than salaried torturers. It was done publicly, not in a dark basement under a military barracks or a police station. It happened in world-class cities like New York and Washington, not in remote villages. It was filmed on live television and replayed over and over again, not covered up.

So it was a shocking event. But that does not make it the most massive event, or the most cruel. Although there is something macabre about comparing terrorisms and barbarities, we must say at the outset that in quantitative terms, it is not the terrorism in New York and Washington that has produced the most innocent deaths. We don't need to go back as far as Auschwitz or Hiroshima, or more recently, to the more than 100,000 deaths in the first Iraq war; already 4,000 civilians have died in Afghanistan. And in terms of cruelty, think of the people who during the wars of national security in several Latin American countries were dropped into the sea from airplanes and helicopters; the massive decapitations and faces scarred by acid; the more than one hundred children—average age, six years—killed at El Mozote; the Indians murdered at San Francisco, Huehuetenango, Guatemala[3]; or the people murdered in a church at Acteal, Chiapas. Remember, too, the routine torture of members of grass-roots and human rights movements by governments imposed or supported and approved by the United States, trained at the School of the Americas.

It is not its massiveness or its cruelty that makes the terrorism of New York and Washington a benchmark, the maximum symbol of evil in our time. It's something different. This time terrorism was unleashed, not against the human beings and the peoples of the Third World, but against the maximum expression of Western democracy, the one held up for everyone else to watch. It was done on that country's own soil, easily brushing aside all its security measures, heaping ridicule and

---

[1]"Clamor de los pueblos por la justicia, la solidaridad y la paz," *Carta a las Iglesias* 484 (October 16-31, 2001), p. 10.

[2]"Infinite Injustice," an address given at the Massachusetts Institute of Technology, October 18, 2001, p. 1.

[3]There were innumerable massacres of incredible cruelty in Central America during the 1970s and 1980s. San Francisco 1982 is only one example. There it is reported that the soldiers "returned to kill the children who were still crying and screaming, separated from their mothers, in the church. They killed them by cutting open their bellies and flinging them against hard poles. The horrified eyewitnesses saw the spectacle through holes in the courthouse window" (R. Falla, "Masacre de la Finca San Francisco, Huehuetenango, Guatemala, July 17, 1982," *ECA* 417-418 (1983), p. 643.

humiliation on a powerful nation unaccustomed to such setbacks. In a way it was a metaphysical affront to "the quintessential reality" of our world; it follows that the perpetrators are by definition "the greatest evil," and everyone is obligated to combat it. This is the interpretation being conveyed to the rest of the world, at least to the affluent world, apparently with considerable success.

In addition to this unprecedented propagandistic discourse, the *oikoumene* of democracy is invoked: the common destiny of Western democracies. On the one hand the fear is raised that something similar might happen at the Tower of London or the Eiffel Tower. Thus "freedom and security" becomes the prevailing slogan, although from a universal perspective, in comparison with the tragedy of most of the world's people, London and Paris are more symbolic of "the good life." By means of that conscious or nebulous fear of a loss of quality in "the good life," it was not difficult to secure the support of the Western democracies for the war in Afghanistan—even if some leaders, once it started and seeing how it was being conducted, began conditioning their support in order to ease their conscience and restore the good name of democracy.

On the other hand, a crusade mystique is created; out of devotion, or for reasons of convenience, or by imposition, governments have had to join the world crusade against terrorism. Governments and countries are forced to take an "anti-terrorist oath" although ironically they have never been invited, let alone forced, to take an "oath" against poverty, injustice, concealment, contempt for the poor. The former clearly expresses structural egoism, while the latter would express generosity, equality, and brotherhood. But it is the former that prevails over the latter. It follows that by invoking September 11, October 7 is presented as noble, just, and necessary in order to combat the greatest of all evils. There are dissenting voices, of course, but this is the dominant interpretation because it comes from the sanctuary of democracy.

Having said that, I want to explain two things.

First, what happened on September 11 and what is happening now in Afghanistan are indeed a benchmark for understanding the reality of our world, but only if New York and Afghanistan are taken as one event, and only if we speak accurately of the reality of Afghanistan and what is happening to it.

To consider the two things as one is to denounce the gross mutilation of reality that is going on now. The dates themselves are ideologized, so when we speak of September 11 we must also mention October 7. The same with language: we must speak of both terrorism and barbarity. But what is most important, I believe, is to consider Afghanistan as a reality with its own identity—not as something that becomes real only to serve the interests of the United States and its allies. As it stands now, reality is reduced to "September 11" because that is what affects the West. Afghanistan itself, like black Africa, does not affect the West; therefore it does not exist.

Second, of course, what I have said does not make what happened in New York and Washington any less abominable, any less worthy of absolute condemnation. To go beyond the surface of the events does not mean ignoring the immense pain of the victims; it does not devalue the sometimes heroic compassion that was shown in New York and Washington; it does not leave us unmoved by the reconciliation offered by some U.S. citizens. It does mean setting the barbarity of terrorism and human suffering in the context of the greater barbarity and suffering that permeate our whole world. I think this is urgently necessary, because it is not usually done.

I would like to add that those who have suffered from terrorism, especially in the Third World, can better appreciate the suffering of the victims than people anywhere else, including the United States. It is they who can best express solidarity with the victims of the Twin Towers, a solidarity full of humanity, a far cry from routine words, from diplomatic courtesy, from any alliance motivated by self-interest or fear. Salvadoran peasant men and women have already done so, sending letters of solidarity to U.S. citizens who once, in a time of repression, showed solidarity toward them. Margaret Swedish, director of the Washington-based Religious Task Force on Central America and Mexico, wrote shortly after the tragedy:

> Many of us have been moved by the many messages of solidarity from communities in El Salvador, Peru, Nicaragua, etc. That solidarity, now in reverse, shows an empathy, a fine sensitivity to our people's suffering, a profound understanding of things, which comforts us enormously.[4]

WHO WE HUMAN BEINGS ARE, WHO GOD IS, WHAT BRINGS SALVATION

Although most of this book is devoted to the earthquake, we have begun by mentioning the events of New York and Afghanistan, because they are more recent and, as we said, they affect the world in general more noticeably.

---

[4]"Lecciones de solidaridad," *Carta a las Iglesias* 481-482 (September 1-30, 2001), p. 14.

The purpose of the book as a whole is to help people think, especially those who live in the affluent world, and to encourage everyone to show compassion and solidarity. Earthquakes, terrorism, and barbarity are symbols, and in Paul Ricoeur's felicitous, oft-quoted expression,"a symbol invites us to think." When the symbol is a cross—central as that is to Christian tradition—then it "moves us to change our way of thinking, it invites us into conversation," as Jürgen Moltmann says in the prologue to his book *El Dios Crucificado*.[5] Earthquakes, the New York towers, the barbarity in Afghanistan, the AIDS pandemic make us think and force us to wrestle with ourselves. There is nothing dilettantish about such thinking; rather it demands personal conversion and structural change. It can offer hope and utopia. But above all it challenges us and raises questions that cannot be ignored.

a) The first question is: *who are we human beings?* The Greeks formulated the task well: "Know yourself," but I'm not sure it is practiced these days, even by educated people. So we have to ask, without taking the answer for granted, what it means to be "human beings." More concretely, what it means to be human beings in a world that makes us so unequal, often scandalously unequal and antagonistic to each other, so that in its concrete historicity "human being" is at most an analogous, sometimes equivocal concept—despite the fact that the beginning of Genesis, the United Nations Charter, and many national constitutions proclaim that "we are all born equal."

The differences among human beings are evident, and it is essential that we recognize them. As I have often said, there are human beings—a minority on this planet—who take life for granted, and there are human beings—the immense majority—for whom life is the one thing they can never take for granted. So the most important question is, by what criterion do we measure what "human being" means? In the presence of earthquakes, terrorism, and barbarity, in a way that is more mystagogical and existential than doctrinal, we can ask whether being human means being immune to the consequences of catastrophe or suffering them; whether it means winning wars—with technology and at almost no personal risk—or suffering through wars and even losing them. We have to ask how one measures the quality of being human: is it in being "the most powerful," "the best," "the toughest," showing no weakness in the face of other people's suffering? Or is it in being the little people of this world, the silent and silenced ones, the ones who walk humbly through history, who hold to the primordial

---

[5]Sígueme, Salamanca, 1977, p. 16 (ET, *The Crucified God* [New York: Harper & Row, 1974]).

sainthood of living and sharing? We have to ask about the shape of human utopia: is it like the churches of a past Christendom that is never quite past, like the now-defeated socialisms and the now-prevailing democracies, or like the signs of compassion and solidarity that can spread a shared table? People in the Western world also have to ask what is the best expression of humanity: is it freedom of expression, which requires money, is available to few, and can be manipulated whenever necessary; or is it the search for truth?

These questions, posed as alternatives, are provocative and cannot in themselves offer a definition of humanity; but after years in the Third World I have become convinced that we can only answer these questions from the standpoint of the victims. From their standpoint, by being in some way a part of their reality and letting them affect us, we can overcome two grave dangers, which were always present in the Christian tradition and in secular history. One danger is *Docetism*, denying the reality of Christ's flesh; today it means denying the reality of our world and of the victims, avoiding that reality and taking refuge in appearances, in an unreal reality: the planet's islands of abundance and waste. The other danger is *gnosticism*, joining the intelligentsia (perhaps we might say being "politically correct") and seeking salvation in the esoteric, in sophisticated technology, in cultures that have become industries and commodities (music, sports, politics, even religion and spirituality).

The Greeks also used to say that the human being is the measure of all things. Now, although no one says it this way, the message being effectively communicated is that the Western world—the world of abundance, industry, and democracy—is the measure of all things. Theology and basic metaphysics converge. "Reality is us."

b) The second question, in both religious and secular versions, is this: *where is God, and what is God doing?* It is hard for a reader in a secularized society to understand how, after an earthquake, Salvadoran peasants can talk of God as they do—fearfully, for it might have been a punishment, or gratefully, because they survived—but without questioning God in either case. Education and secularization lead people to ask where God was and what God was doing in the earthquake. Another earthquake, in Lisbon in 1755, sharpened the question of theodicy: what kind of God do we have? A mean God who does not help people in their misfortunes, or a powerless God who cannot do so? But the question remains relevant for believers, too, especially those who are rooted in Christian tradition. What kind of God is this, who does not respond to Jesus' cry from the cross: "My God, my God, why have you abandoned me?"

The terrorist attack on the towers launched a different debate, centered directly on religion. On the one hand, there was discussion of the common core of the Abrahamic religions, the possibility and need of ecumenism; and also of old grievances, and the need for mutual forgiveness, between Christianity and Islam. But the prevailing debate in the affluent countries has been about fanaticism as an almost universal characteristic of religion—the "God" factor made famous by José Saramago—which stands over against the democratic value of tolerance.

I see a lot of truth in all this, though not the whole truth, as we shall see in the final chapter. For now, from the standpoint of the victims, I want to make three brief points to orient our debate about religion.

The first is that tolerance is opposed to fanaticism, and tolerance is a good and necessary thing—as we know well in El Salvador, where bombs were set off in the archdiocesan offices, in universities, in labor and human rights centers, in the homes of priests and politicians, all because they told the truth. So we can talk firsthand about tolerance and intolerance. But when we speak of tolerance, one must be clear that its *subjective* dimension, which deserves praise and encouragement—respect for the freedom of any subject to think and speak differently from oneself—also requires us to analyze the material as well as the abstract conditions that make it possible, in order to avoid falling into cheap idealism. And we must consider the *objective* reality to which the concept of tolerance also, essentially, refers. We have to ask whether or not the reality is tolerable and whether some things are intolerable. This question is necessary if we are to understand what is really at stake in tolerance. There is only a short step between tolerance and indifference, as we know from observing the Western democracies. High officials of the United Nations have said that less and less international assistance is going to the peoples of the Third World, that we are moving from injustice to *inhumanity*. . . . In view of this, whether it comes from God or from the depths of conscience, even tolerance does not permit us to suppress the question from the first pages of Genesis: "Where is your brother Abel?"

The second point is that when religions are rejected or challenged for their tendency to generate fanaticism, we must also ask what other traditions are upholding compassion for the victims and giving them ultimacy and centrality. We live in a world made up mostly of victims, and their cries must find an answer somewhere. In this world we do not see "mercy" regarded as a central value—there is more talk about "freedom"—which means that "the other" is not central, but "myself." So the debate about *religion and fanaticism* is all well and good, but it is wrong to use it as an excuse for not taking seriously another, equally or even more important debate: the one between *democracy and com-*

passion. In other words, there is a real need to combat the terrorism caused by fanaticism, but it is at bottom a self-centered need: terrorism has affected or endangered "what is ours," without concern for the human family and for victims. Once more the human family, the other, the victim, will have to wait their turn. Certainly they will not be given the resources they need to eliminate terrorism.

From a Third World standpoint, this structural selfishness—not the role of religion—is the main concern of the Western democracies. Some analysts have rejected utopia because it fails to fit together what does not easily go together: individual and society, freedom and justice. But now they are giving it another look: their formulation, as we have said, is "freedom and security." That is understandable, but thought-provoking. It reflects an educated social selfishness, which sets aside the utopia of life and *living well*, which would mean justice and dignity for the poor, in favor of *the good life*, which historically has entailed a comparative injustice and suffering.

The third point, on which the theology of liberation has shed new light, is that the problem of God is about more than whether or not God exists. Whether God exists or not, we still face the theologal—ultimate—problem of idols. By "idols" we mean historical realities that do exist, and that promise salvation and demand worship and orthodoxy. Their existence, and the worship they demand, are decisively verified by the victims they inevitably produce. There must be many idols in our time, because their victims are millions of human beings. We have to take a stand for or against these idols; unless we do, our debate about God and religion is inadequate and banal, ideologized and self-interested at the very least. And it does nothing to help us face with honor the danger of fanaticism.

Right now I am thinking about idols of religious origin, which have produced victims ever since the Old Testament, through the crusades, through the cross that came to Latin America with the sword. But one also finds secular idols in objective structures, idolatrously shaped by social and personal greed. The idols of our Western world—identified in recent decades by the bishops at Puebla, and by Monsignor Romero and Ignacio Ellacuría—include capitalism and national security, among others. So the surprise is not that religion has become controversial in these days of terrorist crisis, but that the idols are not mentioned or debated: the oil that is sought by the powerful in Asian countries, the coin whose face bears the message "In God we trust," the markets, global pseudoculture, and so on. If these idols are not controversial, it is because they are untouchable. And just like religious deities, they generate their own type of fanaticism.

c) The third question, finally, is about *salvation and how to achieve it*. The search for salvation is especially urgent in the face of such a diversity of evils: the injustice that appeared in the earthquake, the terrorism of the towers, and the barbarity of war. In Ellacuría's words, we have to "take responsibility for reality." To do that we must struggle against evil in history, but that is done, so to speak, from outside the evil itself. That "from outside" can be expressed in legitimate ways: in just economic policies, international courts, the development of a collective conscience. It can also be expressed in many illegitimate ways: unjust, cruel wars, counterterrorist terrorism, deceptive propaganda, and so on.

What we must emphasize now, though, is that this struggle against evil—whether by legitimate or illegitimate means—is carried out "from outside" the evil. But history shows that we cannot eradicate evil at its roots, simply by staying outside; there must also be a struggle "from within," a "bearing the burden of reality." This is the consummate act of "being in reality"; the Christian word is incarnation, the definitive victory over Docetism. It is central to the Christian biblical tradition, which relates salvation to the figure of the suffering servant of Yahweh and to the crucified Christ: they bore the burden of reality.

We're not talking here about masochism or the cult of sacrifice, but about being honest with reality. Honest about the facts, certainly, but also honest about the salvific meaning of reality. "Bearing the burden of reality" lends credibility as nothing else can; thus it lends effectiveness to whatever humanizing and liberating ideal one is working and struggling for. It injects self-giving love into a selfish and greedy world. It expresses solidarity with the victims, and thus, from the underside of history and its suffering, it builds the utopia of the human family.

Why this should be so is a perennial question, to which there is no purely rational answer. It can be partly explained in psychological terms, but in the end it resists analysis: something good happens when human beings love to the very end, with the greatest love. That kind of love is *also* necessary in the struggle against evil. By itself it cannot achieve liberation from evil, but without it neither science, technology, reason, raw materials, nor money—to say nothing of weapons—has the power to eradicate evil, to pull it up at the roots. In the language of tradition, without that kind of love there is no redemption.

To bear the burden of reality expresses the mystery of love as a response to the enigma of iniquity. In traditional language, the *mysterium salutis* (love) is the other, mysterious face of the *mysterium iniquitatis* (evil). This view of things is, of course, an option clearly available in the Christian biblical tradition, which is true to the mystery of reality. Some people may say we can do very well without mystery, which can become a bulwark of obscurantism. But others disagree. "You cannot have life without its mystery. We have to keep the aroma of the freshly cut wood."[6] Mystery is not an explanation, but without it we don't know what to do with such profound realities as love, reconciliation, forgiveness, salvation—all of them so necessary for a human world, especially in a time of barbarity and terrorism.

This leads us to one last reflection. Those who bear the burden of reality to the very end are called martyrs. This is very well understood in El Salvador, but the West has a hard time understanding it. In Spain, "martyrs" refers to those who died in the Civil War—and only on one side—or in communist countries, or in the first centuries of the Church.

It is not easy to change that understanding of martyrdom, but the change has occurred in the Third World. Martyrs are those who live and die as Jesus did, defending the poor and oppressed. We call them "Jesuanic martyrs." And martyrs are also the majorities who are massacred in their innocence and defenselessness, almost without regard to their religion; this is a new insight, almost always overlooked.[7]

Along with this underlying conceptual problem there is another, more specific one in our present situation. The attack on the towers was carried out by suicidal believers, who might well be considered "martyrs" by their people. Certainly they gave up their lives voluntarily for what they considered a noble cause. But this "martyrdom" is different from the love-inspired, nonviolent acceptance of death, or from the self-immolation of Buddhist monks during the Vietnam War, for example; it is an abomination because it takes innocent lives.

As a result, to speak of martyrs today in the West sounds suspicious and strange. It smacks of fanaticism, and in any case seems to glorify death when we should be glorifying life—in the affluent world, glorifying the good life.[8] That world doesn't know what to do with martyrs, not only the fanatical ones, but even the Jesuanic martyrs and the massacred majorities. That is unfortunate, because it is the martyrs who "go to the roots" of evil, who are capable of redeeming it. To remember this is not masochism. Rather it means two important things,

---

[6]Pedro Casaldáliga, "El misterio," in *El tiempo y la espera* (Sal Terrae, Santander, 1986), p. 75.

[7]See our article, "Los mártires jesuánicos en el Tercer Mundo," *Revista Latinoamericana de Teología* 48 (1999), pp. 237-255. See *Witnesses to the Kingdom: The Martyrs of El Salvador and the Crucified Peoples* (Maryknoll, NY: Orbis Books, 2003), pp. 119-133.

[8]See Teresa Okure, Jon Sobrino, Felix Wilfred, eds., *Rethinking Martyrdom, Concilium* (2003/No. 1). This review analyzes the various historical, cultural, and theological understandings of the word, the reality of martyrdom in today's world, its positive and ambiguous aspects.

which are not usually considered together. The martyrs remind us that in this world evil causes the death of the best people, the most compassionate and generous, and also the most innocent and defenseless—and that this can happen in any type of human society, religious or civil, socialist or democratic. And they firmly remind us that love exists in this world, the greatest love, love to the very end.

A WORD FROM EL SALVADOR

The reflections in this book are based on these questions about human beings, God, and salvation. They are based on grace and sin, freedom and justice, deception and comparative disadvantage, falsehood and the will to truth, primordial saintliness and countercultural kindness, poverty and utopia . . .

We have formulated them from the standpoint of the Christian biblical tradition, profoundly historicized by the theology of liberation. We raise them in the context of El Salvador; theologians know the decisive importance of place in interpreting reality (understanding place not only as a categorical *ubi*, or geographic space, but as a substantive *quid*, in this case as a reality of unjust poverty and life-affirming hope). Because they come from El Salvador, these reflections set a specific tone of powerlessness and hope.

A word about powerlessness. With respect to the earthquake: haven't there been many other earthquakes, floods, famines, without causing any substantial change in this world? The earthquake in El Salvador struck a poor country, not an important part of the world; everyone knows that the fate of the poor is suffering, neglect, and abandonment. The people here are not only excluded, but nonexistent.[9]

With respect to New York and Afghanistan, nothing has changed there either. We talk a lot about Afghanistan but say little about the country itself, its history, its poverty, its refugees, its civilian deaths. All that has been said and reported is what helps to explain—and jus-

---

[9] A Spanish journalist has bitterly complained that El Salvador no longer exists in the Spanish communications media; only Afghanistan exists. I understood perfectly what he meant. But I said without irony that I wished it were so: if the truth of Afghanistan were told in depth, its truth as a poor country, it would help people to understand the rest of the Third World. The problem is that despite all appearances, people are not learning about Afghanistan and are not much interested in it. What we are learning about, again, is the United States and its allies. As Ellacuría said about the 500th anniversary, it wasn't America that was discovered then but the voracious appetite of Spain, Portugal, and the countries that would come later. The reality of the Roman church of the time was also uncovered, but Latin America remained hidden. "Quinto centenario de América Latina. ¿Descubrimiento o encubrimiento?" *Revista Latinoamericana de Teología* 21 (1990), pp. 271-282.

tify—another U.S. war. That is nothing new. The United States has bombed Iraq in recent times, and closer home it has bombed Grenada, Nicaragua, Panama, and through its puppet armies, produced millions of victims in Honduras, Guatemala, and El Salvador. That is nothing new, and they got their way pretty cheaply. All that has apparently been forgotten.

In view of all this, I often think of the parable of the rich man and Lazarus (Lk 16:19-31). It begins horribly: the poor man Lazarus lies at the gate, covered with sores, waiting for crumbs to fall from the table of the rich man. This is the most realistic parable of our world: the few who live in abundance and the many beggars, whether in normal times or in times of war. It is the insulting "comparative disadvantage" of our day.

But the end of the parable moves me more every time I read it. After his death, the rich man suffers great torment and asks Abraham to send Lazarus to his brothers, to warn them of the suffering that awaits them if they continue to live in such insulting opulence. Abraham says no and explains why: the brothers already have Moses and the prophets, and they pay no attention to them. The ending is sharp: "Neither will they be convinced even if someone rises from the dead."

This reminds me of two great thinkers of our time. Rahner used to reflect on the way theology "used" the mystery of the trinity, that is, the mystery of God, and his judgment was: "That cannot be." Marcuse said, "The irrational has become rational." This is something like what we are trying to say. "It cannot be" that the world is as inhuman and cruel as it is today. We cannot ignore and devalue the victims. We have come to confuse them with the executioners. It cannot be that this is "normal." That's what the feeling of powerlessness does to people.

But there is always hope. Hope does not mean the realization of selfish desire, but rather grows out of compassion and love. In our time it grows out of reconciliation, forgiveness, the immense reserve of primordial saintliness that exists in the Third World. And it grows out of the solidarity of people and groups who live in the world of abundance but have never given in to its logic; who have instead found life by trying to give life to the victims of this world. These are small gestures, but they help to set history back on course.

Let us close with a word about the structure of this book. It has three sections of unequal length. The first five chapters are about the earthquakes in El Salvador; the sixth chapter is about New York and Afghanistan; the last is about God, and God's absence or presence in the various tragedies. We will add a brief epilogue about redemption from violence and utopia.

The book will discuss the earthquake and New York and Afghanistan without trying to be systematic, so the reader will notice some repetition. The reader may also notice that I have quoted some things from memory, since in the flood of information it is not always possible to find the right references.

Sometimes I refer back to my writings on christology, which contain the underlying theological reasoning that is only mentioned in passing here. The reader will also notice how often I quote Ellacuría. It is unusual for theology to place its Christian reflections on sin and victimhood, salvation and redemption, in a sufficiently historical context. Ellacuría gave a lot of thought to those things, with outstanding results. He brought an exceptional intelligence to the task, but he succeeded because he did it "from within" the reality of tragedy and compassion.

San Salvador, December 2001

1

FIRST REFLECTIONS
AFTER THE EARTHQUAKE

I would like to begin by recalling my first thoughts, when I was still under the impact of the earthquake;[1] it seems important to me, as a way of getting into the reality. Obviously one doesn't need to be in an earthquake to be able to reflect on it. But unless we somehow become enfleshed in the reality and in what it produces—death and damage, destruction and desolation, responsibility for things done and not done, the demand for solidarity and the abomination of corruption, and incidentally also the good that has come out of the earthquake—if we close our eyes and soothe our conscience, and life goes on as before, then the earthquake simply will not have existed for us, it will never have been "real." We would be living in what may well be the greatest danger of our time: living in *Docetism*, in appearance, in a fantastic, self-imposed *apartheid* that we never want to leave. In a word, we would be accepting the trivialization of existence that is imposed on us.

And since this is to be a *Christian* reflection, I also want to say that unless we somehow live the reality of the earthquake, we are turning away from the cross of the crucified peoples—whether the cross takes the shape of earthquakes and other natural disasters, or of wars, repression, injustice, and barbarity. And we are turning away from the paradoxical light that can come from these things, and even from the hope and solidarity that can grow out of suffering.

What I have just said should be obvious, but I am afraid it is not always so.[2] Therefore this first chapter aims to help the reader "be in

---

[1] There was one earthquake on January 13, 2001, and another on February 13, along with many other tremors. Together they were the strongest earthquakes to hit Central America in the past twenty years. For El Salvador, the January 13 earthquake was one of the most powerful in the country's history.

[2] It is surprising, and sometimes scandalous, how people and institutions can talk about poverty when they have never in any way known the reality of poverty, and

the reality" of the earthquake, and from there to "think through," to wonder about the reality of our own world and about our own reality, to wonder about grace and sin, and above all, about the victims.

The following is an almost word-for-word copy of what I wrote three days after the first earthquake.[3] What I said then forms the seed of what I shall develop in greater detail in this small book.

THE TRAGEDY OF THE POOR

To live in El Salvador is always a heavy burden to bear. Officially, half the population lives in serious or extreme poverty. Most of the other half live with serious problems and difficulties, which are aggravated by catastrophes: two other earthquakes devastated the country in 1965 and 1986, hurricane Fifi struck in 1974, and hurricane Mitch two years ago. And let us not forget the fifteen years of repression, war, destruction, massive emigration and migration, on top of the everyday poverty and injustice that have always been here.

Now a powerful earthquake has caused deaths that are counted in the hundreds, but will soon reach the thousands. Many more than that are injured, and many, many more have suffered damages. The ruined houses have left hundreds of thousands of people homeless, at the mercy of the weather, suffering the nighttime cold, with many small children among them. The earthquake also leaves behind the anguish of an uncertain future: how and where will people live during the coming weeks, months, and years, where and how will they get the credit they need to rebuild their houses and their lost livelihood, and always the additional fear—sometimes panic—that the earth might start trembling again. Many areas have been evacuated and are now desolate, while refugees crowd into other areas. The scenes are terrifying: unconsolable grieving and weeping for the dead, whole families missing: "My neighbor lost five children," "The whole family was buried in the house." And as the days pass and news arrives from the interior of the country, there is a growing conviction that the catastrophe was worse than people thought.

So, to live in El Salvador is a heavy burden, but it is not borne equally by everyone. As always, it weighs more heavily on the poor majorities.

---

have no experience of it—not even of austerity; who are not the least bit interested in eradicating poverty or in sharing their wealth with others; who never make the effort to lower themselves or to suffer any conflict, risk, or persecution for having confronted the monopolists and oppressors who create poverty. That is, they talk about poverty without ever, in any way—not even by remotely analogous experience—having lived "in the reality" of poverty.

[3]"Primeras reflexiones," *Carta a las Iglesias* 466 (January 16-31, 2001), pp. 10-14.

The earthquake has destroyed houses, especially the ones built of mud and sticks or of adobe, which is where the poor live because they can't afford cement and iron. The floods and mudslides have buried people and homes—simple middle class homes among them—but always the poor, because the steep and barren hillsides are often the only place they can plant their crops, never on a fertile plain. It is the same as in military conflict: the immense majority of those who suffered repression, most of it from the state, and the majority of those who died in the war on both sides, were poor. And so it is in every type of tragedy. The earthquake is not just a tragedy, it is an X-ray of the country. It is mostly the poor who get killed, the poor who are buried, the poor who have to run out with the four things they have left, the poor who sleep outdoors, the poor who live in anguish over the future, the poor who face enormous obstacles trying to rebuild their lives, the poor who cannot get financial credit. Certainly other people suffer losses in the earthquake; sometimes they suffer the painful and irreparable loss of family members. But in general, once the scare is past, they rebuild what has been damaged, they get credit, and go back to normal. Some of them are able to go on living in luxury, as if nothing had happened.

An earthquake, like a cemetery, reveals the iniquitous inequality of a society, and thus also its deepest truth.[4] Some tombs are huge, sumptuous pantheons of luxurious marble, in prestigious locations. Others, almost without names and without crosses, are piled up in hidden places and consigned to anonymity. They are the majority.

So earthquakes remind me of cemeteries, but they also, tragically, re-enact the parable of Jesus (Lk 16:19-31): there was a very rich man who feasted sumptuously every day. And at the foot of his table lay a poor man, Lazarus, waiting for crumbs to fall from the table. Only the dogs would come and lick his sores.

THE INJUSTICE THAT SHAPES OUR WORLD

Tragedies like an earthquake have natural causes, of course, but their unequal impact is not due only to nature; it stems from the things people do with each other, to each other, against each other. The tragedy is largely the work of our own hands. We shape the planet with massive, cruel, and lasting injustice. We think of the planet as belonging to 25 or 30 percent of the human family; the rest—the poor, victim-

---

[4]Something similar can be said of the unequal consequences of catastrophes that occur in rich countries and in poor countries. It has been estimated that in Switzerland, an earthquake of the same seismic dimensions as those in El Salvador would have produced only five or six deaths.

ized majorities—have to wait for the leftovers, the crumbs that fall from the rich man's table. This iniquitous inequality is evident even in normal times, and even more in an earthquake.

There is no point in establishing safety standards for housing construction, when the poor cannot possibly afford to comply with them. It is an insult that we are not even close to achieving livable housing conditions for the majority, while skyscrapers abound and freeways, hotels, airports are constantly being improved. Even in El Salvador. And people take pride in them as a sign that things are going well.

According to the experts, in this new and celebrated millennium of globalization, two billion human beings have no place to live with a minimum of dignity and safety. When Gustavo Gutiérrez wants to shake up the complacency of our world, he asks this simple question: Where will the poor sleep in the twenty-first century? These data and this question are even more painful and disheartening when an earthquake strikes. "Capitalism was born without a heart," says Adolfo Pérez Esquivel. It has been building slums and shacks for over a century, and thus makes a mockery of the poor who, by turns, lose their houses every twenty years.

But the experts are also mocked, as we have recently seen in a cruel example. Earlier, Salvadoran and foreign technicians and ecologists had warned of the dangers caused by the deforestation of the Bálsamo Mountains. They were ignored and hundreds of houses were built, and what happened was inevitable: about 270 houses and several hundred people were buried four meters deep in the ensuing mudslides. Clearly the deforestation alone did not cause the tragedy of the earthquake, but it helped. The next day President Flores went to the site of the tragedy, on one of those official visits that are sometimes sincere and sometimes just to save face. People came up to him, surrounded him, booed and insulted him—a most unusual occurrence—until finally an official had to stand in front of a television camera so the scene could not be filmed. The people's indignation and sorrow can be deduced from their response that day. And a cruel sign of barbarity was found in the rubble of the mudslide. Months before the houses were built, there were demonstrations with posters and banners of protest. By a macabre coincidence, a little girl's body was dug out of the ruins with one of those banners in her hands.

One last reflection on the injustice that stalks our world, fearless and cruel. Earthquakes generally occur every fifteen or twenty years in Central America, but the politicians, government officials, soldiers, oligarchs, even the international community of opulence never seem to learn from the ensuing tragedy. Nothing effective is done to avoid or minimize, as far as possible, the next tragedy. After the 1986 earthquake there was no search for an effective solution to the general situation of the poor in the country—who will automatically become even poorer if some other catastrophe occurs; nor have effective steps been taken to prevent and alleviate the consequences of inevitable catastrophes. In the fifteen years between the last two earthquakes, the country has cleverly devised ways to privatize nearly everything, in order—they say—to provide better service. It has invested abundant resources in improved weaponry for the armed forces, in technology for the banking system, telecommunications, and the Internet. But after an earthquake we still dig through the ruins with a pick and shovel, especially in small towns and remote villages.[5]

The tragedy has been great for the poor. Today people still talk about it, but soon it will be upstaged by other, everyday interests. Already there is talk about whether or not the earthquake will stimulate the economy, which is like discussing the distribution of a dead person's possessions before the body has been taken away. It's not exactly the same, but it reflects a great deficit of compassion and objective concern for the victims, and even less for justice.[6] The owners of the country seek to alleviate the damage, but they are not much concerned with guaranteeing a future for the poor, their survival, their homes, their belongings. What is more shocking is that it seems natural for things to be this way, as if such matters belonged to the natural rather than the historical order. And if it is a matter of history, no wonder people are crowing triumphantly over "the end of history."

THE SAINTLINESS OF LIVING

It is easier to write about tragedy and evil than about life and kindness. But let us say at least briefly that in the midst of tragedy life still forcefully pulsates, attracts, and moves. There is no more fundamen-

---

[5]Mozambique periodically suffers flooding, with no possible escape in some regions except by helicopter. Shortly after the Salvadoran earthquakes, chilling scenes were shown on television of men and women desperately reaching up to the helicopters, but there wasn't room for everyone. NATO helicopters, of which there were so many in action during the Balkan war, were waiting in "peace time" hangars despite the pleas of human rights institutions for NATO to make them available in "catastrophe time."

[6]In our world, so cruel and detached from the victims, we have polite ways of handling these situations. It is no longer done, as it was in the movie *Zorba the Greek*, that everyone waits for the precise moment of death in order to claim as booty some of his poor belongings. But in September 1997 the secretaries of commerce of the Group of Seven met in Denver, without ethical hesitation, to divide up trade with Africa. The U.S. secretary of commerce complained that his country came away with only 17 percent of that trade.

tal expression of life than a procession of people, on foot or in shabby vehicles, women with sacks on their heads and children clinging to their hands, as we saw so dramatically in the African Great Lakes region. That life flows from the best that we are and have. These are poor people, often very poor and with very little knowledge, but all they are and all they have is placed at the service of life, often because they have little else to give. At crucial moments they do not seek help from the government, nor do they expect it to be effective. And they do not expect much from the democratic principle that we call accountability: a willingness by officials to give an accounting, because the people are entitled to ask for it, and to solve the problems they are responsible for solving.

In the Third World, secular experience has taught the poor to distrust governments, authorities, and officials, even though there are responsible people among them. It's not that they don't know, at least vaguely, that they have human rights. In times of catastrophe they know they have a right to be assisted and helped. If help comes they appreciate it, of course, and when it doesn't come, they protest its absence as best they can. But they don't expect much, so their basic response is to use their own creativity, their strengths, and their intelligence in the service of life. The force of life imposes itself in the midst of tragedy, and the magic of the human comes alive in spite of everything. In Armenia, a village of Sonsonate that was totally destroyed, the power of life is preserved forever in a photograph. An old man is sitting amid the ruins, and beside him is a sign held up by a stick: "Armenia lives."

Along with the impulse of life itself, there is the power that comes from solidarity among people. Emergency assistance from many places has begun to arrive, and it will keep coming; there are rescue technicians, doctors, engineers. They provide a great service, offer encouragement, and deserve our sincere gratitude. But I'm speaking now of a more fundamental solidarity; to describe it let us go back to what happened in the Bálsamo Mountains.

Not many power shovels were available to dig up the bodies, and in any case they would have increased the risk of tearing the bodies apart. So long lines of men, passing buckets back and forth, tackled the job of removing thousands of cubic meters of earth. For days they hoped for the miracle of discovering someone still alive. That is the primal power of solidarity: it seeks the living in order to rescue them, or the dead in order to bury them in dignity.

In this primal solidarity, women stand always and everywhere as the focal point of life: caring for the children among the ruins, making and sharing whatever food there is in the refugee camps, always encouraging by their presence, never giving up, never tiring. They are the ultimate, irreplaceable, ever-present focal point of unfailing life. They are not "the pastor of life" (if I may quote Heidegger at this point), but they are the ones who "take responsibility for life."

I like to think that in that fundamental decision to live and give life we see a kind of primordial saintliness, regardless of whether it is a virtue or an obligation, whether it is freedom or necessity, whether it is grace or merit. It is not the saintliness that we acknowledge in canonizations, but anyone with a clean heart can appreciate it. It is not the saintliness of the heroic virtues, but rather of a truly heroic life. We do not know whether or not these poor who cry out to live are intercessor saints, but the heart is moved when we see them. They may be "sinner saints," so to speak, but they splendidly fulfill the primordial purpose of creation: God's call to live and give life to others, even in the midst of catastrophe. This is the saintliness of suffering, which has its own logic, more fundamental than the saintliness of virtue.

Finally—although this may sound exaggerated to believers, and crazy to nonbelievers—these poor may inspire us to repeat what the centurion said at the foot of the cross, watching Jesus die, bloody and asphyxiated: truly, these are the sons and daughters of God.

THE PRIMORDIAL DEMAND:
TO BE AFFECTED BY TRAGEDY

There is a lot to do when an earthquake strikes, but the first thing—without which nothing else we do is enough—is to let ourselves be affected by the tragedy, not to turn away or soften it. This is not a way of promoting masochism, or demanding what is psychologically impossible. It simply requires an initial moment of honesty toward reality. To turn away from tragedy, subtly or blatantly, is a way of escaping the reality of our world. But we must be aware of the consequences: unless we become fully present in the reality we cannot help the people in need around us, nor can we meet our own internal needs. To let ourselves be affected, to feel pain over lives cut short or endangered, to feel indignation over the injustice behind the tragedy, to feel shame over the way we have ruined this planet, that we have not undone the damage and are not planning to do so, all this is important. It motivates compassion and immediate emergency assistance, but more importantly it sheds light on the most effective way to help in the tragedy.

There is also a salvific aspect to truly letting ourselves be affected by tragedy. It roots us firmly in the truth and forces us to overcome the unreality in which we live. So institutions like churches and uni-

versities would do well to analyze and proclaim the truth of these tragedies; one might wish that governments, multinational corporations,
armed forces, and international banks would also do so, but there is
little hope of that.

In this context it is especially important that the communications
media make a "preferential option for the truth," beginning at a su-
perficial but very important level with true information about the
events, and going more deeply into its causes. The view offered by the
media is often notoriously inadequate.

By way of a small excursus, a football player's million-dollar salary
becomes news—scandalous news—when it is publicized in the media;
without them it would not be news. But we should be aware that this
is not a matter of real reality, but of a factual, scandalous, stupefying
anecdote in a world that is dying of hunger. The "news" becomes "reality" when we compare the salary figures for athletes, singers, or movie
stars, with what a human being has to live on in Africa, or Bangladesh,
or in the impoverished community of Guadalupe, which was destroyed
in the earthquake. Then we will at last learn about comparative disadvantage, about injustice and inhumanity, about reality. To make
this comparison challenges the imagination and can produce dizziness,
but it needs to be done. It becomes an insistent demand: "Is a world
like this human?"

Let us return to the earthquake. Tragedy has an immense educational potential. If we analyze and do not conceal its truth, it leads us
into our own truth and that of our world. This is not easy to do. In the
aftermath of the Salvadoran earthquake, it was easier to see what
was happening in the cities than in the remote towns and villages. But
we have to make the effort. As Ellacuría said, if the First World wants
to see itself, it should look at the Third World. Today we might say: if
we want to know the truth of the capital city, we should look at the
villages and towns.

Finally, letting ourselves be affected by tragedy generates solidarity, at least sometimes. Sometimes a family misfortune will unite the
family—*felix culpa!* people used to say—and it may be the only thing
that unites them. Or to put it differently, if even suffering does not
bring unity, there is no solution. Human beings always have hidden
reserves of kindness, often dormant, but they can be activated by other
people's suffering. We are not always, entirely, selfish. An earthquake
in El Salvador, a famine in Calcutta, AIDS in Africa may well help to
build awareness of the human family.

There is something in the suffering, crucified peoples that appeals
to us, that draws us out of ourselves; that is the beginning of solidarity. Along with ethical feelings of obligation, along with the struggle

against feelings of guilt, something deeper and more decisive may appear: a feeling of closeness to other human beings. Material solidarity comes later and is badly needed: food, clothing, tents, medicines, money, technical assistance of all kinds, debt forgiveness . . .

But all this, the quality, the consistency, the "foreverness" of solidarity, comes from the discovery of something good and humanizing in being close to the victims of this world. Perhaps that is when the human miracle happens: the miracle of holding each other up, of giving and receiving the best that we have. And the even greater miracle of loving one another as members of one family. Christians say it more simply and radically: to love one another as sons and daughters of God. That is when the miracle of the shared table happens, the joy of belonging to the human family.

WHERE IS GOD IN THE EARTHQUAKE?

There are many different types of religiosity in El Salvador, but overall it is a religious country, especially in these days of earthquake. In contrast to what might happen in other countries, here the question about God is inevitable. But it comes up in different ways.

Some people, the fanatics, have said that the earthquake was a punishment from God—as happened in the Guatemalan earthquake of 1976, when the cardinal archbishop at the time said that the sins of the priests had caused it. Others, a majority, prayed to God in gratitude (thank God we are alive); in hope (with God's help we shall go forward); and in submission, to find some meaning in the catastrophe (may God's will be done). These expressions are close to what Salvadorans typically say: "With God's help," meaning "Only God can help; we don't expect much of men." Or in less religious terms, suggesting the cumulative skepticism with which the poor understand the meaning of life: "Who knows?" That is, there is not much logic in reality by which they can predict the future, certainly not a future favorable to them.

One seldom hears the question that led to classical theodicy: "God either cannot or will not prevent catastrophes, and God doesn't look good in either case." But the question remains: "Where is God?" Jesus asked the same thing, and Paul had the audacity to reply, "On the cross." These days someone has said, "God is in El Cafetalón," a refugee center for impoverished survivors.

There is no logical, rationally convincing answer to the question about where God is in suffering.[7] Without discussing it further now,

---

[7]We shall return to this at the end of this book. We mention it now only to complete the spectrum of reactions about God in the Salvadoran earthquake.

let us simply say that God is also crucified. In Europe, Bonhoeffer and Moltmann have made that point very well. Some of us have also thought about the problem.[8] But it is clear that the answer to the question about God can only be found in life: if ultimate mystery, even in a time of catastrophe, can give rise to hope. That is to say, if hope does not die.

IS HOPE DYING IN EL SALVADOR?

Let us close with this anecdote. Several churches were destroyed in the earthquake, among them the church of El Carmen, in Santa Tecla where I live. Sorrowfully the people told their parish priest, "Father, we have been left without a church." And the priest, Salvador Carranza, who came to El Salvador from Burgos, Spain, more than forty years ago, replied, "We have been left without a temple, but not without a Church. We are the Church, and the Church depends on us to keep it alive."

Years ago, in a time when the Church was being repressed and persecuted, Monsignor Romero used to say: "If some day the forces of evil should leave us without this marvel [the radio], which is so abundantly available to them, and if they shut the Church out completely, we can be sure that they have not hurt us. On the contrary, we will be 'living microphones' for the Lord, and we will proclaim his words everywhere."[9]

These words are rhetorical, but they are true and lucid. They help to encourage the Church in a troubled time, and to encourage a people in circumstances like these. They point to something fundamental, as few words do. The greatest tragedy—in an earthquake or any other situation—is not the material damages it causes, but the destruction of what is human. The greatest solidarity is to help rebuild that humanity. The greatest hope is to keep walking, doing justice, and loving with kindness.

Has this died in El Salvador? I don't believe so, but we still need to make it grow. In this sense, I hope the solidarity will help to rebuild

---

[8]See my writing in *Jesus the Liberator* (Maryknoll, NY: Orbis Books, 1993), pp. 233-253, and *Christ the Liberator* (Maryknoll, NY: Orbis Books, 2001), pp. 256-274.

[9]Homily, January 27, 1980. Monsignor Romero spoke these hopeful words because in his three years of ministry, the archbishop's radio station was interfered with and dynamited several times. Something he said earlier inspired his listeners with an even more vigorous hope: "If some day they take away our radio station, suspend our newspaper, forbid us to speak, kill all the priests and the bishop too, and if you were left as a people without priests, every one of you would have to become a microphone for God, every one of you would have to become a messenger, a prophet. The Church will exist as long as there is one baptized Christian!" (Homily of July 8, 1979).

houses, but above all it must help to rebuild persons, to rebuild the people, or even better, to build a new people. I hope it will help to repair roads, but above all it must help people find pathways for walking through life. I hope it will help to build churches, but above all it must help to build up the people of God.

Most certainly, I hope the solidarity will give hope to this people. Once they have hope, they will find ways to fend for themselves. And these people will repay what they have received with interest, in the form of light and spirit.

These are the things that came to my mind in the days immediately following the earthquake, which I wrote down on January 16. Now we shall begin to conceptualize more precisely some of what in those days was all impact and intuition.

But other, global, crucial questions also occurred to me in the presence of the earthquake: the kind of questions that inspire reflection as one reads them through the years, but which suddenly take on new and special power, not only as academic but as uncontainable, existential questions. "What really inspires us to think?" Obviously it was the earthquake, but beyond that answer there were other, more theoretical ones. It might be "the admiration that leads to knowledge" (Aristotle), or "the suffering that comes before thought" (Feuerbach). And the earthquake led us back especially to the question we had so often asked in El Salvador. Heidegger had asked, "Why is there being, and not nothingness?" and Ellacuría replied: "Why is there nothing— not-being, unreality, untruth, etc.—instead of being [entity]?"[10]

And in the midst of all these clamoring questions and our silent, stuttering replies, in the presence of the earthquake something came on me, more as a feeling than as an idea: a sense of *indignation* that "the same thing" always happens and "the same people" always suffer; a *yearning* for things to be different some day; and a kind of *veneration* for the life of the poor, for what I have called their primordial saintliness before, during, and after each catastrophe.

---

[10]"Función liberadora de la filosofía," *ECA* 435-436 (1985), p. 50.

2

THE EARTHQUAKE SEEN FROM
A CHRISTIAN PERSPECTIVE

We have said that to understand the reality of an earthquake, and to react appropriately to it, we must "let ourselves be affected" by the tragedy. This is not a problem for the victims. But it is hard for those who hear about the tragedy second hand, from a distance, no matter how moving the first images and reports may be. That is why tragedies are so quickly forgotten.

A scandalous example of this forgetfulness is occurring in the African Great Lakes region, with massacres, refugee camps, and extreme poverty continuing in the Democratic Republic of the Congo. For the past two or three years an average of 80,000 human beings per month have been dying in that country, under invasion by Uganda, Rwanda, and Burundi—the great protegés of the United States—in a struggle to control the supply of coltan, a strategic material in new technologies. Forgetfulness like this[1] is truly a scandal and a shame to humanity, but it happens routinely wherever there are earthquakes, floods, droughts (also repression and war) in the Third World.

It is perfectly normal to forget and remain unaffected by an act of will. Obviously the human psyche cannot bear the burden of so much tragedy. But there are other historical and structural reasons for forgetfulness and detachment. One reason is subjective: human beings

---

[1] Joan Carrero Saralegui complains bitterly, not that people forget but that they don't want to know what is happening in the Democratic Republic of the Congo. Although at first one might have attributed their ignorance to the small size of the organizations that were denouncing the situation, Carrero says, now the United Nations and large NGOs like Amnesty International have spoken out; people have had to accept the reality of the war, the incredible number of deaths, and the fact that the coltan has been seized as spoils by mining and financial corporations from the United States and its African allies. "It is clear now that these spoils are responsible for the great massacres. But almost no one seems to care" ("¿Aún hay tiempo? Reflexión desde África," *Carta a las Iglesias* 483 [2001], p. 18).

are severely lacking in the will to truth, and therefore in concern for "honesty toward reality." On the objective side, the global information system does not fully communicate the truth of reality and its tragedies. Worse yet, it does not provide an adequate framework in which to interpret what is really happening and why; rather, the frameworks it offers often lead to misinterpretation and facilitate deception.

In the next chapter we shall look at the problem of honesty toward reality. Here let us consider an appropriate framework or perspective from which to see and interpret a tragedy like the earthquake.

THE BATTLE OF DEFINITIONS: WHAT IS AN EARTHQUAKE?

As we know very well, the communications media offer us the reality of the tragedies that happen in the world. But in addition to transmitting more or less objective images and words, the media also—subtly or sometimes crudely—tell us how to think about, analyze, interpret, and feel the reality, and how to react to it. Language—in images and words—thus becomes decisive, not only to "present" the reality of things, but to "impose" a normative understanding of them. "The powerful global media machine has transmitted the canons of necessary and right thinking, knowing that they are almost impossible to resist."[2] Controlling language is a way of controlling the mind, the will, the feelings, and the heart of human beings for the benefit of certain, mainly economic interests. Moreover, human beings are defenseless and even unaware of what is being done to them.

Thus to choose and impose language is a fundamental task. To speak for example of "labor flexibility" or of "developing countries" is an efficient way of saying "unjust layoffs permitted" or of ignoring that there are "countries with cruel, inhuman, and demeaning poverty." To speak of "globalization," the "global village," or the "end of history" is to use high-sounding words (*euphemisms*) that subliminally describe false utopias: equidistance (which suggests *equity*) among everyone and everything; the human family at its most natural and least artificial; the goal accomplished. Even more dangerous, of course, is to control the language that defines "the human," "religion," "democracy," "happiness"[3] as the media corporations, cultural or religious ideologies, etc., now do.

---

[2]Manuel Vázquez Montalbán, "Prólogo a Susan George," *Informe Lugano*, Intermón-Icaria (Barcelona, 2001), p. 10.

[3]For example, it would never occur to the makers of television commercials and most entertainment programs that there are very different concepts of happiness,

Returning to the earthquake: in order to "be affected" and react appropriately, after the first instinctive reactions have passed, we have to know *what an earthquake is*. Thus the problem is, *what do they tell us an earthquake is?* As we might expect, how people "speak" about an earthquake is a relevant concern, even if it does not involve the kind of interpretive aberrations we have mentioned.

The media usually describe an earthquake more or less as follows: it is a natural catastrophe, which causes overwhelming physical as well as personal and psychological damage; we must react with emergency assistance to alleviate the basic suffering of the victims, and with reconstruction assistance, usually from the international community. This is often followed by vague reflection on the need to avoid risks in the future. There may also be some mention of the religious reaction of the victims and other believers. In my opinion, this conventional description poses two serious dangers.

In the first place, the conventional view tends to be *reductive*, as if the cause of the destruction and misfortune were strictly natural, involving no historical-social responsibilities. Certainly much has been learned about how to prevent and mitigate the consequences of a catastrophe. But the pace of theoretical learning has been extremely slow in comparison with the destructiveness of the earthquake. And by not taking historical-social factors seriously, it discourages acceptance of the corresponding responsibility. This happens in small countries like El Salvador,[4] but the international community does not react with policies and resources in proportion to the magnitude of the disasters.

Secondly, the conventional view tends to *conceal* the massiveness of the suffering of the poor, as if it were not essential to the *reality* of the earthquake. It does not take seriously, and certainly does not give priority to, what in the previous chapter we called "the same thing" and "the same people." It mentions that the poor are the most vulnerable, but more as an obligatory comment than as a challenge or a call for conversion. The fact that the majority of victims are poor belongs to the historical *essence* of an earthquake, but it is regularly treated as an *accident*, of little substance. That is why, after a while, the world

---

such as the one expressed in Jesus' beatitudes: *blessed* are you, *happy* are you . . . (Mt 5:3-12; in Lk 6:20-23 Jesus adds the corresponding "woes" to the rich). Without knowing it, television is locked in a perennial struggle with the gospel for the power to put into words, "define," something as fundamental to human beings as the meaning of happiness.

[4]"In El Salvador . . . this failure is reflected in the virtual absence of efforts, either for preparedness among the people most at risk, or to mitigate the negative consequences"(CIDAI, "Consideraciones económicas, sociales y políticas del terremoto del 13 de enero," *ECA* 627-628 [2001], p. 42).

goes on as if the catastrophe and the tragedy of the poor were irrelevant to our understanding of reality and our "definition" of our world. They certainly aren't taken as a challenge to all of us, to examine our own humanity.

THE HISTORICAL ELEMENT OF THE CHRISTIAN VIEW

Our view of the earthquake should incorporate *historical-social responsibility*, so that the consequences are not seen as a product of nature alone but also of injustice; and it should incorporate a *perspective partial to the poor*, which sheds an indispensable light on both natural and historical reality. Both these elements are acknowledged in other ways of thinking, of course, but they also belong and are essential to the Christian view.

The Christian view has little to offer by way of scientific and technical knowledge, and of course it is not the only view that offers useful elements of understanding. But I believe that "the Christian view"[5] can offer something important that other traditions, including the "Western view," do not offer in the same radical way. Most importantly, it adopts a *partial* viewpoint that places victims at the center. By making them central we can better *know* what has happened and unmask the deception. We can more easily *overcome* indifference and even cruelty and *react* more humanely.

This Christian view has undergone changes in the course of history, but it has always referred simultaneously to the historical and the transcendent. In the case of catastrophes, an example of the historical is the requirement of assisting the victims; in the days of the plague, assistance was a truly heroic task entailing the sacrifice of one's own life. Examples of the transcendent range from pleas to God for rain in times of drought to questions about God's existence if he cannot eliminate evil from the world. Both these dimensions are part of the Christian view and equally essential to it.

Let us begin with the historical dimension. We see it in the tradition of Jesus of Nazareth, as we have received it from the hands of Medellín, Monsignor Romero, and Ignacio Ellacuría. This dimension shows the earthquake from the viewpoint of the poor, and the dy-

---

[5]Ignacio Ellacuría used this expression to describe the globalizing and essential aspect of the historical-transcendent reality that we call Christianity, which permits and requires us to act in the world through praxis, hope, and celebration. He specifically focused on "the Christian" at the personal level in terms of following Jesus, and at the social level in terms of the Kingdom of God. I have written about this in "Ignacio Ellacuría, el hombre y el cristiano," *Revista Latinoamericana de Teología* 32 and 33 (1994), pp. 131-161 and 215-244, especially pp. 215 ff.

namics of dehumanization but also of humanization that the earthquake produces. I want to analyze the earthquake specifically, dialectically, in the context of the realities of truth and concealment, responsibility and injustice, solidarity and selfishness, utopia and resignation. And in the context of victims and sacraments of God, who reflect the very depths of Christian faith.

Truth and Concealment: The Earthquake Is a Catastrophe and an X-ray of the Country

The earthquake is a *catastrophe*, but it is also a *bearer of truth*. It is an *X-ray* of the country in its many dimensions: physical, economic, social, political, cultural, religious. To pursue the X-ray metaphor, it reveals the truth that people would rather keep hidden. We know—or should know—more about the country today than we did before the earthquake, although efforts will soon be made to conceal or forget that new and truer knowledge.

The fundamental reality revealed by the earthquake is the poverty and vulnerability of the Salvadoran society, produced by injustice and by a national leadership that cares little about eliminating it. That reality is certainly "known" by the people who suffer it, but it is not effectively "recognized" by the powerful inside and outside the country.[6] The powerful may react to the catastrophe in some degree, but at bottom they do not usually act in accordance with the demands of the reality. That is why I insist that the earthquake is not only a tragedy but has an immense "epistemological" potential for understanding reality, and an immense "educational" potential for showing the truth to all who "love the truth" (Jn 8:37). The earthquake brings out the truth and unmasks the lie. Together with its consequences, it is prophecy in action against those who falsely boast of progress, "who put darkness for light and light for darkness" (Is 5:20). It is a denunciation against "those who suppress the truth" (Rom 1:18).

Christian faith is quite insistent about that. The earthquake shows the truth of reality and unmasks it as a fundamental scandal. Even before we ask about the injustice that an earthquake reveals, it forces us to put into words the primary realities (the iniquitous comparative harm that human beings, sons and daughters of God, do to each other),

---

[6]Monsignor Romero used to say that his homilies were intended as the "voice of the voiceless." He added something that was not so evident: "That is why they are disliked by those who have too much voice." In the same way, it is "the voiceless" who "know the reality," and it is "those who have too much voice" who refuse to "recognize it."

and primary feelings (the deep shame we should feel as a result). The earthquake tragically enacts Jesus' parable: the few rich (Dives) coexisting with the majority poor (Lazarus). It reveals many other things, as we shall see, but above all it gives unappealable proof of the scandal of our country—and of our world. And it raises the fundamental question: are we living in the reality of El Salvador, now earth-quaked but always poor? Are we enfleshed in it, in our *sarx* (weak flesh), or do we live outside reality, outside the real El Salvador?

The official reactions, national and international, sometimes leave the impression that as Jesus said in the parable of the rich man and Lazarus, there is no solution "even if someone should rise from the dead" (Lk 16:31). Even an earthquake usually cannot cause the scales to fall from people's eyes (Acts 9:18). And the power of evil, the Evil One, who is a liar and the father of lies (Jn 8:44), is acting in the world. Concealing the truth is the essential task of the Evil One.

Despite all this, the Christian view insists on looking directly at reality: at the earthquake, its consequences, and its victims. Perhaps this will show us the way of true science and human erudition.

Responsibility and Injustice: The Earthquake Is a Natural and Historical Catastrophe

The earthquake is a natural catastrophe, but also *historical and social*.[7] Nature (or God) alone does not cause the catastrophic damage; it is also the result of what we humans do to one another, of the way we have shaped reality "in normal times." More specifically, it is the result of what we could have done—but didn't—to foresee the magnitude of the earthquake and to mitigate the damage. And the tragedy widens after the earthquake when the assistance and solidarity are not effectively managed, and worse, when infighting, lies, corruption, and larceny begin and are half-reported, masked, in political discourse and the media. But the Christian view, which affirms the sinfulness of all human beings, is able to speak of it clearly.

To reflect on the historical and social aspects of the earthquake is a decisive change of perspective—a paradigm shift, we say today. It shows the injustice that prevails in the country and the planet, which people have spared no effort in hiding, but which the earthquake has clearly

---

[7]There has been some movement in this direction. After a recent earthquake in India, an Oxfam publication described India as "one of the greatest theatres of tragedy, both natural and human-made." By this they mean that governments are more concerned with helping the victims than with preventing catastrophes (Henar L. Senovilla, *Vida Nueva* 2267 [February 3, 2001], p. 33).

revealed. Is it right to learn so much about other planets and not about how to make our own as safe as possible? To spend astronomical sums on lethal weapons, and on such trivial things as cosmetics, manufacturing, and marketing offensive entertainment, music, sports? This reflection leads us to *demand accountability* (as the Enlightenment did with God), with all the seriousness that the situation entails. It does not let us shift the blame to nature, or hide behind mere emergency aid.

Let us come back to the Christian faith. While accountability is essential in the democratic tradition—even in natural catastrophes—the *Christian tradition* is even more radical. It grows out of the great, inescapable question: "Where is your brother?" (Gen 4:9). God's question to Cain is anthropologically and socially foundational; in the Bible the murder of Abel ranks beside the sin of Adam and Eve as "original sin."

Today in the presence of all victims—including those of natural catastrophes, in which much of the damage is avoidable—that remains the fundamental question of faith to us all, and especially to the forces that shape society: capital, government officials, politicians, military leaders, and also the communications media, religions and churches, the intelligentsia and universities: "What have you done with this world?"

Solidarity and Selfishness: The Need to "Bear One Another's Burdens"

Aid is absolutely necessary in an earthquake, but to be effective and humane (the latter is important) the aid should take the form of solidarity, which is not the same thing. As we know, aid (especially official, international aid) can be a quasi-mechanical, unilateral reaction immediately after the catastrophe. It can be a way of soothing the conscience, maintaining social control, and evading the responsibilities of justice, because it will not challenge us to overcome selfishness, especially structural selfishness. Aid is an excuse not to face the real need that a catastrophe poses: solidarity. Worse yet, it can be an opportunity for the donors to build personal or institutional prestige and power, and to enrich themselves.

Let us begin with a simple clarification. *Aid* means giving from what one has to alleviate another's suffering; that is good, necessary, and urgent, despite the above-mentioned dangers. But *solidarity* goes much further. Understanding the difference will not only help us develop humanitarian skills—to respond to human sorrow not with a spirit of geometry but of finesse, as Pascal said—but make our aid-giving more effective, in an earthquake or other situations. Solidarity means not only giving but self-giving; this is not only or mainly an ascetic or romantically voluntaristic approach, but rather presupposes a fundamental anthropology.

Solidarity means *letting oneself be affected* by the suffering of other human beings, sharing their pain and tragedy. This—not *a priori* political, ideological, partisan, religious, or ecclesiastical considerations—is what must guide the assistance process. It means giving priority to building up the human side: individuals, communities, peoples. Physical building efforts must serve people, not the other way around. It is necessary to build houses, schools, town halls, and churches, but it is more important to help in the building of communities and peoples, the fabric of fraternal human relations. It also means giving "assistance" without time limits. "Solidarity forever," as I have heard it said in U.S. solidarity committees.

From the viewpoint of Christian faith, the most important part of solidarity is that it expresses the ideal of bearing one another's burdens, as exemplified in the first Pauline communities. Solidarity is *helping one another*, those who give and those who receive. This means several things. Giving must be judged not only by the donors' criteria, but with the recipients in mind. Above all, the givers must be open to receiving—the victims' will to live, their dignity, creativity, and hope, and often their forgiveness—with the joy that comes from belonging to one human family. Perhaps if people have not "received," we should ask if they have really "given," or what it is that they have given. Solidarity, in the end, is "unequals bearing one another's burdens" (when "equals" do it, it is more an alliance of self-interest), fully aware that the dynamism and strength that make this process possible come from the "weaker unequals," who should not be seen as victims.

It is necessary to ask what kind of "assistance" is needed in the world, but that can be deceptive, especially in times of earthquake when the hearts of many people of good faith—though not necessarily their governments, the multinational companies, the banking system—are truly moved. It can also be deceptive because the word "assistance"—in a kind of semantic blasphemy—is also used to describe what is really colonization, the perpetuation of dependency. Worse yet, a macabre manipulation of the language allows people to speak of military "aid"—often to criminal military armies, like that of El Salvador, to which the U.S. government gave a million dollars a day in "aid" during the recent war.[8] Until assistance is transformed into solidarity, avoiding aberrations like these, it will always be a self-deception to some degree. Remember also that aid without solidarity lacks the

---

[8]We must not forget this. The Atlacatl Battalion, perpetrators of the massacre at El Mozote and the assassinations of six Jesuits and two helpers at the Central American University, were trained in the United States. And that is only one example.

mystique and dynamism that lead to the formation of the human family. More importantly, it lacks the mystique of mercy and justice that is needed for the survival of the *species*, not in a random way but as a human *family*.

Even in the broader meaning of the word solidarity, in its normal usage as assistance to the needy, can there be real solidarity on a planet where a few people have appropriated secure land for themselves, multiple homes, and abundant capital (some of it in foreign countries, in case they ever need to emigrate)? These examples of insolidarity are especially relevant in a time of earthquake. Is there solidarity on a planet where one child in the First World consumes as many resources as 400 children in Ethiopia? This is a paradigmatic example of reality on this planet, of insolidarity even in normal times. Can we say that these human beings, brothers and sisters, are "bearing one another's burdens"?

These words are written out of helplessness, but also in hope. They are written, in spite of everything, to offer a truer vision of what an earthquake reveals and what it demands. The Christian tradition, in its helplessness and impotence, proclaims solidarity as the only way to be human. Micah adds the challenging "forever" to the concept of solidarity, and the challenging "humbly" to "walking in history." For Paul, "bearing one another's burdens" is essential. For Jesus, it is "celebrating the shared table."

These are the givens, and at the same time utopias: that assistance will be transformed into solidarity, and that it will be *human* solidarity. It is important that solidarity be "for each other," but it has a higher goal, to be "with each other"; higher still, to be "partnership and joy among unequals." The earthquake and its aftermath reveal how much of this there is, and how much is lacking in our world. Either way, the earthquake demands this kind of solidarity.

Utopia and Resignation: Rebuilding and Building Something New

It is necessary to *rebuild* what has fallen, but this must be guided by a desire to *build* what does not yet exist. For us it is not a matter of rebuilding the *old El Salvador*, where some part of the country will be destroyed every ten or fifteen years. It is about building a *new El Salvador*, and this is more than a play on words or childish naïveté— although it is utopian.

To rebuild obviously requires realistic steps, but unless there is a horizon in which to build something new, everything stays the same: poverty, iniquitous inequality, injustice, lies, concealment, disregard for the poor. When people want only to rebuild, it is not because they have not heard about the biblical value of hope, of promise, of something new. It is not that they have never read *The Principle of Hope* by Ernst Bloch.[9] It is because they have not yet seen that the old world they are trying to rebuild is inhuman; they think of it as good because they are familiar with it and are therefore set on rebuilding *that* world. At most they may say hopefully that now they know the right and effective path toward progress. Don Pedro Casaldáliga sees it very differently. He candidly addresses St. Francis of Assisi in these poetic and prophetic words:

> Compadre Francisco,
> the world is so old,
> we'll have to make another
> to see it renewed.[10]

That is the great truth, and we have to see clearly that *rebuilding* and *building* require different dynamics and mystiques. Aid alone may be enough for rebuilding—although the aid would have to be voluminous—but more than aid is needed for building. *Qualitatively*, building requires the human, social, and political will to *turn history upside down*[11] in this country, and in the world.[12] *Quantitatively*, the international community would have to decide at last to *make life possible* on this planet, certainly in places like El Salvador, Honduras, India, the African Great Lakes . . .

If we want the human family to survive, much more is needed than the niggardly, dwindling aid given by the rich countries. We need an anthropological and social conversion to the primacy of "the human family," surpassing the ideas of nation, continent, or bloc as the absolute, unchallenged center of self-interest. We need the decisiveness of a "Marshall Plan" for the poor world, the majority of the planet, with

---

[9]Trotta, Madrid, 2002.

[10]"Oración a San Francisco en forma de desahogo," in *Cantares de la entera libertad,* Managua, 1984, p. 38.

[11]"El desafío de las mayorías pobres," *ECA* 493-494 (1989), p. 1078. These were the words of Ignacio Ellacuría on November 8 in Barcelona, and they stand as a countercultural testament, especially in this age of postmodernity *lite*, of a quasi-mechanical globalization as the good news, of a single discourse . . .

[12]Unfortunately, the trend is in the other direction. In 1999, in Geneva at the publication of the annual report of the United Nations Development Program, UN Secretary General Kofi Annan severely criticized the fact that "official development aid had reached its lowest level in the last 50 years" ("La globalización de la pobreza," *Carta a las Iglesias* 431 [1999], p. 14). More recently, in September 2000, World Bank ex-president James Wolfensohn said in the Czech Republic: "Assistance from the West to the Third World has only declined, and I believe this is a crime." History has continued to show this pattern.

the same magnitude and breadth of assistance and the same purpose (the same combination of altruism and selfishness) that marked that plan. Half a century ago people understood very well that unless they built a new Germany, the whole Western world was at risk. They made a virtue of necessity, and Germany rose out of the ashes. Whether it is necessity or utopia, we need to build a new world, not just rebuild the old one. Unless we "build" the Third World, the whole planet is at risk.

Utopia has fallen on hard times in the affluent world. We are said at last to have come to the end of history,[13] with nothing left to hope for. But the biblical tradition speaks knowledgeably about a utopia that does not spring up overnight and does not come from on high like David's power, but remains constant throughout the tradition, emerging from below, from the hope of victims. Centuries before Jesus, the school of Isaiah proclaimed: "For I am about to create new heavens and a new earth; the former things shall not be remembered or come to mind. . . . They shall build houses and inhabit them; they shall plant vineyards and eat their fruit. They shall not build and another inhabit; they shall not plant and another eat" (Is 65:17, 21-22). And the New Testament concludes: "Then I saw a new heaven and a new earth" (Rev 21:1). That is utopia, the mystique of difference and contrast, of justice and newness. "The world becoming a *home* to humanity," as Ernst Bloch put it in language that is once again relevant to our time.

What we have said about the earthquake as a bearer of truth, about the largely historical responsibility for the catastrophe, about the need to transform aid into solidarity, about the utopia of a new (not patched-up) world: we need these perspectives in order to deal with the reality of an earthquake. They express a Christian vision, although to varying degrees they may be shared and supported by others. In any case they must be historicized by institutions and by every kind of knowledge: technical, juridical, psychological, educational, economic, and political. The Christian vision is weak and helpless without the support of these bodies of knowledge. But it can open minds, wills, and hearts to realities that are overlooked in the conventional understanding of what an earthquake is.

At this point something comes explicitly into action that lies deep in every human being and is at the center of the Christian vision, giv-

---

[13]We are at "the end of the evolution of human thinking about guiding principles. . . . This is the end of human ideological evolution, and of the universalization of western liberal democracy as the ultimate form of government," F. Fukuyama keeps saying. Pedro Casaldáliga has replied that we are still in the prehistory of a human humanity.

ing it its ultimate depth: faith in mystery, which may be any kind of mystery but is especially relevant to Christian faith.

The Mystery: Victims and Sacraments of God

In the Christian faith, as it was lived among us by Monsignor Romero and Ignacio Ellacuría, *the victims are more than victims.* They are the "crucified people," "the suffering servant of Yahweh," "Christ crucified in our time." These victims demand absolute respect and reverent silence, but in their presence we might also call them (with stammering faith) the presence of God in the earthquake, a hidden, crucified God, and even (emboldened by faith) a God of solidarity.

The important thing is to see the victims with respect, devotion, and veneration, whether we do so in this theologal (faith) language or any other words, because the victims confront us with the ultimate mystery of reality. They may also confront us with the mystery of God, the unexpected one, the hidden source of dignity and hope. In any case, the one thing we must never do with victims is reduce them to objects—not even objects of charity, and certainly not propaganda tools. They are signs and sacraments of a mysterious reality, the reality of a God who participates in their suffering.

THE TRANSCENDENT ELEMENT
OF THE CHRISTIAN VIEW

The Christian view has a fundamentally transcendent dimension, and we must ask what, if anything, that dimension contributes to our understanding of the earthquake. Here I want to do two things. I will describe different religious responses to an earthquake—including an initial description of theodicy and anthropo-dicy, which will be discussed more fully in the last chapter. But first I want to stress how seriously we need to reflect on God when an earthquake strikes. Christian faith does not trivialize that reflection, because at bottom, in God everything takes on a sense of ultimacy.

A Christian view of the earthquake does not offer easy explanations and solutions by simply invoking God, as if faith and reflection were immune to the helplessness of the human condition in a catastrophe. That would be cheap faith, like the cheap grace that Bonhoeffer denounced. Christian faith does not allow us to trivialize the victims' suffering, even by invoking God.

Thus a Christian cannot sugarcoat the earthquake by relating it to God; the God we see in the earthquake does nothing to eliminate the negativity of natural reality. Christian faith does not magically cause the problematic truth of the earthquake, or the problematic truth of God, to vanish. At first, rather, it can lead to confusion, questioning, and even protest. The Christian faith "doesn't make things easy for God" (the perennial problem of theodicy). But the historically positive aspects that this view offers should not be too quickly dismissed, as if it were based on falsehood or dishonesty.

To say it from the beginning, although it belongs more logically at the end: an earthquake forces Christianity to face the problem of God without easy answers to solve it. But in a mysterious way, that same God is bearing the burden of the earthquake. The earthquake expresses the reality of God, no longer as power but—scandalously—as solidarity, love, and hope.

Differing Religious Responses to the Earthquake

God is very present in countries like El Salvador; therefore, we cannot fully understand the earthquake without considering the relationships between the human beings and that God. It is clear that when a catastrophe strikes in predominantly religious countries, the people look to God as the best way to understand what has happened, to bring some kind of logic to the absurd, and even to find some kind of "salvation" in the midst of the catastrophe. In this type of piety the people may consider the earthquake a just punishment, requiring them to placate God and beg his forgiveness. Or they may look to God and find mercy, protection, and hope. Behind both these attitudes, even in the midst of tragedy and even when they can do nothing to overcome it, is the ability to seek and find "reasons why," and above all "meaning," in God. The earthquake, therefore, does not only express death and destruction. Understood "in God," the earthquake is more than absurdity and negativity.[14]

There are different ways to follow this logic of understanding negativity in terms of God, and thus making it more than pure negativity;

---

[14]Although the following reflection may seem remote from the subject at hand, let us remember that the first Christians had to look for "meaning" in the tragedy of Jesus' cross. Although they developed different models to understand it (a pleasing sacrifice, vicarious atonement, etc.), they concluded that the cross had been "God's plan," that is, that its meaning lay entirely "in God." From this we learn that in the presence of a catastrophe—the crucifixion of a just, innocent man—those human beings sought understanding and meaning "in God." And that's not all. After the resurrection, when they asked why the cross was God's plan, rather than something else, they answered that the cross was something extremely positive: it had become the expression of love, God's love, and so it had brought salvation. Thus they came back to the unattainable, scandalous mystery of God.

it is an important part of all religions, and it can help to understand why people in our countries talk about God in the way they do when an earthquake strikes.[15]

But sometimes that is not obvious; then God is not part of the solution, but of the problem. The earthquake forces many believers today, like Job throughout history, to contemplate a questionable mystery (one that does not dazzle with its brilliance but casts a shadow with its terrible darkness) that becomes an enigma: the ineffable God becomes a "mute" God, like a sphinx. In order to hold on to faith, the believer has to assume that God is (also) the inactive, silent one.

On the other hand, if agnostics ask about God even hypothetically,[16] they will probably see the earthquake as confirmation that they were right to suspend judgment about God. That would not have been the case in the days of radical theism and antitheism. The people of the Enlightenment were not detached from God, but held God accountable for the world's evils and, with their "intellectual honesty," drew their own conclusions about the existence (or not) of God. Perhaps the time for such avatars is past; it is more common to treat God with detachment than to confront him. But let us remember that it was an earthquake—the one that destroyed Lisbon in 1775—that put an end to Leibniz's rationalist optimism and provoked Voltaire's bitter reflections on God.

Theodicy and Anthropodicy

Later we shall see what God has to say and do, positively, in the earthquake. For now I want to stress that faith does a great service to our world by not minimizing the problem of God. The benefit is that the victims can and must demand an accounting. And those responsible—whoever they are—must render accounts.

The meaning of *theodicy*, holding God accountable, questioning God about evil in the world, is the *religious* formulation of something much deeper. Its secular equivalent is *anthropodicy*, that is, justifying human beings in view of evil in the world. The parallel I am suggesting with the word "anthropodicy" may seem strange. In theodicy the formal problem is that if God can overcome evil but does not, or wants to but cannot, then God is not as godly as we think; human beings are not to blame for that. But it is not that simple. Fifty million human

---

[15]The problem, obviously, is to talk *appropriately* about God in the earthquake. For us the earthquake is not, for instance, a punishment from God.

[16]In our day, wherever secularization and agnosticism are prevalent, people are most likely to treat God with detachment in times of earthquakes and catastrophes.

beings die every year from hunger or hunger-related illnesses. We know that today hunger can be overcome. So humans have no excuse—just as we might say God has no excuse in the case of earthquakes—since they would need only to dedicate one percent of the gross world product to eliminate hunger.

There is not an absolute parallel between *theodicy* and *anthropodicy*, but there are important similarities. Humanity today must also face the question, "Do we want to, and can we?" The enlightened people of today must follow the same logic and the same *pathos* as those of the past: if they can eliminate hunger but it still exists, then they do not want to do so. And they should come to the same conclusion: if they say that God's only excuse for evil in the world is that God doesn't exist, that may also be humanity's only excuse. Humanity doesn't exist; what exists is inhumanity. Fifty million human beings do not just die; they are killed. By the critical logic of theodicy, it may be that "the human species" exists—but not "humanity," not "the human family."

In times of earthquake, there is nothing rhetorical about these reflections. There is something analogous between death from hunger and the destructiveness of an earthquake, although in an earthquake the natural component is still involved. If it is technically possible to build earthquake-resistant housing, if we have the knowledge and resources to build it but do not, then humanity does not want to do it. What political language we use to disguise that "not wanting" is another question. But the question of anthropodicy still stands, with growing urgency. Is it that we can't, or don't want to, do away with (some of the important) evil in the world?

So by examining the transcendent dimension of the Christian faith, we are not setting aside the serious questions that an earthquake poses to "God," and therefore also to the believer. The view from faith does not exempt us from honestly questioning and/or challenging God. In a time of natural or historic catastrophes, believers too have to wrestle with the God they believe in, who apparently cannot or will not prevent the catastrophes. But the same transcendent dimension also challenges human beings. It may well be that the world of believers, who ask transcendent questions whether or not they find answers, is the best—perhaps the only—vantage point from which to ask about negativity and evil. Other worlds put a higher value on detachment, the *carpe diem*, the "lite," even blind euphoria.

To put it more positively, believers cannot evade the question, "Where was God in the earthquake?"[17] In our opinion, unbelievers also

---

[17]We should say, at least in a footnote, that the religiosity of the simple people can perhaps benefit from a small dose of theodicy in order to avoid trivializing the reality

cannot evade the question, "Where was humanity, democracy, global-ization in the earthquake?" without being essentially dehumanized. In other words, a naive faith may emphasize *anthropo-dicy*—what hu-manity does—in order to excuse God from being responsible for evil. But it is also a naive humanism that emphasizes *theodicy*—what God fails to do—in order to excuse human beings from their responsibility for evil. We cannot cancel either side of the equation. And since we have described both attitudes as "naive," we should add that at bottom they are not naive at all; they are defending particular interests. Some are reluctant to question God so as not to diminish the power con-ferred by religion and the churches; others are reluctant to question humanity so as not to diminish the power conferred by science, democ-racy, etc.

And as we know well, this is not just about the Salvadoran earth-quake. The challenge to God, and to human beings, is where were they *both* in Auschwitz, Hiroshima, the Gulag . . .? Where are they today in the African Great Lakes, Haiti, Bangladesh, countries that live, as we do, side by side with the scandalous profligacy of the North? The prob-lem of evil and negativity in the world will be with us forever,[18] and that "forever" is essential to the Christian faith. It *never* lets us trivialize the question. And it forbids us to treat evil as something transitory, not really serious, as we have been told in a thousand ways.

In this chapter we have outlined a few points that will be discussed in greater detail later on. The important point is that there are differ-ent ways of looking at an earthquake, and at the world in general. Today everything—even assistance in natural catastrophes—is col-ored by the neoliberal-globalizing (capitalist) view, although voices are

---

of God, making that reality ahistorical, unverifiable from any viewpoint. In our opinion, what we call popular piety has nothing to lose by asking seriously about God in the earthquake; indeed it will gain if at least it stops its present slide toward infantilizing religiosity. This infantilization serves the interests of neoliberalization and globalization, not only in the religious sphere but in other human endeavors: politics, entertainment, sports, music, etc. Perhaps in this context the question of theodicy, which comes from the deepest roots of Christianity, can help recover the old sense of "popular conscientization," at least under the rubric of anthropodicy.

[18]*Historical* catastrophes, as the product of human will and freedom, seem better able to *excuse* God; it is good that God respects our freedom, although the question remains as to why an omnipotent and omniscient God could not create a world and a human being in which freedom would not lead to such atrocities. But earthquakes and other natural catastrophes place us in a different framework, in which God's good act of respecting human freedom does not exempt God from responsibility: it is God's creation, even before the (sinful) exercise of human freedom, that causes destruction, suffering, and death to human beings. Why did God create an earth whose tectonic plates shift so destructively?

being raised against that view in Seattle, Prague, Porto Alegre, Barcelona, and Genoa. But there are other ways of looking at the earthquake. We have mentioned the Christian view, or at least some important elements of that view. Certainly the Christian view respects and is open to all that the physical and social sciences are discovering about the physical reality of an earthquake and the social behaviors it elicits. But the Christian faith does something different: it places the earthquake, its aftermath, and people's responses to it in the context of grace and sin, responsibility and hope, hard facts and mystery. And all from the viewpoint of the victims.

3

BEING HONEST TOWARD REALITY

The immediate reaction to a tragedy is to help the victims, moved by compassion and mercy. In Christian tradition, that is the measure of a "true human being" (as exemplified in the parable of the good Samaritan, Lk 10:29-37); it is also a mark of definitive salvation (as seen in the parable of the last judgment, Mt 25:31-46). But in Christian tradition we must react to reality, first and foremost, by hearing the *word*—and in the case of catastrophes, hearing the *cry* of reality. For that we need a will to *truth*, or what I have called "honesty toward reality." Just as in theology we insist on "letting God be God"—as Barth never missed a chance to say—on not manipulating God, now we insist on "letting reality be what it is," in order to grasp it and hear it as it is. We need the integrity not to manipulate reality, the decisiveness to proclaim it, and an adequate reaction to the demands that spring from it, even when they often go against our own interests.

We shall dwell on that in this chapter, because while catastrophes clearly call attention to the need for compassion and mercy, we seldom insist—in practice, almost never—on the importance of listening to the word that springs from reality itself. Although it may seem surprising, it is often easier to respond with some act of mercy than to face the truth that the earthquake uncovers and proclaims, "cries out," for those who have ears to hear.

It is hard to face reality, not only in an earthquake; the problem is more universal than that. It comes from the dark side of the human condition, and sinfully permeates our world. It is extremely difficult to see and hear reality, to let it be without manipulation, even when the reality is expressed by an "outcry"—as it was in the earthquake, or in the massacres of the African Great Lakes region, or in the 1.3 billion human beings who live on less than a dollar a day, which Pedro Casaldáliga has called "the macro-blasphemy of our time."

The underlying reason is easy to see: certainly, reality "speaks" to human beings in many different ways. But it always speaks, challenges, and demands a deep and integral conversion in the realms of knowing, hoping, doing, and celebrating. In this context the primary demand of an earthquake, and in the long term the most decisive, is not merely to do acts of mercy but to be honest toward reality. This honesty necessarily leads to acts of mercy, but not the other way around. That is why the powerful do not want the truth of reality to come out; it requires a subjective conversion and an objective revolution, so they put all their effort into keeping it hidden so everything will remain more or less the same. In the end the truth is dissembled or annulled, and the reality is covered up.

This sobering fact becomes manifest in many ways, earthquakes among them. So we don't claim to be saying anything new in this chapter, but simply insisting without apology on the need to be honest toward reality. This argument is based primarily on the Christian tradition, which we shall analyze in greater detail than we have done in the previous chapters.

DEFICIT IN THE "WILL TO TRUTH"

There is a lack of honesty toward reality in our world. The time-honored *pathos* has been domesticated to establish the truth of social and historical reality;[1] the masters of suspicion, although they do exist, have not prevailed. At least they seem to have lost some of their old relevance in shaping the collective consciousness. And we do not lack for prophets[2] and protesters,[3] but there has been a head-on, worldwide struggle to co-opt, discredit, or silence them—so far, within the democratic rules protecting freedom of expression. In today's enlightened democracies, what I have called "honesty toward reality" does not carry the same weight as what used to be called "intellectual honesty," which in those days was seen as the *stantis vel cadentis humanitatis* in the world of philosophy.

What has happened is that an ironclad dictatorship has been imposed on reality, which at present is only visible through small fissures:

---

[1] We refer here to historical-social reality, including its economic, military, political, religious, and cultural aspects.

[2] To mention only a few: Mario Benedetti, Eduardo Galeano, and in the Church a whole generation of bishops: Monsignor Romero, Leónidas Proaño, Monsignor Gerardi, Don Pedro Casaldáliga, Don Samuel Ruiz.

[3] In the past two years there has been a qualitative jump in protest demonstrations, especially against globalization: Seattle, Bangkok, Prague, the World Women's March, Porto Alegre, Barcelona, Genoa. These marches are also a protest against the hypocrisy of calling the present world economic order "democratic."

Every day we experience more forcefully the contradiction between a world regime beyond any democratic control, powerfully
able to defend the economic, political, and cultural interests of a
small fragment of humanity, and on the other hand the persis-
tence of a certain debate and democratic give and take within the
political framework . . . which has less and less influence on the
most vital issues.[4]

In this dictatorship,[5] in contrast to democracy whose most obvious
presupposition should be "the free expression of reality," one of the
important casualties is truth; just as it is said that in war (as in Iraq
or Afghanistan) "the first casualty is truth." It is in the spheres of
economic, military, political, cultural, and religious power that truth
is oppressed; but to be effective, all of these must go through the communications media. What the media say or don't say, and how they
say or don't say it, helps to conceal the reality and effectively render it
invisible.[6]

As a whole, the present concealment of the reality of our world is
truly scandalous, and it has led to the current process of dehumanization; this directly affects the affluent world, which is shamelessly trying to control the poor world. Never has so much knowledge about the
reality of our world been so accessible: poverty and waste, disease and

---

[4]J. Corominas, "¿Cancelar el pasado? Tolerancia y oscurantismo en la sociedad
mundial," *ECA* 629 (2001), pp. 241 ff.

[5]J. Comblin believes that the present system is becoming fearful. "The 1990s were
a triumphalist decade; the neoliberal leaders were optimistic, promising a paradise
and believing in it. Now they are finding out differently. The establishment is no
longer so self-confident" ("América Latina 2001. Análisis de coyuntura [II]," *Carta a
las Iglesias* 473 [2001], p. 12).

[6]Three examples from the days following the earthquake:

1) The government of India was criticized for buying $60 million worth of weapons
soon after an earthquake, but there was no mention of the government or governments that profited greatly from the sale, or of the fact that the five members of the
UN Security Council control, manufacture, and sell 85 percent of the weapons (cf. V.
Fisas, *El desafío de Naciones Unidas ante el mundo en crisis*, Icaria, Barcelona,
1994).

2) I have just read that "in terms of news coverage, a kidnapped white person is
worth more than 10,000 Congolese tortured or murdered" (Gerardo González Calvo,
director-chief of the magazine *Mundo Negro*.)

3) At a soccer game between Real Madrid and Lazio—played, by coincidence, on
February 13, the day of the second earthquake in El Salvador—the market value of
the 22 players on the field was 125 billion pesetas (US $650 million); the press
reported this fact not only without irony or shame, but with an air of satisfaction and
enthusiasm. The press naturally did not mention that this amount would equal a
significant part of the national budget of a black African nation; it is perhaps two or
three times the budget of Chad.

luxury, weapons sales, government corruption. And we might add that never has the *goodness* of this world been so accessible: the heroic struggle for survival of billions of poor people, the dedication of many people to serving the rights of the weak, the utopias and hopes expressed in many small grass-roots communities, the cloud of witnesses, martyrs of humanity, unconditional generosity, forgiveness, and the victims' steps toward reconciliation.

We shall come back to this point, but for now I want to emphasize that there is no will to truth,[7] no desire to take seriously either the aberrations or the goodness of human beings. There is no will to put into words either the sin or the grace of reality. And something worse happens, as we can see in the manipulation of the word "globalization"[8]: a harsh, often cruel reality is turned into an appealing consumer commodity.

Luis de Sebastián brilliantly points out that in itself, "globalization is the present state of the world economy," but in fact the term "globalization" is used to describe very different realities: the universalization of the marketplace, almost instantaneous communications around the world, the homogenization of cultural environments, hopes for a new human *oikoumene*.[9] So the term is complex and ambiguous, and even more so in its broadest sense, when we remember how long people have thought of reality as global. The year 1492 (America) gave us a round planet for the first time. The year 1945 (Hiroshima) introduced the idea of global responsibility, because now the whole planet was in danger.

Certainly there are positive aspects in this internationalizing trend, such as the growing internationalization of communications that can foster solidarity, make it harder to claim impunity for human rights violations, and open new horizons of thought. But the defenders of globalization, especially in the economy, have tried to surround this vague, ambiguous term with a splendid halo. They present it as salvation (*euaggelion*) in its definitive state, which is taken to mean "the arrival of the end of history." The metaphor also lends itself to hopeful expectations: *inclusiveness*, because there is room for everyone in the

---

[7]We often say that "freedom of expression" is not the same as "will to truth." Democratic countries have the former to some extent, for those who can pay for their expression, although they are formally granted freedom to do so. The latter is unusual where institutions are concerned, although as we have seen, there are prophetic exceptions.

[8]The following three paragraphs are taken from my article "La redención de la globalización. Las víctimas," *Concilium 293* (2001), pp. 801-811.

[9]Luis de Sebastián, "Europa: globalización y pobreza," *Concilium 293* (2001), p. 743.

global world, and the existence of a *powerful center* that will generate goodness. It suggests perfection, *roundness*, and even *equity*: every place on the surface of the globe is *equi*-distant from the center. In a secularized but nonetheless effective way, it echoes the Advent Liturgy: "Rejoice, Jerusalem, for your salvation is near."

But even with the positive aspects that we have noted, the facts do not support this optimism. It is still true that in contrast with the "ideal essence" of globalization, it is not "inclusion" but "exclusion" that has increased and become global. It has not produced the homogenization of the truly human, but a threat to the identity of peoples and groups; has not deepened human foundations, but produced more triviality; has not embraced the planetary family, but opened a cruel abyss among peoples. So now many are asking: is this internationalism or conquest?[10] And the anti-globalization demonstrations are answering with a utopian demand: "A different world is possible."[11]

The important part of these reflections is the conclusion. We live in a culture of concealment, of distortion, and thus in effect we are living in a lie. There is not only *structural injustice*, not only *institutionalized violence*—as the bishops emphasized at Medellín—but also *institutionalized concealment, distortion, and lies.* And vast resources are used to maintain that structure.

Truth is oppressed, both environmentally and structurally. The spiritual ecology is seriously damaged. Not only the air the body breathes, but also that of the human spirit is contaminated by half truths, pretense, propaganda, subtle and blatant lies. And all this is encouraged, sometimes imposed, by international institutions, governments, political parties, and civic institutions, all praising democracy. Other cultural, academic, religious, ecclesiastical institutions fail to react in proportion to the level of concealment—and sometimes are directly complicit with it.

"We have touched bottom," one often hears in El Salvador in view of the accumulated evils that plague the country. Personally, I would say the same about the powers of this world, their indifference to truth

---

[10]*¿Mundialización o conquista?* is the title of a book published by Cristianisme i Justicia, Barcelona, 1999.

[11]See also the reflection by J. Moltmann, which reviews—with great wisdom—centuries of progress in the West: "The burial fields of history, which we have seen, do not allow us . . . an ideology of progress and pleasure in globalization. If the accomplishments of science and technology can be used to annihilate humanity (and if they can, some day they will be), it is hard to get enthusiastic about the Internet or genetic technology" ("Progreso y precipicio. Recuerdos del futuro del mundo moderno," *Revista Latinoamericana de Teología* 54 [2001], p. 245).

and their calculated interest in oppressing it, although there are always worthy exceptions. Here let us pause briefly to remember some moments in recent history when there was more will to truth.

One such moment was at the beginning of the Enlightenment, although the situation is not exactly comparable to ours—and the comparison does not flatter the Christianity prevailing at the time. In the midst of so many human failings, there seems still to have been a will to truth. A certain passion for truth was essential to the Enlightenment; with it came a sense of independence and a combative attitude toward structures of authority (churches, religions, monarchies). This turned the search for truth into an existential matter; life was a struggle, which gave it a mystical flavor. There was a determination to know and spread the truth. That meant accepting the risk of ostracism, persecution, excommunication, defamation, imprisonment, and even the gallows. Ideally, "honesty toward reality" seemed to be an ethical-mystical corollary to enlightened reason. This *pathos* was also nourished by the conviction that the truth would make human beings free, not only from ignorance but from obscurantism; that alone was an achievement. And it was nourished by the hope that the truth would lead to a political, global, humanizing liberation.

In the Western tradition, this *pathos* led historically to questions about even the truth of God,[12] with all the headaches that entailed for the churches, theologies, and believers. A secular, partly atheistic vision emerged, citing reasons why humanity had remained so long in the dark.[13] Atheism too was presented as a new, liberating gospel for a humanity that no longer needed God, but should rather ignore God for the sake of progress—although as history shows, the most lucid thinkers soon saw that progress did not automatically follow.[14]

All this is well known, but I mention it now to point out—and la-

---

[12]In the Christian biblical tradition the *pathos* of truth maintained the reality of God, of course, but it also carried an anthropological interpretation associated with the Enlightenment: "the truth will make you free" (Jn 8:36).

[13]"God? That is nothing but a human projection (Feuerbach), the opiate of the people (Marx), the resentment of the frustrated (Nietzsche), a childish illusion (Freud)" (Introduction to "Dios de vida, ídolos de muerte," *Misión Abierta* 5/6 [1985], p. 5).

[14]"Either build a God or rebuild man," said Rostand. "Theology will be liquidated. But what we call meaning will disappear with it," said M. Horkheimer ("El anhelo de lo totalmente Otro," in *Anhelo de justicia. Teoría crítica y religión*, edited by Juan José Sánchez [Trotta, Madrid, 2000], pp. 165 ff.). Metz often recalls—also out of intellectual honesty, in this case honesty toward Nietzsche—that Nietzsche's proclamation of the death of God was accompanied by a prediction of the death of humanity ("¿Qué pasó con Dios? ¿Qué pasó con el hombre?," *Revista Latinoamericana de Teología* 14 [1988], pp. 207-217).

ment by way of contrast—the lack of *pathos*, of honesty in knowing and spreading the historical-social reality of our world and efforts to conceal it, certainly in the great centers of power and sometimes also in the centers that make use of reason and the word, while boasting of their roots in traditions that once struggled to liberate the truth. In some ways these traditions are more about maintaining, absolutizing, and celebrating "freedom"—with its ties to enlightened self-centeredness, which easily degenerates into selfishness—than about "truth."

The situation today is clearly different from that of the early Enlightenment. A different truth was involved then, at least at the beginning: the status of faith and reason, which was essentially a question of how all truth should be known—although the socialist movement, especially in its Marxist version, focused mainly on the truth of social reality. But it is still surprising that today, societies shaped by "the enlightened" and "masters of suspicion" not only fail to suspect that reality is not what it seems to be, but have actually—out of self-interest and cynicism—become "credulous." They preach and proclaim the new gospel: the end of history, the global village, globalization, in short, the gospel of the marketplace—without any sign of suspicion that this proclamation is not true, and without attempting to verify it as the canons of scientific knowledge require.[15] And we might add that the argument from authority, no longer the authority of ecclesiastical but of political dogmatism, still prevails.[16] In today's context, it has been easier to apply suspicion and critical judgment to God, whom we do not see, than to the reality that human beings have created, which we see very well.

What we have just said is true to different degrees, of course, and there are important exceptions. But in general it is true that the collective consciousness has been injected with somnolence, ignorance, forgetfulness, avoidance of reality. It is also indifferent to reality and the accompanying truth. J. B. Metz rightly said a few years ago that "a routine postmodernity is spreading, among hearts that have been forced

---

[15]The Enlightenment was "suspicious" of the New Testament gospels and subjected their good news to verification. In retrospect, that was very positive. It helped us to understand the reality of Jesus, to find a "more real" Jesus. Something similar might happen today if people *seriously* suspected that our historical, economic, social, political, and cultural reality is not the end of history but—from the standpoint of the poor—a prehistory waiting for history to begin.

[16]The governments of Western democracies, and many of their political parties, their communications media, and their ideologues, unblinkingly accept the definition of "democracy"—now of "terrorism"—*imposed* by Washington and act accordingly.

into an unprecedented apathy by the poverty and misery of the so-called Third World."[17]

Let us return to the earthquake. These days, alongside truths that are inherently unconcealable—ruined houses, mudslides, deaths, and injuries—the deepest truth of what happened and why is still being concealed. People lie when they need to, even hiding the real number of deaths; outrageous arguments are used to protect the good name of some institutions; with some exceptions, political parties, and sometimes even universities and churches, keep silence with respect to the global interpretation of the earthquake. Worst of all is the cover-up of the secular history of capitalism, which has made El Salvador vulnerable because it is poor, and poor because it is a prisoner of capitalist injustice. The fact that this capitalism is still on the same course is also concealed.

It is not easy to be honest toward the true reality of the earthquake; we have to go against the flow. But for those who have eyes to see, the earthquake gives us a better understanding of the truth of the country, as the UCA declaration makes clear.[18] At the existential level, the earthquake can also shed light on our truth as human beings. Who are we, victims or victimizers? Did we suffer damages, or were we untouched, untouchable, indifferent, or moved to help others?

The earthquake can also show us the goodness that inspires hope: it is possible to live as decent human beings, although that fact, too, is often concealed. Again, we shall return to this in another chapter, but here we insist that it is an aberration to pretend that goodness does not exist.[19] It's not that people don't talk about it. In times of catastrophe there is official discussion, even propaganda, about awe-inspiring heroic actions, but other good things are kept quiet: an increase in social awareness, in demands and protests, in community awareness to overcome individualistic approaches, in grass-roots consciousness against the omnipresence, centralization, and heavy-handedness of the state, in recognition of the weakness, one-sidedness, and self-centeredness of international society and its institutions.[20] Some people

---

[17] "Teología europa y teología de la liberación," in J. Comblin, J. I. González Faus, and J. Sobrino, eds., *Cambio social y pensamiento cristiano en América Latina* (Trotta, Madrid, 1993), p. 268.

[18] "Clamor de justicia y esperanza. Pronunciamiento de la Universidad Centroamericana José Simeón Cañas," *ECA* 627-628 (2001), pp. 3-10. The declaration begins with and focuses on the truth revealed by the earthquake.

[19] The clearest example of this aberration, which we protest every year, is the silence and forgetfulness that the powerful have imposed on Monsignor Romero for the past twenty years.

[20] The popular and social reaction after the earthquake in Mexico is a clear

want to hide these good things, which lead not to pure charity but to the transformation of reality and its structures, reducing goodness to human interest anecdotes associated with the earthquake. This is another, flagrant and tragic, way of concealing reality.

THE LIE AND THE TRUTH
IN THE CHRISTIAN TRADITION

For the Christian tradition (meaning the tradition that began with Jesus, and meaning to our community the one that continues with Medellín, Monsignor Romero, Ignacio Ellacuría), truth and lies are central realities in human life, both personal and social. Christian tradition therefore has important things to say about them, things that are still useful and necessary in our time. Humanity has progressed in many respects since the time of Jesus, but in fundamentals, like truth and lies, grace and sin, we should keep those traditions in mind; we need them badly.

The Primordial Sin: "Oppressing the Truth"

We remember that Jesus of Nazareth was a man of mercy and faithfulness, of good news for the poor and protest against the oppressors, of hope for the coming of the kingdom, of strength all the way to the cross. But here we must remember something that is often forgotten: Jesus was "enlightened" with respect to God's truth, a "master of suspicion" about the ways God is used.[21] In the language of this chapter, Jesus was honest toward reality and unmasked the lie that oppressed that reality.

This was not just one dimension of his praxis, among others; it was a central dimension, perhaps the historically best documented aspect of Jesus' character.[22] The purpose of this task was to de-ideologize,

---

example. Some people believe it was the beginning of the end of the then-ruling PRI.

[21]Certainly the Enlightenment of Jesus' time moved in a different direction from that of modernity, when the main issue would be the existence or non-existence of God; here it is concerned with God's relevance to justice in the world, when the main issue was the idols of death or the God of life. Despite this difference in its meaning, I use the term "Enlightenment" because I believe that the biblical tradition of Jesus and the Israelite prophets "deconstructs" any oppressive conception of what is considered ultimate, and "demands" interhuman justice so that the ultimate can be fulfilled in history—whether in our time that ultimate is accepted in its religious form (God, the kingdom of God) or in secular forms (utopias, humanisms). On this subject see my discussion in *Jesus the Liberator*, Trotta, Madrid (2001), pp. 180-192.

[22]Juan Luis Segundo makes this affirmation in *La historia perdida y recuperada de Jesús de Nazaret* (Sal Terrae, Santander, 1991). J. I. González Faus picks up and extends that insight in "Jesús y la mentira," *Sal Terrae*, May (1992), pp. 347-361.

that is, to liberate human beings from the trap of justifying unjust and inhuman situations in the social consciousness. Jesus carried it out through a double denunciation: against *culpable blindness and hypocrisy* (violations of the eighth commandment, not to lie), and against *the manipulation of God* (a violation of the second commandment, not to take God's name in vain). Thus Jesus explained and denounced the things that lie behind and lead to dishonesty toward reality. The problem of honesty toward reality stems from the problem of being honest toward one's own reality. And lies that conceal reality are intended to conceal one's own sin.

Culpable Blindness. According to Jesus, human beings tend to behave *as if* they were blind, and he denounces that behavior in moments of conflict with his adversaries. The blind do not see, but human beings do not want to see. Sometimes he explains this with simple, easy to understand examples: "Why do you see the speck in your neighbor's eye, but do not notice the log in your own eye?" (Mt 7:3). It is evidence of a lack of honesty.

Sometimes the context is more sublime, the lesson more profound. Jesus heals a man blind from birth (Jn 9:1-41), which in John's theology is a sign of Jesus' truth: he is the Son of Man. The "Jews," however, see the sign but do not see the reality. That is not because of a natural handicap (blindness), but because they do not want to see (a matter of will) the truth that is right in front of them. Jesus says, "If you were blind, you would not have sin. But now that you say, 'We see,' your sin remains"(Jn 9:41).

So the problem is not "seeing," but "wanting to see." If people do not want to see the reality in front of them, there is no solution. Because knowledge and will are linked together, "not seeing" is sin. This culpable blindness leads to the falsification of reality, to the *lie*; existentially it leads to a self-interested way of understanding reality, to *selfishness*.

Hypocrisy. In Jesus' view, human beings conceal their true reality from others—and probably from themselves—by pretending to be the opposite of what they are. This is *hypocrisy*. Matthew 23:1-36 and Luke 11:37-53 are collections of anathemas against the scribes and Pharisees, and Jesus also anathematizes the scribes in Mark 12:38-40.[23] Directly, Jesus is denouncing their vanity: they show *external* signs of fulfilling God's will, so as to be *well looked upon* by others. But what concerns us now is his denunciation of the Pharisees' hypocrisy, and to a lesser extent that of the scribes.

---

[23]For a more detailed analysis, see *Jesus the Liberator*, pp. 160-179.

This hypocrisy is one of the more repugnant ways of concealing reality. In the anathemas Jesus unmasks it by contrasting inside and outside. He condemns it not because it expresses a "disproportion" between the two, but because it expresses a "contradiction," that is, because it communicates a lie. He accuses the Pharisees of purifying the outside of the cup while inside they are full of greed; of tithing mint and abandoning justice; of being like graves, white on the outside, filled with death inside (Lk 39-44).[24] The outside "contradicts" the inside, conceals and distorts it. The reality remains hidden, and in this case, perverted. Hypocrisy not only refuses to be honest with (one's own) reality, but glorifies that lack of honesty.

Manipulating God. According to Jesus, it is hard for human beings to be honest toward the reality of God; they have different ways of manipulating it.

Jesus is especially forceful in denouncing the creation of new religious traditions to bypass the real tradition that comes from God, because these new traditions seem to be innocent or maybe even good.[25] He gives a clear example in Mk 7:10-13: God's will—the real tradition—is to attend to the needs of one's parents and not turn away from them (the fourth commandment). But human beings had created another *religious* tradition: to set aside the resources for attending to a parent's needs as *Corban*, to which only God has rights, in order to avoid that filial obligation. Thus a divine tradition is supplanted and prostituted by a human tradition. In religious language, God's will is bypassed; in anthropological terms, the example Jesus used—caring for one's parents—clearly shows how honesty toward reality has been prostituted.

Jesus (and even more the prophets of Israel) unmasks another way of manipulating God: using the outward fulfillment of religious rites and practices to replace right relations with God. The manipulation enables them to justify themselves and obliges God to reward them for fulfilling their duty. This entails a double error, or evil. In the first place it annuls grace, God's loving initiative, which is central in the whole New Testament. But here we shall focus on the second, which is more complicated.

On the one hand, in human relations with God there is always a risk

---

[24]He doesn't accuse the scribes of hypocrisy so much as oppressive evil, although in his scheme of antagonisms, he points out a double evil: they impose heavy burdens without moving a finger themselves; they build tombs for the prophets, but approved of their ancestors who killed them; they have taken away the key of knowledge and kept others from entering (Lk 11:46-52).

[25]See *Jesus the Liberator*, pp. 162-170.

and temptation to hide behind what is "invisible" and "unverifiable" in the religious world. Jesus says, in simple but crystal-clear words, that although the religious sphere is invisible it is not unverifiable. Certainly religious people are not allowed to invoke the invisible in order to avoid verification. "Not everyone who says 'Lord, Lord,' will enter into the kingdom of heaven, but only the one who does the will of my Father in heaven" (Mt 7:21). "I desire mercy, not sacrifice" (Mt 9:13, 12:7).

These words of Jesus, simple and clear, bring us to a more general and fundamental problem. When faced with God's reality, religious men and women may claim that it is a matter of "faith," and thus historically unverifiable. So an appeal to "faith" or "belief"—to the unseen—can be used to avoid facing the truth of what is seen; to evade reality.

But that is not what faith means in Scripture. Scripture requires not only "belief" in God but "knowledge" of God. Faith in the ineffable mystery of God is accompanied by a visible praxis that brings us into relationship with God. "Knowledge" verifies the existence of "faith." And this knowledge is described in very real, historical, and visible terms. In the Old Testament, Jeremiah and Hosea—men of faith—demand the knowledge of God, and measure it by a clear, unequivocal, and profoundly human criterion: doing justice and righteousness, "Is not this to know me?" (Jer 22:15-16; cf. Hos 6:6). In the New Testament, John's theology gives centrality to "knowing God," and his criterion of verification is equally clear: "everyone who loves is born of God and *knows* God. Whoever does not love does not *know* God . . ." (1 Jn 4:7-8).

If we now ask why we humans are so given to the lie (blindness, hypocrisy) and to the manipulation of God, the answer is not so much our desire to distort reality or to distort God, but to conceal what we are doing to reality (in violation of the eighth commandment) and sometimes to give ultimate justification to the unjustifiable things we are doing to reality (thus violating the second commandment). The Pharisees are not only hypocrites and liars; they have abandoned justice. That can be said even more forcefully of the scribes: they lay heavy burdens, they do not put knowledge to the service of the people, they applaud those who killed the prophets. Sometimes they justify, even sanctify oppression and injustice in God's name. Those who ignore their parents' needs (Mk 7:11-13) are taking God's name in vain. And while saying long prayers the scribes devour widows' houses (Mk 12:40).

Lying and using God's name in vain are not the fundamental problem. The eighth and second commandments are violated for the sake of something even more basic: to conceal and even sanctify sin. Let us begin with a word about "concealing."

Human beings are capable of good, but they are also sinful. That sin involves several ways of "killing": by assassinating, impoverishing, hurting, insulting.[26] Killing necessarily involves concealment and lying.[27] Sin and concealment go together, both personally and socially.[28] And the size of the concealment is a measure of the sin.

That is what the biblical tradition affirms. Evil has its own dynamic and requires concealment and lying. In John's theology, the devil is a murderer and a liar (Jn 8:44), *in that order.* The violation of the eighth commandment (against lying, concealment, manipulation) necessarily follows the violation of the commandments that protect life: not to steal, not to kill.[29] They are primary dimensions of human sinfulness. As we have said, the *cover-up* and the *institutional lie* go along with *structural injustice* and *institutionalized violence.*

In the Pauline tradition, "to oppress the truth with injustice" is a fundamental sin with profound consequences. Reality loses its transparency and its ability to be a sacrament (of God); the human heart is darkened, and it is given up to all kinds of vice (Rom 1:18-32).

We have already said that although sin is usually kept hidden, it sometimes seeks to be sanctified, justified in God's name; this is the most sophisticated lie.[30] In the religious sphere, the lie becomes sharper and expresses a radical distortion of reality. Religious men distorted Jesus' reality by presenting him as crazy, a glutton and drunkard, and they killed him as a blasphemer. In John's gospel, Jesus dramatically denounces the religious distortion of reality: "An hour is coming when those who kill you will think they are offering worship to God" (Jn

---

[26]This is strong, not common language. We seldom use it, not because the word "sin" has "religious" connotations—other words and concepts can be used, although the religious language carries weight, and it is hard to find adequate equivalents—but because "sin" refers to a *radical* human failure. Facing that fact is always unpleasant. But there is a tendency in our time to avoid facing whatever is radical and goes to the *root* of human nature.

[27]"In order to do evil, human beings almost always need to lie, and especially to lie to themselves" (J. I. González Faus, "Jesús y la mentira," p. 349).

[28]Jesus indicates the social side of sin by using the *plural* form to address his adversaries, when he accuses them of blindness and hypocrisy. Joaquín García Roca describes this more analytically, in our own time, in "Mentiras institucionales. ¿Se puede recrear la verdad en la Institución?" *Sal Terrae,* May (1992), pp. 363-373.

[29]See my article, "La honradez con lo real," *Sal Terrae,* May (1992), pp. 377-379.

[30]It has always been and is still common to invoke one god or another to make wars, and to present the killing of human beings as something good, even religious. Sometimes the invocation is not of a religious but a secular god (gold, oil, more recently coltan, strategic territory), but something is always needed to bless depredations and death: the crusades, the conquest of the Americas, holy wars, prayers before the bombing of Iraq. And let us remember that in many Latin American countries, Western terrorism is not blessed by invoking "God," but "democracy."

16:2). This, he says, is "because they have not known the Father or me" (v. 3).

These days religion is manipulated differently, and the second commandment is violated in a more secular fashion.[31] But others co-opt religion, sometimes in incredible ways, and use it to serve an unjust, cruel, and criminal economic system. In the context of honesty toward reality in the religious sphere, we offer two now-classic quotes from the world of economics; the reader can judge their meaning. Michael Novak, the theologian of neoliberalism, says:

> For many years one of my favorite scriptural texts was Isaiah 53:2-3: "For he grew up before him like a young plant, and like a root out of dry ground; he had no form or majesty that we should look at him, nothing in his appearance that we should desire him. He was despised and rejected by others; a man of suffering and acquainted with infirmity; and as one from whom others hide their faces he was despised, and we held him of no account." I would like to apply these words to the modern business corporation, an extremely despised incarnation of God's presence in this world.[32]

Michel Camdessus, when he was president of the IMF, said in a famous lecture to representatives of the world banking system in Lille on March 27, 1992, that neoliberal capitalism fulfills the words of Jesus in the synagogue at Nazareth, announcing the good news to the poor (Lk 4:18):

> Today, that Scripture is fulfilled for you who hear it. That today is our today, and we who are in charge of the economy, are the administrators—at least in part—of this grace of God: alleviating the suffering of our brothers, and working for the expansion of their freedom. It is we who have received this Word. It can change everything. We know that God is with us in the task of building brotherhood.[33]

---

[31]God is more often "made useless" than used, "co-opted" in the economic and social sphere. Monsignor Romero never fell into the trap of the second commandment; in the economic and political sphere he spoke well of God, in line with God. "We need to restructure our economic and social system, because this idolatry of private property cannot continue; frankly, it is paganism" (Homily of September 30, 1979).

[32]In M. Novak and J. W. Cooper, eds., *The Corporation: A Theological Inquiry* (Washington, 1981), p. 203.

[33]From J. M. Castillo, *Los pobres y la teología* (DDB, Bilbao, 1999), p. 11. In Bangkok, February 2000, in his farewell address after thirteen years as president of the IMF, he spoke differently: "It still is not clear that globalization is sufficiently

Let us come back to the earthquake. Obviously, to be faced with the reality of Jesus (as the "Jews" were, according to John's gospel), or with the social reality of Palestine (like the scribes and Pharisees in the gospels of Matthew and Luke), or with our own reality (as Paul analyzes it in the letter to the Romans) is not the same as being faced with an earthquake. But they have one thing in common: there are human and inhuman, honest and corrupt ways to face any reality. To face and live reality in an adequate, human way, we need a "will" to truth; we must want to know the reality and not conceal it.

That is the lesson of the New Testament tradition. It asks some existential questions, which are fundamental for today's world: How can one not see the tragedy of this world, given the incredible amount of knowledge that is available? And it offers wise answers: we human beings, even after the Enlightenment, often fall into culpable blindness; not only blindness but often concealment, hypocrisy, and manipulation.

Letting Reality Speak

The answer of Christian faith to concealment is honesty toward reality. That requires *hearing the word of reality* and *giving voice to reality*.

Hearing the Word of Reality. Karl Rahner wrote in a memorable article[34] that "reality wants to have a word" (to speak). If I may use a pun: "the word was made *reality* (flesh, *sarx*); now reality wants to become *word*." If that is so, the dynamism of reality forces us to listen to its word. Then reality ceases to be merely factual, silent, and above all oppressed and distorted reality, and it becomes "real" reality, reality that can speak freely—as is affirmed at decisive moments of the Christian tradition.

Above all we must remember that the history of revelation began when God listened to the word of reality, listened to the "cry" of suffering human beings (Ex 3:7). That the word becomes a "cry" is an important hermeneutical aid for us, as we seek out and listen to the word spoken by reality throughout history—a task that theology has neglected, in my opinion.

---

concerned about the most serious problem of this epoch, poverty, or capable of resolving it. The growing breach between rich and poor, and the abyss that separates the richest and poorest countries, are morally inadmissible, economically inefficient, and socially explosive."

[34]"The Theology of the Symbol," *Theological Investigations IV*, 1974, pp. 221-252.

A second moment worth remembering is at Vatican II, when it insisted on "discerning" the signs of the times;[35] this presupposes that reality is able to break its homogeneity and monotony, able to "speak." We have repeatedly pointed out that "signs" has a double meaning in Vatican II, although I believe the Church and theology are not very aware of the distinction and its significance. The council speaks of signs of the times as "the characteristics of an epoch" (GS 4), which bring together important elements of its reality. We call these the historical-pastoral signs of the times. But it also speaks of "true signs of the presence or plans of God" (GS 11); that is, of the theologal sacramentality of reality. We call these the historical-theologal signs.

In both cases, especially the second, "discerning"—hearing the true word of reality—is not an easy task for human beings; objective reality is opaque and complex, and human beings are subjectively sinful. To make it easier I would suggest taking seriously not only the "historical epoch," but also the "geography" in which we hear the word of reality. History shows clearly that we do not hear or discern "the same things" in one place as in another. Bartolomé de Las Casas *in* Latin America and Sepúlveda *in* Castilla, Cardinal Ratzinger *in* Rome and Desmond Tutu *in* South Africa have heard different words of reality. (The advocates of globalization have not raised this problem, and I doubt that they are interested in it.)

Recognizing the existence of "signs of the times" means accepting that reality speaks throughout history.[36] It means that some real things deserve more attention than others. In my opinion it also warns against falling into a kind of hasty and facile dilettantism, as if a "changing epoch" or a "new paradigm"—real as they may be—could annul the word of reality that may be recurrent and perennial, hard as a rock. Ellacuría, as we shall point out in the next chapter, said that one sign of the times is *always* the most important: *the crucified people.*[37]

A third moment to take seriously—because it is currently being ignored, as if there were more interesting topics in the marketplace—is

---

[35]See my article, "Los 'signos de los tiempos' en la teología de la liberación," in José María Lera, ed., *Fides quae per caritatem operatur*, University of Deusto-Mensajero, Bilbao, 1989, pp. 249-269.

[36]In theological terms, this contradicts what we might call "Christian deism," according to which God spoke in Jesus at the beginning of Christianity and then fell silent; we have to go back to this lifeless beginning to hear God's word.

[37]Taking the signs of the times seriously also means that theology is necessarily contextual. How to integrate the signs into the tradition, how the signs move the tradition forward or jeopardize it, is a different issue. But it seems to me that separating "systematic"(universal) theology from "contextual" theology constitutes a denial *in actu* of the signs as "the place of God's presence or God's plans" (GS 11).

the Latin American tradition of Medellín and Puebla. They identify the irruption of the poor as the great sign of the times; it is an appropriate description of reality on the one hand, and on the other, it shows the place of God's presence. Moreover, they understand the word of reality as a cry, and in this profound sense they come back to the Exodus tradition. Thus Medellín, in 1968, began its analysis of the continental reality with these words: "That misery, as a collective fact, is an injustice that cries out to heaven" (*Justicia* 1). And Puebla, in 1979, said:

> The Medellín Conference, just over ten years ago, already pointed to proof of this fact: "A voiceless *cry* is arising from millions of men, asking their pastors for a liberation that refuses to come" (*Pobreza de la Iglesia* n. 2). The cry may have seemed voiceless back then. Now it is clear, growing louder, impetuous, and sometimes threatening. (nn. 88 f.)

Giving Voice to Reality. If reality speaks and God can speak in it, especially when it *cries out*, then listening to it is a necessary way of realizing our humanity: to be "hearers of the word."[38] By doing so, we start moving toward our own humanization.

But to be human also means giving voice and word to reality, when reality is silenced and oppressed; to help its stammering become a clear, demanding, and promising word. We must also understand the beautiful and profound words of Monsignor Romero, which we have quoted before: "These homilies seek to be a voice for the voiceless."[39] They are voiceless because they are not allowed to speak, although they have much to say about reality, and reality is prevented from speaking through them. That is what Monsignor Romero did: he gave voice to reality. Ignacio Ellacuría put the same insight in different, conceptually precise words when he spoke of what a university should be and do:

> The university should take flesh intellectually among the poor, to be the knowledge of the voiceless, an intellectual support for those who have truth and rightness in their own reality even when it has been stolen from them, but who do not have the academic reasons needed to justify and legitimate their truth and rightness.[40]

---

[38]If reality is this way, then metaphysically the human being becomes human by becoming a "hearer of the word," as Rahner put it in his analysis of human openness to transcendence. It can also mean openness to the whole of reality.

[39]Homily of July 29, 1979.

[40]"Discurso de graduación en la Universidad de Santa Clara, 12 de julio de 1982,"

This insight from Christian faith on "the word and the cries of reality" is often rejected in history. We human beings don't want to see reality as it is but to cover it up; we don't want to hear its word, but to ignore it. We don't even want to listen when it takes the form of a "cry." Then comes the anguish, which we might describe as follows, paraphrasing Paul: "Who will free us from this world of lies?" (Rom 7:24). And then comes the protest, to paraphrase Antonio Montesinos: "How can they be in such lethargic sleep, that they do not see a world of cruel inhumanity?"

Perhaps we have dwelt too long on this idea. It is simple but fundamental, and it is urgent because the world is sliding down the slope of indifference, concealment, and lies.

Now we can come back to the earthquake. In material terms, the earthquake is a word cried out by reality. By itself and by the thundering reality it expresses, the earthquake should be able to awaken people to the true reality and liberate us from the lie. But the human struggle to avoid seeing reality, especially among the powerful, reminds us of the parable mentioned earlier: if the rich man's brothers were not moved by seeing Lazarus, they will not be converted "even if someone rises from the dead."

We speak out of our helplessness. Just as the cries from Auschwitz and Hiroshima were ignored, so today people do their best to hide or remove from the collective human consciousness the powerful cries of people with AIDS in Africa, of those suffering bombing raids in Iraq and Afghanistan, of the millions who have been excluded from society.[41] To underline the importance of "returning" to honesty toward reality, let us remember two thinkers who faced reality more honestly.

J. B. Metz repeats endlessly that we must *remember*. He is talking mainly about Auschwitz, but he makes "remembering" a central category in Christianity. He combines the "Remember, Israel" theme from the Old Testament with "Do this in memory of me" from the New, and insists on remembering in order to "restore *reality* to the victims," in order not to condemn them to permanent unreality. In this sense, forgetting is a kind of intellectual dishonesty, while remembering is intellectually honorable. And when the reality in question is human suffering, then it should be remembered not only for humanitarian reasons but because it is a necessary constituent of thought. "Suffering comes

---

Carta a las Iglesias 22 (1982), pp. 11-15. "The Task of a Christian University," in Jon Sobrino et al., *Companions of Jesus* (Maryknoll, NY: Orbis Books, 1990), pp. 147-161.

[41]No such effort is made to silence the cries from the barbarity committed in New York and Washington on September 11.

before thought," said Feuerbach. "The need to let suffering speak is a condition of all truth," says Adorno.[42] And of all theology.

Ignacio Ellacuría is another of the great forgotten ones, with regard to honesty toward reality and the will to truth. He spoke passionately about the need to know the truth of reality, and how hard it is to know it, not mainly because of the limits of human understanding, but because of a will to oppress the truth. Impacted by the lies of the powerful, locally and among the nations, he worked with determination to know reality and make it known; he even said that the national reality was the most important subject taught at UCA.

This is widely known, and some people will remember it. What has perhaps been forgotten, and not by accident, is that without abandoning scientific ways of knowing, Ellacuría appealed to the Christian tradition—it was his deepest, most paradoxical trait—to offer an effective way of knowing the truth of reality: the example of the suffering servant of Yahweh, as presented in Isaiah 52-53, destroyed by the historical catastrophe produced by the powers of this world. "We know who we are by what we produce," he used to say. "By looking at the devastated servant, we will know the truth of the world that produces him."[43]

Along with this biblical-historical reflection, he used two metaphors that made history in their day. He said that if the First World wanted to know itself, that is, know its own reality, it should look at what it is making of the Third World; there it will see its own true figure as if in a carnival mirror, disfigured. The other metaphor is even stronger. He used it several times, the last time in a speech he gave in Barcelona, ten days before he was assassinated. It was about coproanalysis, the use of stool samples to analyze a patient's health. "Coprohistorical analysis, that is, the study of the feces of our civilization, seems to show that this civilization is gravely ill; to avert an ominous and fatal outcome, the civilization will have to be changed from the inside out."[44]

Carnival mirrors, coproanalysis—these are vigorous literary devices for encouraging people to face reality. An earthquake is even more vigorous.

In a Christian vision, the truth is central. It is enough to remember John's theology. Jesus is the way, the *truth*, and the life (Jn 14:6).

---

[42]Quoted in J. B. Metz, "Hacia una cristología después de Auschwitz," *Selecciones de Teología* 158 (2001), p. 112.

[43]See "El pueblo crucificado. Ensayo de soteriología histórica," *Revista Latinoamericana de Teología* 18 (1989), pp. 305-333. "The Crucified People," in Jon Sobrino and Ignacio Ellacuná, eds., *Systematic Theology* (Maryknoll, NY: Orbis Books, 1996), pp. 257-278.

[44]"El desafío de las mayorías pobres," *ECA* 493-494 (1989), p. 1078.

Those who do what is *true* come to the light (Jn 3:21). The word lived among us, full of grace and *truth* (Jn 1:14). Now we shall begin to analyze that truth. To put it in classical terms, we want to analyze what the word of the earthquake says about sin and about grace.[45] More specifically, we shall analyze the reality of the crucified people (chapter 4), primordial holiness (chapter 5), and the question—from the viewpoint of hope—about where God was in the earthquake (chapter 6).

---

[45] We want to insist on this, because covering up grace and goodness is worse than covering up sin. Hope, grace, and blessing are also given to us by reality, and it all appears—sometimes very clearly—in times of earthquake, as we shall see in chapter 5.

4

THE CRUCIFIED PEOPLE

THE SINFULNESS OF REALITY

The earthquake has revealed the sinfulness and the grace of reality. Let us begin with sin. El Salvador is a vulnerable country; it is vulnerable because it is poor, and it is poor because of injustice. Along with poverty and injustice, the earthquake has also revealed inequality, arrogance, hypocrisy, disrespect, and other evils.

Of course an earthquake is not the only thing that reveals the sinfulness of reality. Wars and terrorism, famines and AIDS epidemics, the economic state of the world in general, all show the same thing—sometimes even more forcefully. This chapter adds nothing to what we already know: we are not living in a world of justice and life, but of injustice and death. The earthquake reveals a reality hostile to the majorities, and shows that those who have shaped this country—people and structures—have shrugged off and failed at the task of building a humane country. The earthquake has simply made that fact more obvious to anyone willing to see the truth. To put it in more radical Christian terms, the earthquake has shown that there is a great "sin" in the country, not occasional but permanent sin, which shows its face regularly and without pretense.

Whether or not people accept the word "sin," I use it to show the depth of the tragedy and the fact that it is largely due to what we human beings are doing. In the Christian tradition, "sin" has a specific, radical meaning: it was sin that killed Jesus of Nazareth, which means it is able to kill even God, and it is still killing the children of God. Thus sin means "killing," which—throughout history and especially in today's world—is anything but a metaphor.[1] So to speak of sin

---

[1] In wartime this is clear from all the Auschwitzes and Hiroshimas. In "peacetime" we see it in the 50 million human deaths every year from hunger, which could have been avoided.

49

as deadly is not masochism, but honesty toward reality.

This idea and language are not new. For centuries the tradition has spoken of "mortal" sin, but with reference to the subjective state of the sinner: the death of the soul. That language has gone out of style, but without its obsolete, macabre connotations it still has something to say about human acts of commission and omission today. Sin is *subjectively* "mortal" because it "dehumanizes"; it kills the humanity in the human being. And it is *objectively* "mortal" because it actually "kills" the other. Those who reject or are uncomfortable with the language of "sin" and "death" should look back at the twentieth century, which Hannah Arendt called "the cruelest in history"—and there are no signs that the twenty-first century will be much different. In the final analysis, our discomfort and rejection are not a response to exaggeration or obscurantism in the language itself, but to the fact that it reflects the truth of the world—and therefore accuses us.[2]

In our circle, here in El Salvador, we do not hesitate to use that language. Those who live at the center rather than the margin of tragic human realities (especially oppression and repression), who have given their lives to turn the history of death upside down, use the language of "sin" and "death." They draw from the biblical tradition, which has more forceful language than other (even democratic) traditions for doing justice to reality.

Thus Monsignor Romero, looking for words to describe the reality of repression that had erupted in the country even before the war, told the horrified survivors of a peasant massacre: "You are the pierced body of the divine."[3] These are dramatic, eloquent words. They are fitting, not only in a homily but as a conceptual expression of the reality, if by *divine* we mean *ultimate* in either its religious or secular meaning.

Ignacio Ellacuría also used this language, more theoretically. He saw the Salvadoran reality as poverty, injustice, oppression, repression, and war. He saw the people bearing the burden of it all. He called them "the crucified people." And turning it into a theory, he said that the true reality of this world "is nothing more or less than the exist-

---

[2] Those who seek to control reality through language will dismiss these words as "politically incorrect," but that is a different problem. We shall continue using words like "sin" and "death," precisely in order to win the language battle and avoid whitewashing the reality.

[3] Homily in Aguilares, June 19, 1977. Aguilares had been under military siege for a month, during which countless peasants were killed. After the soldiers withdrew, Monsignor Romero went to celebrate the eucharist. In the homily he was alluding to the prophecy quoted in the Gospel of John about the crucified Jesus: "They will look on the one whom they have pierced" (Jn 19:37).

ence of a large part of humanity, literally and historically crucified by the oppression of nature and, above all, by historical and personal oppression."[4]

This way of describing reality was not a sudden stroke of genius, but a central and permanent part of their view of history and their understanding of Christian faith. Moreover, the idea of the "crucified people" was not at all rhetorical but deeply rooted in their concept of God's revelation and their theological understanding of reality. Ignacio Ellacuría said about the crucified people:

> Among all the signs we see—some of them obvious and some barely perceptible—in every age there is always one that stands out, in the light of which we can discern and interpret all the others. That sign is the historically crucified people, which is always present although the historical method of crucifixion constantly changes. This crucified people is the historical successor of the servant of Yahweh, still deprived of human form by the sin of the world; still robbed of everything by the powers of this world, which snatch away even his life, especially his life.[5]

Some readers have noticed how often I quote these words from Ellacuría. I keep coming back to them for the following reasons.

First, they are *vigorous*—with an almost unmatched passion; such vigor has almost disappeared from today's descriptions of reality, which increasingly tend to trivialize it.

Second, they are conceptually *rigorous*—which is also seldom true of so-called progressive theologies.[6] "Crucified" means that the people are: a) really dead, not merely hurt, impaired, or deprived; b) "killed,"

---

[4]To the best of my knowledge, the term "crucified people" came from I. Ellacuría (see "El pueblo crucificado. Ensayo de soteriología histórica," published posthumously in *Revista Latinoamericana de Teología* 18 [1989], pp. 305-333. The quote cited here is on p. 305). It was first published in *Cruz y resurrección. Presencia y anuncio de una iglesia nueva* (Mexico, 1978), pp. 49-82, a collaborative book prepared for the bishops' meeting in Puebla. We have seen that Monsignor Romero used the idea in 1977, but I cannot say which of them inspired the other, or whether they reached the same insight by coincidence, based on their own historical and faith experience.

[5]"Discernir el signo de los tiempos," *Diakonía* 17 (1981), p. 58.

[6]J. I. González Faus shows this kind of rigor; that is also one of the great contributions of I. Ellacuría ("Mi deuda con Ignacio Ellacuría," *Revista Latinoamericana de Teología* 21 [1990], pp. 255-262, especially pp. 260-262). But in general, even the theology that defends and yearns for Vatican II has not taken very seriously Ellacuría's *theologoumenon*, with all its Old and New Testament flavor. Progressive theology rightly appeals to the council to demand the Christian democratization of the people of God, but it has never fully examined the historical situation of the people

not dead of natural causes; c) "a shameful, undeserved death"; d) connected to Jesus and his fate, which is important from the perspective of faith because it makes an ultimate—theologal—reality of the reality lived by a large part of the human race.[7]

Third, *theologoumena* like these, which fully deserve to become "classics," are not noticed or valued as they should be; rather they are ignored by the academy and by theology, shaped as it is by postmodernity and new paradigms. This is surprising from the viewpoint of Christian sensibility—which ought to pervade theology—as if weightier, more Christian *theologoumena*, more expressive of reality, had been discovered in the twenty-first century.

Finally, I quote these words to point out a danger that may be present in Ellacuría's case, although it is broader than that. Ellacuría is remembered and cultivated in the academy as a *thinker*, a philosopher and theologian,[8] while in civil society he is remembered as a *negotiator* working to end the war. That is all well and good. But I am concerned that if utopianism and prophecy[9] disappear or are marginalized in his philosophical and theological thought, if his social and political praxis is only remembered for its pragmatic realism without his broader view of justice and injustice, then we may be passing on a somewhat watered-down Ellacuría—which we also risk doing with the traditions of Medellín, of the martyrs, etc.

The danger is in not presenting the whole Ellacuría, who was both thinker and negotiator, with both aspects shaped by his character as a human being and a Christian. Today this *whole* Ellacuría can teach us ways of *living* in our world, in the Church and the academy, which are discomforting now as they were in his lifetime. To be specific: we must hold together his demand for objectivity and realism with his prophecy and utopianism, which were central in both his theoretical work and his praxis. Otherwise I doubt that we can either do justice to Ignacio

---

of God—a "crucified people"—which would also be the best way to recover the idea of the (crucified) "body of Christ."

[7] See what I have written in "Los pueblos crucificados, actual siervo sufriente de Yahvé," *Concilium* 232 (1990), pp. 497-508. "The Crucified Peoples: Yahweh's Suffering Servant Today," *The Principle of Mercy* (Maryknoll, NY: Orbis Books, 1994), pp. 49-57.

[8] Several doctoral theses on his philosophical and theological ideas have already been published, and centers for the study and promulgation of his thinking have been established in several places. I am personally aware of such programs in Madrid, Boston, Berkeley, Nicaragua, and San Salvador, which of course I consider very positive.

[9] This was the title of his last, long theological work: "Utopia y profetismo. Un ensayo concreto de soteriología histórica," *Revista Latinoamericana de Teología* 17 (1989), pp. 141-184.

Ellacuría or focus properly on the reality of our own world—beginning with the earthquake.[10]

This brings us back to the main point of this section. An earthquake like the one in El Salvador forces us to ask whether or not reality is truly permeated by sin, and the people truly crucified; whether or not this earthquake (and the one in India, and the floods in Mozambique around the same time) prove Ellacuría right, not only as a thinker but as a human being and a Christian; whether these events do not at least support his audacious affirmation that the crucified people is "always" the sign of the times. We shall now briefly analyze these questions.[11]

INIQUITOUS POVERTY: THE DESTRUCTION OF "HOME"

It is impossible to describe Salvadoran reality without speaking of *injustice* and of *structural* injustice. Injustice crucifies; there are "different forms of crucifixion" according to the circumstances. An earthquake has its own way of revealing how injustice crucifies, by showing what happens in an earthquake. Let us take it step by step,[12] beginning with what happens first: the vulnerability that comes from poverty of all kinds.

Vulnerability means weakness, and at its height, defenselessness against all kinds of attacks and threats. The earthquake showed unequivocally the country's vulnerability at basic levels of human exist-

---

[10]Some years back I wrote that Ellacuría required four things as conditions for dealing properly with the processes of reality. On the one hand: *objectivity* in addressing, understanding, and analyzing reality as it is, and *realism* in taking appropriate steps—which means they must be possible, but must also be steps followed by other steps in order to reach a goal that must never be lost from view. On the other hand: *prophecy* to denounce the evils of reality and never be conformed to it, and to do so categorically because evil presents itself as ultimate; and *utopianism* to propose whatever is needed to abolish those evils, and beyond that, to envision the horizon of personal and social fulfillment. In other words, Ellacuría's genius was to seek *justice* and *justness* at the same time. See "Ignacio Ellacuría. El hombre y el cristiano" (I), *Revista Latinoamericana de Teología* 32 (1994), pp. 135 ff.

[11]In the next chapter we shall look at the other dimension expressed by the crucified people in a time of earthquake: grace, the ability to bring salvation, which Ellacuría analyzed even more insightfully.

[12]The data in this section are from J. M. Tojeira, "Reflexiones sobre el terremoto," January 24, 2001, on the Internet; CIDAI, "Consideraciones económicas, sociales y políticas del terremoto del 13 de enero," *ECA* 627-628 (2001), pp. 29-57; IDHUCA, "Vulnerabilidad . . . ¿hasta cuándo?," *ECA* 627-628 (2001); José Miguel Cruz, "Terremotos y salud psicosocial," *ECA* 629 (2001), pp. 279-282; Mauricio Gaborit, "Desastres y trauma psicológico," *ECA 631-632* (2001), pp. 473-495; María Santacruz Giralt y José Miguel Cruz, "El impacto psicosocial de los terremotos: una aproximación empírica," *ECA* 631-632 (2001), pp. 497-517.

ence: *physical, psychological, economic, cultural,* and *religious* vulnerability. Together, these aspects reflect the image of an extremely poor country.

Physical vulnerability. The physical destruction has been enormous. It covered two-thirds of the country, including the most densely populated areas. According to tentative official data from February 15 (two days after the second earthquake), there were 1,159 dead, 7,538 injured, 37 missing, 1,452,608 people suffering material losses, 68,777 evacuated, 106 hospitals and clinics damaged, 286,471 homes destroyed or seriously damaged, 1,179 public buildings damaged, 1,597 schools damaged and 91 destroyed, 405 churches damaged or destroyed, 43 boat docks damaged. For a small country like El Salvador, this was an enormous disaster.

Except in the landslide at La Colina, the destruction of homes mainly affected those built of straw and mud or adobe. This type of construction is found in old urban areas, rural towns, and peasant villages; thus the people most affected are the poor. "The earthquake showed that the quality of housing is another decisive risk factor, especially the informal and marginal housing available to most of the population of the country."[13]

Psychological vulnerability. The earthquake has manifested—and intensified—the psychological vulnerability of the country, which was already at a high level. According to the Medical College, the various forms of psychological depression constitute one of the ten most important reasons for medical visits. The Institute of Legal Medicine has registered a growing suicide rate. Aggressivity and violence, which reflect a lack of adaptation to the environment, are endemic especially among young people. The homicide rate for males, twenty to forty years of age, is now 166 per 100,000 inhabitants, according to the Institute of Legal Medicine.[14] This psychological fragility was not caused by the earthquake, obviously, but the deterioration of and lack of treatment for mental health have exacerbated the effects of post-traumatic stress from the earthquake.

For example, according to research in one community,[15] more than 65 percent of medical visits after the earthquake were due to psychological trauma: anxiety and anguish, sleeplessness, "body tremors," "wanting to scream and run out," headaches, etc. In some places there

---

[13]CIDAI, "Consideraciones económicas, sociales y políticas," p. 34.
[14]Cf. J. M. Tojeira, "Reflexiones sobre el terremoto," pp. 2-3.
[15]Cf. José Miguel Cruz, "Terremotos y salud psicosocial," pp. 279 ff.

was increased alcoholism, intensified social and community conflict, and a heightened awareness of personal insecurity. And I repeat, this type of psychological reaction developed especially in poor communities with scarce resources, with a long history of victimization in their living conditions, with no effective action by national institutions to address their most basic needs. This already was causing psychological disorders, which were intensified by the earthquake:

> Thousands of citizens, already anxious about daily food and more or less dignified clothing, were suddenly faced with the loss of a safe place to live, of the basic resources for subsistence, and in some cases, of support from family members who were now dead. Thus the tragedy shattered the precarious balance of subsistence and led to fears of a greater tragedy. This has aggravated the already precarious mental health of the population.[16]

Economic vulnerability. The earthquake has deepened the country's economic vulnerability. Without counting the direct costs (loss of basic infrastructure, machinery, transportation equipment, damage to agricultural land and irrigation systems) and indirect costs (goods not produced), the total estimated costs from the January 13 earthquake are about a billion dollars. If we add the costs from sectors of production for which data are not yet available, the total costs will probably reach about $1.65 billion, about 13 or 14 percent of the gross internal product. Since the earthquake affected a population sector with very little capital accumulation, the damage in some cases may represent 80 to 100 percent of what the poor sectors possessed.[17]

All this increases the enormous inequality in income distribution; today the richest 20 percent of the population make sixteen times as much as the poorest 20 percent. Neoliberalism further impoverishes the poor, it does not guarantee a minimum standard of living, and it does not allow for savings. The earthquake has led to an additional increase in layoffs and unemployment.

Socio-cultural vulnerability. It is hard, especially for the poor, to accept the truth of what happened in the earthquake, the use and misuse of the aid, the decisions made. It is also harder for them to evaluate the information and the pseudoculture that people try to impose on them.

---

[16]*Ibid.*, p. 281.

[17]CIDAI, "Consideraciones económicas, sociales, y políticas del terremoto del 13 de enero," pp. 37 ff.

Furthermore, through the *religious* component of the culture, in a macabre way they may become the victims of psychological oppression when preachers tell them that the earthquake is a divine punishment.[18] This may increase their panic, since if that is the cause, there could easily be more punishments. It also deepens their sense of guilt and decreases their self-esteem and dignity, all of which adds to the psychological disorders mentioned earlier.

To this litany of vulnerabilities we may add that "the country lacks the appropriate juridical instruments to regulate both the functions of the State and individual responsibilities with respect to situations affecting the common good, such as disaster prevention and risk reduction; there has been very little progress in this sense."[19]

We could analyze these vulnerabilities in more detail, but the important thing is the conclusion described at the beginning of this book: life is always a heavy burden, and for the poor it is especially hard to bear. The poor are always more vulnerable to life's hardships, and more helpless in the face of social dangers and ills. In "normal" times they are less protected against bank fraud, controllable diseases like dengue and diarrhea, and death from adulterated beverages.[20] In "earthquake" times the poor are less able to secure the credit they need to rebuild their homes.[21] They are more exposed to corruption, arbitrary action, and cruelty.[22] This is why—although 1.5 million Salvadorans (a quarter of the population) have emigrated to the United States and other countries in the past twenty years—since the earthquake many thousands more have come to see emigration as the only solution.

Of course an earthquake does not have an electronic eye, to seek out and destroy poor people and their homes. All it needs is to strike a structurally poor country, and we can take as given that it will destroy

---

[18]According to a survey by IUDOP, almost 40 percent of Salvadorans draw a connection between the earthquake and the divinity; 26.7 percent of the total (54.2 percent of Evangelical church members, 14.8 percent of Catholics) believe that the disaster "was foretold in the Bible"; 12.8 per cent of the total (12.1 percent of Catholics, 11.4 percent of Evangelical church members, 19.4 percent of members of other religions) believe it is God's punishment for human behavior. See *Carta a las Iglesias* 473 (2001), p. 6.

[19]IDHUCA, "Vulnerabilidad . . . ¿hasta cuándo?" p. 117.

[20]I mention these deaths from dengue, diarrhea, and poisoning from industrial alcohol because they have occurred recently.

[21]Some banks require that a family member have a monthly salary of 5,000 colones or more as a condition for credit; that is impossible for most earthquake victims.

[22]For example, some farm workers who lost their rundown houses were given building materials donated by international solidarity groups. But they have not been allowed to use them because the land under their houses did not belong to them, but to the landowners. They now have wood and corrugated roofing, but the landowners do not let them use it.

mostly poor homes and injure mostly poor people. Around the same time as the earthquake in El Salvador, another struck Seattle without tragic consequences. Another in Japan left twenty people injured and caused much less damage. Apart from the likely differences in magnitude, we can predict in advance that the consequences of an earthquake will be very different in poor and rich countries. Just as it happens with human rights: we are not all equal.

From the consequences of the earthquake we can deduce that El Salvador *is* a poor country, more so since the earthquake. The United Nations Development Program recently reported that the earthquake had caused "a serious increase in poverty."[23] Thus the earthquake reinforces a kind of macabre tautology: it impoverishes the country because the country is poor. Thus an earthquake not only causes damage, but unmasks the lie and reveals the fundamental truth: El Salvador is an extremely poor country. It also shows the truth of Ellacuría's words: there are "crucified peoples," not only individuals or groups but immense majorities of poor and vulnerable people. We must hold on to these words, because people are trying to hide or trivialize the prevalence of crucifixion in today's world, in spite of reports like the ones published annually by the UNDP. This is the truth of our world.

An earthquake causes many kinds of damage. What happened first in El Salvador was the destruction of the homes of poor, simple people, the "houses" of many families, the most basic human grouping. I want to reflect briefly on that.

The earthquake demolished the "houses" of the poor, their physical domicile. But the falling walls revealed an even greater poverty. The poor have little, almost nothing, of the wherewithal needed to live, to prevail in life. Not only the "house," but the home is poor. The earthquake has revealed the vulnerability of the Salvadoran *house* and *home*. If an earthquake can leave a quarter of a country's population homeless, a sin is being committed against life in that country.

Remember that the Greek word for home is *oikos*, from which come the words *oiko-nomia* (economy: to manage the house, make possible the basics of life); *oikoumene* (ecumene: the whole *inhabited* earth,

---

[23]The earthquakes caused "over 225,000 persons (3.6 percent of the total population), who were not previously poor, to fall into poverty; over 200,000 persons (3.3 percent of the total population) fell into extreme poverty. The national poverty rate is estimated to have increased from 47.5 to 51.1 percent, and extreme poverty from 20.3 to 23.6 percent" (PNUD, *Informe sobre desarrollo humano. El Salvador 2001,* San Salvador, p. 52).

although contemporary usage is limited to the ecclesial sphere); and
oiko-logia (ecology, a neologism reflecting the cosmos as a habitable
home). Remembering this will help to clarify an important point.

We said in an earlier chapter that an earthquake is not only a natural but a historico-social reality. In an earthquake what happens to
the economy, the *ecumene*, and the ecology of the country partly determines what will happen to the *oikos*, the home. If there is massive
destruction of family homes in an earthquake, it indicates that the
economy is not doing well, that is, not prepared to protect the *oikos* of
the poor. That clearly is the case: the Salvadoran economy was not
designed to make possible the homes of peasants and slumdwellers. If
mother earth has been injured more than was necessary in an earthquake, it indicates that the ecology is not being taken seriously; Las
Colinas showed that to be the case. In a more metaphorical sense, if
the people have nowhere to go in an earthquake, it indicates something wrong with the *ecumene*: its universality is failing.

Not building a human economy and destroying the ecology are ways
of collaborating with earthquakes and other natural catastrophes in
the destruction of the *oikos*, the home. Economic and ecological destructiveness often work together against the majorities:

> Economic-ecological conflicts today are mostly conflicts between
> the great foreign companies and local inhabitants; thus they are
> conflicts of interest between the exploitation and the habitability
> of nature.[24]

The future of the *oikos*? International organizations had already
predicted that by the year 2000, two billion people would be living in
shacks or other structures unworthy of human habitation. Gustavo
Gutiérrez wonders about today's world: "Where will the poor sleep in
the twenty-first century?"

With respect to physical housing in El Salvador, the UNDP study
cited earlier[25] reported that it would take about eighty-nine years to
eliminate the housing deficit. According to the government's National
Emergency Committee (COEN), 186,444 housing units were destroyed
and another 153,011 damaged in the earthquake. By figures published
in August, the most optimistic short-term projection would allow for
the building of 12,439 new housing units. That leaves a deficit of

---

[24]J. Moltmann, "Progreso y precipicio. Recuerdos del futuro del mundo moderno,"
Isidorianum 18 (2000), p. 252. The reason for this is well known.
  [25]*Ibid.*, p. 140.

174,005.[26] This is the state of the Salvadoran "house," which also speaks eloquently about the state of the "home," or what living means to the Salvadoran people.

INIQUITOUS INEQUALITY: COMPARATIVE HARM

We have seen how the earthquake shows the reality of a crucified people. We have also said that an earthquake does not crucify everyone equally, and this leads to a second reflection: an earthquake reveals the fallacy of human *equality* and *universality* that is often portrayed as the reality of our world. Let us be clear: that all human beings possess equal dignity and came into the world with the same rights is hopefully true as a utopia that might be realized as an end result of humanization in history. But in the present historical reality it is absolutely false to say that we all have the same rights; the way to that humanization is not even visible on the horizon—although by speaking of equality we may be able, in some small way, to avoid giving more power to those who threaten the life of the poor. It is good to declare equal rights as a utopia, but not to act as if it were true.

We are not equal when it comes to the basic necessities of life. We are not equal when it comes to enjoying dignity, respect, consideration, being taken seriously, being able to speak for ourselves, to make choices. For the enjoyment of life and human rights it helps to have been born in Bonn or in Boston, rather than in Rwanda or Honduras.[27]

Being human does not necessarily mean being able to have everything one needs to survive, to have a simple home, to get simple medicines for one's sick children, etc. One must also be North American, European, Soviet, or Japanese in order to be able to count on sufficient resources to survive and to enjoy the resources that God, through nature and reason, put in the world for everyone. Indeed it is more important to be a citizen of a rich, powerful country than to be human; the former offers more real rights and effective possibilities than does the latter. This is a breach of human solidarity.[28]

Neither are we equal when it comes to an earthquake; rather, an earthquake shows how unequal we are. To escape the destructive ef-

---

[26]Cf. "El drama de la vivienda," *Carta a las Iglesias* 480 (2001), p. 7.

[27]Cf. what we wrote in "Los derechos humanos y los pueblos oprimidos," *Revista Latinoamericana de Teología* 43 (1998), pp. 79-102, especially pp. 96-98.

[28]I. Ellacuría, "Subdesarrollo y derechos humanos," *Revista Latinoamericana de Teología* 25 (1992), pp. 5 ff.

fects of an earthquake—and to rebuild what has been destroyed—it is more important to be rich and powerful than to be Salvadoran or simply human.

"We are not equal" is itself a euphemism that does not convey the real meaning of that inequality. There is nothing well-sounding and well-spoken (euphemistic) about that reality; it is terrifying. We shall come back to this from an evangelical perspective, but for now let us say that this abyss of inequality was magnificently described in the parable mentioned earlier:

> There was a rich man who was dressed in purple and fine linen and who feasted sumptuously every day. And at his gate lay a poor man named Lazarus, covered with sores, who longed to satisfy his hunger with what fell from the rich man's table; even the dogs would come and lick his sores. (Lk 16:19-21)

The story juxtaposes the rich man and the poor man, without explicitly mentioning the causal relationship between the two situations: the rich man's injustice creates Lazarus' misery. But here let us focus on the *juxtaposition* itself, the mere coexistence of Dives and Lazarus, because it produces something in the human conscience that may be— I'm not sure—even more primordial than the indignation we feel toward injustice. It is the ultimate shame that humanity feels—or should feel—in the face of that iniquitous inequality. It is the affront to decency of taking for granted that "that's the way it is." It is the offense to our intelligence when people try to dampen the protest by "explaining" things to us.

That coexistence of Dives and Lazarus, chronic and permanent, tolerated and accepted, should cause all humanity—at least everyone with a human heart—even before we ask why, to lower our heads in shame, indignation, and anger. Without these primary emotions there may be no solution for the world. Certainly we must insist on analyzing the causes and seeking solutions, but unless we see something deeply wrong in the mere coexistence of Dives and Lazarus—so wrong it means the difference between simple humanity and inhumanity— then there is no solution. In English the word "obscene" harshly describes an unnatural, repulsive situation (with or without sexual overtones). The coexistence of Dives and Lazarus is obscene.

It is obscene, not only unjust, that the affluent world uses 400 times more resources to care for a baby than does Ethiopia. It is obscene that a Salvadoran woman in a *maquila* factory earns U.S. 29 cents to make a shirt that Nike will sell to the NBA for $45.[29] It is obscene that ac-

---

[29]Recently reported by Charles Kernaghan, director of the U.S. National Working

cording to the UNDP, the abyss between rich and poor is growing at a staggering rate: it stood at 1 to 30 in 1960, 1 to 60 in 1990, 1 to 74 in 1997. And still it does not seem to produce a reaction worthy of this metaphysical obscenity. Eduardo Galeano says that "a U.S. citizen is worth 50 Haitians." He adds: "What would happen if a Haitian was worth 50 U.S. citizens?" The question takes us by surprise, but the premise is not at all surprising: we live in a heartless world, in which Dives and Lazarus can live together and nobody cares.

To formulate it as a thesis, the coexistence of wealth and poverty—quite apart from the reasons for it—is a fundamental breach of human solidarity, a negation of humanity:

> The state of underdevelopment, in itself and in comparison with states of development, is a flagrant violation of human solidarity—that is, of the very foundation of human rights, and it brings with it the permanent violation of those rights.[30]

Dives and Lazarus represent an enormous comparative harm in our world. It is an offense to the poor, caused by the mere fact of their poverty alongside the opulence of others.

In conclusion: If we do not see the "harm" of the comparison between Dives and Lazarus, if it does not produce a primal "shame" in us, if it does not "shame" us into overcoming the scandal, then our dehumanization has hit bottom. We must either be restored to a sense of social decency or impassively contemplate the shame of humanity, gaze serenely at the wealthy and the poor—and create more of them in the process.

Scholars say that when Jesus told some of his parables, he appealed to the deepest feelings of his listeners (who were often his adversaries), in order to make them change. Thus in the parable of the lost sheep, or of the hope-starved prodigal son, he was saying to his adversaries: "Have you no compassion for these poor people? Don't they turn your insides out?" We might add that in the story of Dives and Lazarus he may be saying to us: "Aren't you ashamed to live in a world like this, of wealthy and poor, of lavish world championships and African famines?"

Medellín, Puebla, and Santo Domingo[31] spoke of the poor, and—in

---

Committee for Human Rights. Cf. "La vergüenza de las maquilas," *Carta a las Iglesias* 474 (2001), p. 11.

[30]I. Ellacuría, "Subdesarrollo y los derechos humanos," *Revista Latinoamericana de Teología* 25 (1992), p. 4.

[31]Puebla in particular offers an inspiring description of the flesh-and-blood faces

surprisingly ecclesial language—described them as the *product* of the wealthy; that is, they identified the cause of poverty. But before analyzing the causes, they expressed the primal feelings of outrage and shame it causes: "The luxury of a few is an offense to the misery of the great masses" (Puebla, 28).

An earthquake reveals an enormous comparative harm. If we do not recognize it, if we are not shamed by it and do not feel it as an offense to the poor and to all decent human beings, if we do not put an end to it, then shamelessness is stalking the planet along with unrecognition, unconcern, disrespect. In short, a negation of the "human family."

THE CHRISTIAN TRADITION: POVERTY, INEQUALITY, AND INJUSTICE

The poverty and inequality we have described are obvious. All human beings should be able to recognize them, but they do not, and it is a serious matter. So let us return to the subject of the poor as it has been discussed since the time of Jesus. To begin with, the tradition of Jesus sets out the great truth: the massive, cruel, and unjust reality of the poor. From there it derives the consequences: a denunciation of those who cause poverty and a defense of the poor.

The Reality of the Poor

Anyone halfway knowledgeable about theology knows that Jesus is the central figure in the gospels. They should also know that Jesus' purpose is to establish the kingdom of God, and that this kingdom is primarily for the poor. This basic fact is enough to make the poor—*a priori* at least—a central feature of the gospels. But their centrality is also clear when we analyze the texts. We can say in thesis form that if the poor were to disappear from the gospels (where they are present not only by name but in many other ways), the gospel text would be greatly diminished. The qualitative element is even more important than the quantitative: without the reality of the poor the person, words, and praxis of Jesus would become meaningless. So would his prayer to the Father and his fate on the cross. Let us look at this very briefly.

---

of the poor, children, Indians, peasants, and the marginalized (nn. 31-39). In the same way, Santo Domingo explicitly mentioned the Indians and African Americans. This was not only a rhetorical device, but provided the basis for their denunciation of injustice in the shocking abyss between poor and rich, between the oppressed and the oppressors.

The *majorities*, "the people," appear frequently in the gospels. The Greek word used to describe them is *óchlos*,[32] and it has a very precise meaning: the *multitude of the people*, implying the insignificant and unworthy sectors of society. Their situation is extremely hard, desperate in many cases. They walk along battered and bent over, like sheep without a shepherd. They are often seen following Jesus, because they cannot find salvation anywhere else; thus the repeated comment that "they came to him from everywhere." So there are *majorities*, and they are *poor*.

Poverty has an inherently historical dimension; that is obviously why we do not find it defined in the gospels. The authors describe it in slightly different ways, although they coincide on the basics. Thus according to J. Jeremias, in the Palestine of Jesus' time the poor are seen in generic terms as bent under the burden of life; the despised and marginalized are identified by their occupation or religious behavior.[33] According to J. M. Castillo, the poor can be classified in four groups: the sick, sinners and tax collectors, the dispossessed, and women.[34] A. Pieris offers a broader description: the poor are the *socially excluded* (lepers and the mentally handicapped), the *religiously marginalized* (prostitutes and tax collectors), the *culturally oppressed* (women and children), the *socially dependent* (widows and orphans), the *physically impaired* (in hearing, speech, mobility, or sight), the *psychologically tormented* (demon-possessed and epileptic), the *spiritually humble* (simple God-fearing people, repentant sinners).[35]

Furthermore, the gospels insist that the poor are in a situation of inequality with the non-poor, the rich and powerful. Since Jesus' ministry took place in Galilee, in a first-century agrarian society, we can clearly see the great inequality between the *óchlos* and other social classes. With regard to economic and social status, there was an "abyss" between the upper classes (leaders, rulers, priests, functionaries, and merchants) and the lower classes (peasants, craftsmen, the *despised*). From a religious viewpoint there was an abyss and a contradiction between the *haber*, pure and untainted, and the *'am-ha'ares*, the impure,

---

[32]Four terms are used in the New Testament with reference to the *people*: *dêmos* (people, country), which is clearly secondary; *laós* (people), with religious connotations; *éthnos* (multitude, people, nation). The most commonly used term is *óchlos* (people, multitude, persons); it appears 175 times in the gospels and the Book of Acts alone.

[33]J. Jeremias, *Teología del Nuevo Testamento* 1 (Sígueme, Salamanca, 1972), pp. 134-138.

[34]José María Castillo, *Los pobres y la teología* (DDB, Bilbao, 1997); *El reino de Dios. Por la vida y la dignidad de los seres humanos* (DDB, Bilbao, 1999).

[35]"Cristo más allá del dogma. Hacer cristología en el contexto de las religiones de los pobres (I)," *Revista Latinoamericana de Teología* 52 (2001), p. 14.

contaminated category, which included the uncivilized and ignorant.

We do not find in the gospels any concept, let alone a clear one, of the poor. But taking the gospels as a whole, the poor have these characteristics: 1) They are on the underside of history and have to bear its weight; their life is a burden, hard to bear; they are *really, materially* poor, not only by choice or spiritually.[36] 2) They are socially segregated and despised, which usually (though not always) coincides with poverty as previously described; they suffer "dishonor," the greatest evil in that society. 3) There is an abyss of inequality between the poor and the rich and powerful. 4) That burden and dishonor are expressed in different ways, but together they distinguish the *óchlos,* the great majorities.

Although poverty must be defined sociologically, from the perspective of different times and places, we cannot escape the conclusion: in the society where Jesus lived there were human beings for whom living was the hardest job, and whose greatest hope was for dignity (overcoming disrespect and dishonor).

Thus the first lesson of the Christian tradition is to take the existence of the poor very seriously, as a massive reality whose life and dignity are threatened. The very way they are presented assumes a rejection of that reality. Sometimes that rejection is interpreted theologically in depth: God denounces poverty, claims the poor as his own, defends them and loves them. This is the good news.

Times and circumstances change, but today also the gospel helps to see what is fundamental: the poor and their poverty are still with us, even in times of globalization and its promises. It is true that the people are "always" crucified, and that only the "form" of crucifixion changes. Gustavo Gutiérrez insists on this, in the context of the present reality of our world:

> The poor person is the "insignificant" one, the one considered a "non-person," someone whose full rights as a human being are not recognized. People without social or individual substance, who count for little in society and in the Church. This is how they are seen, or rather not seen, because they are rendered invisible by their exclusion from the world of our time. There are many reasons

---

[36]In New Testament Greek, *ptochos* is the term most commonly used to describe the poor. Of the twenty-five times it appears, twenty-two refer to the economically afflicted and dispossessed. In the three places where *ptochos* refers to spiritual poverty (Mt 5:3; cf. Gal 4:9; Rev 3:17), further description is added. And in the three cases where Jesus relates the kingdom of God to the *ptochos* (Mt 11:5, Lk 4:18, and Lk 6:20), the meaning is not spiritualized. We can conclude that in the New Testament and for Jesus, the term "poor" is a sociological category.

for this: economic scarcity is certainly one, but also the color of their skin, being a woman, belonging to a despised culture (or one seen as merely exotic, which comes to the same thing).[37]

The faces of the poor and their poverty may change, but they always have something in common. In an effort to put it in formal and dialectical categories, I sometimes think that the poor are above all "those who don't take life for granted" (in a world where others do take it for granted); "those who are close to death" (in a world where others are well protected from death and close to life, sometimes a life of luxury); "those who have (almost) all the powers of this world effectively arrayed against them" (in a world where the minorities who cause the poor have the powers on their side).[38] Playing with the imagery suggested by the destruction an earthquake causes, we might say that the poor are those who live "out in the wind and rain."

The Poor, Product of Greed and Injustice

Let us go a step further. We have said the earthquake shows how unequal we are, and we have reflected on that fact itself—because the first thing people want to do with an aberration, and the comparative harm it causes, is to pass it off as a natural fact. But the Christian biblical tradition also looks for reasons why (as the Marxist tradition, and other theological and ecclesiastical traditions in the line of Medellín, did years ago). Let us review it briefly.

In the biblical tradition there are two interrelated types of answers to the question about iniquitous inequality. The first, fundamental one is *injustice*.[39] A few texts will suffice. The prophets of Israel roar: "They sell the righteous for silver, and the needy for a pair of sandals—they who trample the head of the poor into the dust of the earth, and push the afflicted out of the way" (Amos 2:6-7). "[T]hat widows may be your spoil, and that you may make orphans your prey!" (Is 10:2). In the New Testament, James roars: "But you have dishonored the poor. . . . The wages of the laborers who mowed your fields, which you kept back by fraud, cry out" (Jas 2:6, 5:4). The condemnation of injustice was alive and well in the early church. Listen to St. Jerome

---

[37]"Situación y tareas de la teología de la liberación," *Revista Latinoamericana de Teología* 50 (2000), pp. 109 ff.

[38]This is especially true in times of repression and war. In normal times we might describe them as those whom (almost) no power takes seriously.

[39]I am pointing out the high moments of the biblical tradition, fully aware that for centuries—especially in Christendom periods—the tradition has been absent and even persecuted in the Church.

in the fourth century: "All riches proceed from injustice, and unless one loses, another cannot find" (*Cartas* PL 22, p. 984).

Centuries later, early in the colonial period, Montesinos and Las Casas used equally strong language against the oppression of the Indians by Spanish *encomenderos*. With Marxism and the new social consciousness of the Church (Medellín, social doctrine) there was a profound analysis of injustice. Just before the paragraph that describes the faces of the poor, Puebla adamantly affirms that there are mechanisms that "at the international level make some people richer and richer, by making others poorer and poorer" (n. 30). Monsignor Romero often said to us with crystal clarity: "If we want the violence and all suffering to end, we have to go to its roots. And here are the roots: in social injustice."[40] The problem of poverty is fundamentally one of justice.

But there is a second tradition, related to the first, that emphasizes *greed* as the particular evil of the rich. Strictly speaking, their sin should not be described in terms of *injustice* but of *greed*, ambition, lust for wealth, although the practical consequences are the same: greed generates poverty just as injustice does. This is what Jesus denounced directly, and its macabre outcome is brilliantly described in the oft-cited parable of Dives and Lazarus. This doesn't mean that Jesus ignored injustice,[41] or that he simply brought Dives and Lazarus together, with no relationship between them.[42] But Jesus' condemnation of greed, and the reasons for it, are worth remembering in our time. To put it in today's language, Jesus does not accept the "invisible hand" or the "impersonal laws of the marketplace." Behind them are real human beings, "the interests of the stockholders"—that is, greed, the desire to acquire, even when it means pushing aside the needs of the poor or making them more needy. Wealth, my wealth, is proclaimed as a god (cf. Mt 6:24; Lk 16:13). "I am God." It is important to remember "ambition," so as not to use unjust structures as an escape from the need for personal change as well, change in the high standards of living that people tend to take for granted as normal.

The best way to explain how poverty is "produced" in our world is in terms of the objective injustice that shapes society, because it is a structural reality, fundamentally independent of people's intentions. But it

---

[40]Homily of September 30, 1979.

[41]See J. I. González Faus, *Jesús y los ricos de su tiempo*, México, 1987. Some of the collected diatribes against scribes and Pharisees in Mt 23:1-36, Lk 11:37-53, and Mk 12:38-40 are against injustice as well as hypocrisy.

[42]"The Old Testament dialectic of social class is implicit in this understanding of rich and poor" (G. M. Soares Prabhu, "Clase en la Biblia: los pobres, ¿una clase social?" *Revista Latinoamericana de Teología* 12 [1987], pp. 228 ff.).

is still important to remember that the rich—"rich people," the Group of eight other nations—are "greedy," sometimes insatiably so, although tactically they may moderate their greed in order to sustain it over time. The natural destiny of greed is injustice. Greed is so deeply rooted that it continues in the presence of Lazarus, the beggar. In El Salvador it continues in the presence of the earthquake victims:

> Many merchants have come out ahead: more demand, more supply. Construction companies have done well. Vendors of building materials have raised their prices and are increasing their profits. The banks have benefited from a growing number of new accounts for emergency aid and reconstruction programs.[43]

The lucid words of the New Testament are still true: "For the love of money is a root of all kinds of evil" (1 Tim 6:10). Perhaps those words should replace "In God we trust" on the dollar, since they are a better expression of its purpose.

THE UNCONCEALABLE SIN

Let us come back to the earthquake and take one last step. The earthquake tore off the mask of a healthy, apparently fairly prosperous country, and scientifically—that is, by its results—confirms the truth of the neoliberal policy in this country. After years of post-war demagoguery, the earthquake also shows the deep division, the antagonism within Salvadoran society. It shows a society made up of a few rich people, with every chance of recovering, and a large number of very poor, with very little chance of recovering. The words of the prophet Isaiah still echo against "those who add field to field (bank to bank)—until there is room for no one but you" (Is 5:8). Thus the earthquake also shows that we live in an unreconciled society, and shows the deepest roots of that unreconciliation.[44]

---

[43]Ismael Moreno, S.J., "Reflexión y propuesta eclesial desde la crisis post-terremotos (I)," *Carta a las Iglesias* 475-476 (2001), p. 6.

[44]On the occasion of the visit of Pope John Paul II to El Salvador in 1996 we wrote that it seemed inappropriate, even dangerous, to raise the problem of reconciliation in terms of overcoming the hatred of war, and not in terms of overcoming economic injustice. The earthquake reveals the latter. Of course some powerful people—from the goodness of their hearts, and more or less out of conviction—offered aid in the time of the earthquake. But this brings no substantial change, for it does not change the substance of their lives and the leadership they stamp on the country. See "La preparación de la visita de Juan Pablo II. Breves reflexiones teológicas," *ECA* 567-568 (1996), pp. 17-28.

At times like these, capitalism in any of its forms may come to mind. It threatens or kills millions of human beings, in this country and throughout the Third World, and increasingly also in the First World. And it endures over time, although it tries to disguise its effects. It plunges boldly forward, and for good reason: neoliberalism has no scruples. Some say it doesn't even know what harm it causes; it believes it is proclaiming good news (Hugo Assmann). It shows no signs of effective conversion, although now it uses more polished language; and when confronted with the evidence it has no choice but to admit its limitations (remember the "confessions" of the World Bank and the International Monetary Fund). But this is a long way from heartfelt sorrow, a decision to reform, the acceptance of penalties, and above all restitution, returning what has been taken from the respective peoples. Every two or three years there is a natural catastrophe (earthquake, flood, drought) somewhere in Central America; each successive tragedy fails to teach much of anything, or to contribute effectively to avoiding or minimizing the next one.

The earthquake has torn off the cosmetic mask of the system. Promises of sustainable development collapse because of the country's unsustainable economic infrastructure. The siren songs of democracy have become a cacophony because the majorities are so absolutely unequal before the law, and especially before life. The arrogance of a political leadership that claims to have things under control has also collapsed in the face of its powerlessness, not only to protect against such massive damage, but to manage the incoming aid and especially to look toward the future. What national vision do the local rulers and oligarchies, the empire and the international banking system have to offer? Compared with the gravity of the situation, what we have is laziness and negligence, rivalry and stubbornness. And there are no encouraging signs that the tragedy of the earthquake has helped to build awareness and efforts to root out our other national tragedies: violence, political ineptitude, and corruption, the abandonment of social leadership.

We used to talk about sin, perhaps excessively, often superficially, even masochistically and unfairly. We talked about many kinds of sin, sins against God and against the Church, capital, mortal and venial sins. Luther called the conscientious examination of those sins "human butchery," and he was not far wrong. So it is just as well that the obsession and horror once caused by the language of "sin" have disappeared. But with the language gone, sin itself tends to disappear from the collective consciousness—and has been declared dead, nonexistent, in the sphere of social reality. That is not good.

In times of greater spiritual sophistication, sin was taken more seriously. The psalmist prayed to God in all sincerity: "Clear me from hidden faults" (Ps 19:12). Today we would rather keep sin hidden. The human tragedy is expressed only in *numbers*. In numbers we express the behavior of the economy and the distribution of wealth and poverty; in numbers we report violence, deaths, injuries, and disappearances. The legal and illegal emigrants who have to flee the country are represented in numbers. But we also have words, not only numbers, with which to say things: there is sin, and it is sin to kill human beings.

So the earthquake makes it harder to conceal sin, which is essential to the Christian tradition. John speaks of "the sin of the world," and Paul speaks in the singular of *hamartia*, sin as power. With greater simplicity the synoptics described it as sin to put Jesus to death on the cross. That sin—killing, creating victims, cooperating in the death of the powerless—has not disappeared from this country or from the planet. Quite the contrary.

The earthquake has unmasked all that. It has shown that there are immense majorities of the poor who do not take life for granted; their life itself is threatened. The earthquake has pointed out where sin, poverty, and injustice are most cruelly focused: on women and children, on peasant men and women, on those who have lost jobs and those who cannot get credit, on those who have practically no decision-making power over their own lives and future.

Perhaps now is the time for a final word about the Church and the earthquake, at least on one point. The Church made what was certainly an important, unusual, and difficult decision to proclaim the need for an "option for the poor." It specified that the option is "preferential," not exclusive, in order not to antagonize anyone—but even so, we know well how hard it is for Christians and other human beings to put into practice. Ironically, earthquakes and catastrophes show that there is no option with misfortune and misery. It works with certainty, *ex opere operato*: the poor are vulnerable and attract all sorts of evil and misfortune, simply because they are poor. It follows that the Church should embrace the poor and pour out its life for them just as certainly as catastrophes seize hold of them. An "option" is appropriate in the realm of freedom. But the "option for the poor" also belongs to the realm of necessity. It is a non-optional option. I pray that the earthquake can help the Church to see it that way.

All irony aside, the earthquake again makes clear that most of reality is poor and that taking an option for the poor means taking an option for reality. It means deciding for real participation in reality. So the option for the poor is not something extraordinary, let alone esoteric. It also should not be thought of as the ultimate way of being Christian and human, but rather as a first, fundamental step. Certainly Christian faith gives a qualitative motivation to the option, but the mere fact of its quantitative reality should be enough to show the need for a free acceptance of that option.

In conclusion: the poor are suffering in this country, and the poor countries are suffering in relation to other nations. The "same thing" happens, almost always, to "the same people." "Everyone else" goes on living splendidly. But then comes the concealment: "There has not been any sin here. The crucified people are an invention of feverish, resentful minds unwilling to acknowledge the progress we have made." The people close to reality see it differently:

> After the post-earthquake emergency passes, the tendency has been to seek "normalization," incorporating the rubble and the victims into the everyday dynamic: "Nothing happened here." That tendency is imposed by big capital, by the well-off. Life goes on as usual for them. The poor, as usual, are the losers. Now there are more poor, and those who were poor are poorer than before: "That is all that's happened."[45]

Reality shows how right Ellacuría was. The truth is that there is a "crucified people." The "form of crucifixion" changes, but the crucifixion goes on.

---

[45]Ismael Moreno, S.J., "Reflexión y propuesta eclesial desde la crisis post-terremotos (I)", op.cit., p. 6.

5

PRIMORDIAL SAINTLINESS

Out of the midst of the earthquake came the force of life, the longing to live and the decision to live, and the situation endowed it with a unique, primal power. The only way to describe it is in nonconventional language; that is why we speak of "primordial saintliness." By that we mean that life is *holy* [saintly], and defending it is *holy*; it is *fascinating* to see life struggling to survive, and *fascinating* to see people devoted to strengthening it. In these acts of defending and strengthening life, we can also see the primordial saintliness of "human nature."

We also use "primordial saintliness" as the antithesis of "primordial sin," taking life, giving death. We referred to the latter in the last chapter; looking at them both together makes the meaning of each one clearer.

That is what we want to analyze in this chapter: the goodness that has become apparent through the earthquake and because of it. We shall do so in three steps. First, by analyzing the meaning of "primordial saintliness." Second, by showing how this primordial saintliness can become a "principle of solidarity among unequals." And third, by showing how it can also become a "principle of civilization" from below, how out of the context of poverty it can lead the way to a civilized universalization of the human family. This chapter will close with a reflection on the "countercultural" dimension of goodness, to help us understand a scandalous fact: why this "primordial saintliness" is so often hidden, and so little used, when it is so needful and beneficial.

PRIMORDIAL SAINTLINESS
AND PRIMORDIAL MARTYRDOM

In this section we shall focus on what happens as a *direct* result of an earthquake: the will to live and the struggle for life. As we said in the first chapter, the earthquake showed life in all its primacy: the parade of people struggling for survival, women carrying "what is left of the house" on their heads and leading their children by the hand; the old man sitting beside the sign, "Armenia lives." It also showed primordial solidarity: women cooking and sharing what little was left after the earthquake, men moving mountains of earth to search for buried human beings. . . . The force of life imposed itself on the tragedy, and human goodness made its presence known in spite of everything. Those women and children, men and old people, cooking and sharing, sifting through the rubble together, become an ever-present signpost pointing to the primacy of life.

To say this is not to make a virtue of necessity, but rather to let the *mystery* of life show through. In the famous words of Rudolf Otto, the earthquake showed the mystery as *fascinans et tremens*, as simultaneously fascinating and horrifying. The earthquake clearly expressed the element of *tremens* in the mystery, but there was also, despite everything, an element of *fascinans*. There is something *fascinating* in the will to life, and there is something that inspires *veneration* in the victims' suffering and desire; they want simply to survive, and help others survive.

That *primacy and ultimacy of life* is what we want to analyze. We shall begin with the existential impact it produces. Then we shall look at it more conceptually, as a theological and biblical reflection. Although it may seem so, this reflection is not at all superfluous in normal times and for affluent societies, where life in all its primacy is taken for granted and the effects of a catastrophe are softened substantially.

The reason is that the primacy of life as we see it in a catastrophe can help us to focus on the basics, life and solidarity; it helps us to unmask the superfluous, unnecessary, and even dehumanizing elements that a certain civilization and concept of progress have introduced into normal life. And it helps us to denounce the inhumanity and injustice that result when some people gain access to superfluous things at the cost of basic needs for others. We do not deny that there is more to life than primary life, or that primary life can and must always unfold into "more" life. But this primary life can help to establish the conditions for real progress and set a right direction for the "more" that is truly humanizing.[1]

The Saintliness of the Victims

The Will to Live in the Midst of Suffering. Something like a primordial saintliness makes its presence known in the primary decision

---

[1]Years ago I wrote a phenomenology of bread, to explain that "bread—as the primary symbol of life—is always more than bread; it unfolds and situates human

to live and give life, as it was seen in the earthquake. I am consciously using the term "saintliness" [holiness]—in a mystagogical way, for I cannot fully conceptualize it—to emphasize the ultimacy of life, understood here not in its universal and generic sense, but as the life of the victims. In the victims' will to live there is something that fascinates, overwhelms, humanizes, reveals the mystery. There is also something that saves and challenges us in an ultimate way.

That is why I say that we cannot yet look for freedom or necessity, virtue or obligation, grace or merit in that saintliness. Saintliness does not have to be accompanied by heroic virtues—which are required for canonization; it is also expressed in a life of everyday heroism. We don't know whether these poor who cry out to live are saints-intercessors or not, but they have the power to move our hearts. They do not perform "miracles," in the sense of violating the laws of nature, which is also required for canonization. But it is not rhetorical to say that their miracles violate the laws of history; it is a miracle to survive in a hostile world that makes their life exceedingly hard.

What we call primordial saintliness is the will to live and to survive amid great suffering, the decision and effort that it requires, the unlimited creativity, the strength, the constancy, defying innumerable problems and obstacles. Even in the midst of catastrophe and daily hardship, the poor and the victims—especially the women, and their children—put into practice and fulfill with distinction God's call to live, and to give life to others.

This is the saintliness of suffering for the will to live, which is different from—more fundamental than—the saintliness of virtue. The poor and the victims do not want us to "imitate" them, as official doctrine tells us to imitate the saints. People seldom imitate them; almost everyone, including the official experts on sainthood and blessedness, tries to avoid imitating "these saints." But their lives inspire humanizing feelings of veneration, wherever there are people of good heart.

These saints also are not mediators across the infinite distance between human beings and God: rather, they are the presence of God. With respect to us they maintain the specific "alterity" of the divine and thus, simultaneously and paradoxically, they make the divine

---

beings in the diverse settings of their life: physical and spiritual, personal and social, praxic and celebratory, historical and transcendent. So we are not denying that there are steps forward, but we do insist that they must start right; otherwise they can and often do lead to dehumanization." See J. Sobrino, "La centralidad del 'reino de Dios' en la teología de la liberación," *Revista Latinoamericana de Teología* 9 (1986), pp. 247-281. See "Central Position of the Reign of God in Liberation Theology," in Sobrino and Ellacuría, eds., *Systematic Theology* (Maryknoll, NY: Orbis Books, 1996), pp. 38-74.

"present" in the world. In the famous words of César Vallejo: "The lottery vendor who cries, 'A thousand for one' reflects something of God."[2] In the same way these saints are not exactly the path to Christ, but they are his sacrament. They are "vicars of Christ," as people said in the Middle Ages, in a phrase whose lucidity is way ahead of official church awareness in our own time.[3]

Illustrious "virtues" are made present in this primordial saintliness, timeless traditional virtues, and new ones that emerge in times of commitment and liberation: "Solidarity, service, simplicity, openness to the gift of God," as Puebla put it (n. 1147), strength in suffering, commitment to the point of martyrdom, forgiveness for offenders, which we have often seen.

But it is not an idealized saintliness. These poor people and victims may well be "holy sinners," in the conventional understanding of holiness and sin. The poor are also sometimes overcome by the mystery of iniquity; sometimes it leaves them without words. In my view Africa today is the continent that most forcefully shows the presence of both primordial saintliness and the *mysterium iniquitatis*. Its saintliness is visible in television images, and especially in first-person reports from people on the scene. In Mozambique, human beings with faces of hope and despair reach out to helicopters that are their only possible salvation from the floods. In Biafra, Ethiopia, Somalia, mothers with their starving children: there can be no better representation of the crucified God. In South Africa, majorities are condemned to die of AIDS. In the African Great Lakes region, long caravans of women flee death with nothing but their children and their tales of incredible cruelty and misery in jails and refugee camps—yet miraculously accompanied by dignity, love, and hope.

This is primary saintliness, and like all saintliness, it "saves." There are many stories about it; one comes from a religious sister who spent many years in Africa, who wrote during a spiritual retreat in Spain:

> It is not hard to praise and sing when one lives in security. What is surprising is that people who are rebuilding their lives after a catastrophic earthquake, and the prisoners in Kigali whose relatives are struggling today to bring them something to eat, can bless and give thanks to God. How could they not be God's favorites, from whom we must learn the meaning of thanks?

---

[2]Quoted by Gustavo Gutiérrez, *The God of Life* (Maryknoll, NY: Orbis Books, 1991), p.90.

[3]See the book by J. I. González Faus, *Vicarios de Cristo*, Trotta, Madrid, 1991.

Today I received a letter from them. Perhaps they have no idea how much we have received from them, and how they save us.

But the mystery of iniquity is also here. Melchisedek Sikuli, bishop of Butembo, Democratic Republic of Congo, listed the terrible problems of his country in a recent peace congress. He mentioned many: misery, injustice, refugees, women raped, and villages looted, all set on the background of colonialism, which is still supplying the weapons of death. But he ended the list with "the drama of the child-soldiers," and quoted Kouroma's book *Allah Is Not Happy,* in search of words for a tragedy that seems to allow only silence: "When you have no one in the world, no father, no mother, no sister, and you are still a child in a ruined and barbarous country where everyone is killing everyone else, what do you do? You become a child-soldier in order to eat and kill; that is all we can do."[4]

In my opinion, no concepts can express the reality of these child-soldiers, these poor people and victims. The drama is clear. We clearly must condemn the causes that lead to such a reality. But we don't know what to say about the reality itself. It is an extreme example of the tragedy of the poor, and of their "will to live." It may seem exaggerated, demagogic, or blasphemous to go on speaking here of "primordial saintliness." But perhaps it is less so than any other conceptualization we might make—if anyone wants to try—from the standpoint of a world indifferent to, and co-responsible for, such a tragedy.

Anonymous Martyrdom. This reflection about primordial saintliness in the context of the earthquake is similar to what we said some years ago about the recent martyrs of El Salvador and Latin America. We were not thinking then about the victims of an earthquake. Nor were we thinking of famous and noteworthy martyrs, like Rutilio Grande or Monsignor Romero, but rather of men and women, children and the elderly, innocent, defenseless victims of persecution and repression, murdered massively and cruelly in massacres,[5] usually for the simple fact of possessing "subversive" material (the homilies of Monsignor Romero, even the Bible), for living in areas near to or controlled by guerrilla forces, for providing humanitarian assistance (food, medical care) to rebels and sometimes also to government soldiers. We

---

[4]See the full text of Sikuli's address in *Concilium* 293 (2001), pp. 145-147.

[5]One example. In El Mozote, Morazán, El Salvador in 1981, about a thousand men, women, and children, some only months old, were separated into three groups, sent to different places, and murdered, some apparently by burning. There were many other such horrors in El Salvador and Guatemala.

were thinking about the fact that in general, those men and women have remained unknown, anonymous, without the recognition received by better-known martyrs. They don't have names to rescue them from oblivion; they don't have even a generic name (saints, confessors, martyrs, "good Christians" . . .) to express the "dignity of their death" before God.

This anomaly, to put it gently, or rather this scandal, demands an answer. Here in El Salvador the communities began very early to do what they could to remember their "proper names." And many of us spontaneously gave them the (generic) name of "martyrs." Personally I am certain that this was their response to the powerful logic of faith (which need not be justified to curias or academies). What was important was to give them a name befitting their dignity, because we saw in these victims the servant of Yahweh in our own time, a people crucified like Christ. Together with "primordial saintliness," "primordial martyrdom" was making its appearance in the deaths of these majorities.

Moving from this spontaneous reaction to the concept behind it, to explain the positive and polemical meaning of the expression "primordial martyrdom," perhaps we should say a word about a change in the theoretical understanding of martyrdom that occurred in Latin America, beginning more or less at the time of Medellín. An important first step was to understand the reason for martyrdom—more than just the canonical definition of a martyr—not only as death "for the sake of the faith" but also "for the sake of justice." But a second, more fundamental and programmatic step was to understand martyrdom "from the standpoint of Jesus." In this step a martyr is one who in substantial ways lives like Jesus, promotes the cause of Jesus, the reign of God as good news for the poor; enters into conflict with and struggles against the anti-kingdom, the oppressive powers of this world; and is therefore killed as Jesus was. We have given these martyrs, men and women, the name "Jesuanic martyrs."

As important as this new understanding was, it still does not resolve the anomaly or scandal I referred to, for it ignores the massive deaths. The necessary third step comes when we appeal to the analogy of martyrdom, which must be done carefully, for the massive victims raise some questions about the *analogatum princeps* of martyrdom.[6] In this context it is worth noting that the Church has thought about

---

[6]On the analogy of martyrdom, cf. *Jesus the Liberator* (Maryknoll, NY: Orbis Books, 1993), 254-271. More recently we have written "Los mártires jesuánicos en el Tercer Mundo," *Revista Latinoamericana de Teología* 48 (1999), pp. 237-255. See *Witnesses to the Kingdom* (Maryknoll, NY: Orbis Books, 2003), pp. 119-133.

the possibility that the death of soldiers and combatants might be considered as martyrdom,[7] but it has not thought about—has not known what to do with—the innocent victims of massacres, except in the legend of the Holy Innocents, which remains as a tragic, ornamental-theological element in the narratives of the infancy of Jesus.

So the strongest argument for using the analogy, for referring to those who die in massacres as "martyrs," is their similarity to the ultimate aspect of the servant of Yahweh: the suffering servant (Is 52:13-53:12). They do not necessarily represent the "active servant" of the first servant songs, who comes to impart justice and righteousness, but they do reflect with chilling precision the "passive servant," the anguished servant of the final song.

The important thing is that beyond descriptive words, and beyond the use of analogy to clarify concepts, there is an undeniably primary similarity between the massacre victims and Christ at the culminating moment of his crucifixion. These massive, anonymous victims participate utterly in the reality of Jesus. For that reason we call them "martyrs."

That we also call them "primary martyrs" requires some additional explanation. Their death can be compared with that of the Jesuanic martyrs, including Jesus. In comparison with Jesus' death, the massacre victims' deaths are *less* reflective of Jesus' praxis of defending the poor and actively struggling against the anti-kingdom; they are also *less* reflective of Jesus' faithfulness in the face of persecution, and of the freedom with which he confronted death. On the other hand, they express historical innocence *more* exactly, for they have done nothing to deserve death except to be poor (for instance, they have not engaged in prophetic denunciation); and they represent defenselessness *more* fully, for they often did not have even the physical possibility of avoiding death (by fleeing, for example). And above all their deaths show how these majorities unjustly bear the burden of the sin that has been destroying them bit by bit in life, and has completely annihilated them in death.

These majorities, oppressed in life and massacred in death, are the best expression of the overwhelming suffering of the world. It is they who—without presuming or wishing to do so, even without knowing what they are doing—in their own flesh "complete what is lacking in Christ's afflictions." They express *primordial* suffering, even more than the suffering of other martyrs. For that reason we speak of "primor-

---

[7]St. Thomas recognized this possibility in *IV Sent. dist. XLIX, q. V, a. 3, q. 2 ad 11.* In our day it is considered a *quaestio disputata.*

dial martyrdom," which is not measured in terms of subjective saintliness or their defense of faith and justice, but in terms of their suffering; they are the most self-evident victims of the *mysterium iniquitatis.*

> In the traditional language of analogy, although this type of reflection has not been done, if martyrdom is considered as a response to the anti-kingdom by one who struggles actively for the kingdom, the *analogatum princeps* of a martyr is the one exemplifed by Monsignor Romero. If martyrdom is considered as truly bearing the burden of the sin of the anti-kingdom, the *analogatum princeps* is represented by the defenseless majorities who are put to death innocently, massively, and anonymously. . . . It is they who most abundantly and cruelly complete in their flesh what is lacking in Christ's afflictions, and who most tragically reveal the blackness of the world's afflictions.[8]

When we reach this point in the discussion of what I have called primordial saintliness and primordial martyrdom, although it certainly is not the most important issue, I believe we need to think more deeply about official canonizations.[9] It is not that the saints who are canonized do not deserve it, or that they are not exceptional people in many cases, or that the Church and the world would not benefit by recognizing them (think of the good that could be derived from the canonization of Monsignor Romero or Simone Weil, for example). But I also think that in order to possess the kind of virtues required by canonization processes, one must previously belong to a social and even economic level that makes such virtues possible, and to a priestly, religious, or papal status that makes them recognizable. The suffering servants of Yahweh may not always possess the most exceptional virtues or be in a position to have them recognized, but they are unsurpassed in unjustly inflicted suffering.

Giving Voice to "Anonymity" versus "Elitism." Along with these "arguments" in favor of speaking about "primordial saintliness" and "primordial martyrdom," I would like to add something very personal and existential. Primary life, even after an earthquake, and primary death in massacres, both are very often massive but usually end up

---

[8]*Jesus the Liberator*, p. 27.

[9]There are some obvious problems to resolve: pressures and influence, exorbitant costs, compensatory policies to satisfy religious congregations by canonizing their founders, an equitable geographic distribution so that no countries are left out—a process that has begun to occur in the Third World . . .

very soon in anonymity. What is worse from a Christian viewpoint is that the Church—Christian people—doesn't know what to do with deaths that are so massive, anonymous, and un-newsworthy. We don't even have a name for those millions of men and women.

In the Church, in theology, in the traditions of religious orders, we know how to relate to active saints and martyrs; but with a few exceptions, we almost never know what to do with the poor and crucified peoples. We know how to relate to canonized saints, but not to primordial saintliness. I believe this stems from a certain conscious or unconscious vision of holiness, martyrdom, and the Christian life as something exceptional; we might call it "elitist" without a pejorative inflection, although it can be dangerous. Certainly we are more likely to know, and pay attention to, what some people are and do (Monsignor Romero) than what the majorities are, do, and suffer. There must be underlying reasons for that inclination toward elitist exceptionalism.

In some readings of the synoptic gospels, for example, people show admiration for the disciples and followers of Jesus and are able to relate to them, but less so with the multitudes that came to him everywhere: the poor, the sick, sinners, women, tax collectors. Yet the kingdom of heaven was theirs, according to Jesus. As a Jesuit I sometimes say—not out of irony but to show the tension between elitist exceptionalism and brilliance on the one hand, and the pale monotony of everyday reality on the other—that two or three billion human beings have been chosen to "live in poverty" without ever having known St. Ignatius, or done the *Spiritual Exercises*, or had the vision of La Storta, and yet the Father has "placed them with the Son," as St. Ignatius so tenderly prayed. We can relate to the followers who ask "to be placed with the Son," but we often don't know what to do with those who—without asking—have certainly been placed with him on the real-life cross.

Something similar is true of victims and martyrs. We can relate to the "Jesuanic martyrs," but we often don't know what to do with the "crucified people"—and that is no small problem. Again, it would be ironic if we focused on the exceptional saints and ignored the victimized majorities, because what the saints ask of us is precisely to stand at the cross with the victims; to feel deep respect for their mystery, which both hides and reveals the mystery of God; to let ourselves be graced, forgiven, saved by them. And that we pour out our very lives to bring them down from the cross.

I believe we need to reconsider—not only in terms of the exceptional saints but of the primacy of life and death—the meaning of Christian virtue and heroism, of following Jesus and imitating his life, of love and faithfulness to the people of God, and of the beatitudes and Matthew 25. I think we need to broaden the horizon in which we think about holiness. What do the victims of El Mozote have to say about it, or the people imprisoned—inhumanly, in total poverty, defenselessness, humiliation—in Kigali?

I don't know who loves God more, the canonized saints or these anonymous men and women, these scraps of humanity. We also don't know which of them God loves more—if I may raise such an inopportune question about the mystery of God. But God has made very clear who are his favorites. Curiously, this seems not to be considered in the theory and practice of canonization. What have the Church and its theology done to make clear God's preferential love for the poor and the victims, and to make that love the center of their mission?

However that may be, I think we have to reconsider the very notion of saintliness, not to add more canonical precision, but to allow for the greatest fact of humanity: the primordial saintliness of those who want to live, and the primordial martyrdom of those who are innocent and defenseless victims of the same old powers and of modern-day humanity. We believe the poor—victims of everyday injustice, earthquakes, or repression—belong to a different order of saintliness: a saintliness that is almost metaphysical in its elemental effort and hope to simply prevail in life, and in the mystery of being deprived of life, unjustly murdered. This is primary saintliness.

The Ultimacy of Life and Partiality toward the Poor: Biblical Insight

Can reflections like these be found in Scripture? That must be answered by the scholars. But I think that the central insight of Scripture fits with what we have been saying, and gives it an ultimate theological justification. Therefore let us briefly recall some very basic, though well known,[10] concepts that can serve as equivalents to primordial saintliness.

The primacy of life is multiplied in an earthquake, and the primacy of death is multiplied in a massacre. This primacy appears without regard to the victims' status: poor, middle class, wealthy. . . . But it is the poor who most clearly show the primacy of life.[11] *The poor* are those whose life is vulnerable, threatened, and denied; they are also those who desire and defend life, and from this perspective we can analyze the importance of primary life in the Christian biblical tradition. It is

---

[10]See *Jesus the Liberator*, pp. 79-87.

[11]In Scripture, the oppression of the poor in everyday life appears much more often than their repression in massacres. For that reason we shall refer more to everyday oppression.

important to remember this, because it is not so evident in other traditions, including the democratic tradition that focuses more on the rights and values of citizenship. This may be because in its origins and in the areas where Western democracy prevails, even when globalization has brought poverty, social reality is seen more through the eyes of the citizen than of the poor. In contrast, the Christian biblical tradition, especially as it has been recovered in our day in the Third World, gives ultimacy to *primary life*, because it gives ultimacy to *the poor*. And this ultimacy of the poor appears in God's *partiality* toward them: there is a correlation between the primary life of the poor and God's partiality to them.

In the foundational event of the biblical tradition, God reveals himself to a people who are poor and oppressed at the basic level of life and human dignity and desires to set that people free. That people's suffering is the reason for God's self-revelation and God's desire to liberate them. In this way God shows from the (chronological and logical) beginning his partiality to the oppressed, and it is through that partiality that God's reality would be demonstrated throughout the Old Testament. God is defined in Psalm 68:5 as the "father of orphans and protector of widows." In the prophets he refers not only to all Israel, but to the oppressed within it, as "my people."[12] "God is the protector of orphans and of the poor; he does justice against those who oppress them and take advantage of their weakness."[13] In short, the true *confessio Dei* of Israel focuses on the exclamation, "In you the orphan finds compassion."[14] An essential partiality is expressed in the relationship—a transcendental relationship, we would say today—between God and the poor.

This partiality also appears in the origins of law and the administration of justice in Israel and in the neighboring countries. What is in these origins is partiality toward the poor, not a universal vision of the human being (in theory, of the citizen as such). The hoped-for king is one who is partial to the oppressed; without such partiality, they are more easily victimized by the powerful. The king's justice does not consist in "handing down an impartial verdict, but in the protection he gives to the neglected and the poor, to the widows and orphans."[15] The act of a just king is "to save the oppressed from injustice."[16]

---

[12] J. L. Sicre, *Con los pobres de la tierra* (Cristiandad, Madrid, 1984), p. 448.

[13] J. Dupont, *Les Béatitudes* II (J. Gabalda, Paris, 1969), p. 73.

[14] H. Wolf, *Dodekapropheten* I (Neukirchener, Neukirchen-Vluyn, 1982), p. 304.

[15] J. Jeremias, *Teología del Nuevo Testamento* I (Sígueme, Salamanca, 1972), p. 122.

[16] P. Miranda, *Marx y la Biblia* (Sígueme, Salamanca, 1972), pp. 140 ff.

God's partiality shows what is "ultimate" in God. It is the compassion God feels toward the poor, the little ones, the victims, because their life (in the body and in the soul, in their survival and in their dignity) is threatened or negated. What is ultimate in God becomes clear in relation to what is primary in the life of the poor.

This is what the best thinkers of liberation theology insisted on in their day, in reacting—polemically—against the first instruction from the Vatican on the theology of liberation (1984). According to that document, God liberated a people so that they could worship God and, later, in order to make a covenant with them.[17]

This purely religious interpretation was refuted by J. L. Segundo[18] and Ignacio Ellacuría[19] in favor of a more historical and even political interpretation, although it is based on God's mercy toward the threatened life of the poor. The *Yahwist tradition* says: "I have observed the misery of my people who are in Egypt; I have heard their cry on account of their taskmasters. Indeed, I know their sufferings, and I have come down to deliver them from the Egyptians, and to bring them up out of that land to a good and broad land . . ." (Ex 3:7-8). And the *Elohist tradition* says: "The cry of the Israelites has now come to me; I have also seen how the Egyptians oppress them. So come, I will send you to Pharaoh to bring my people, the Israelites, out of Egypt" (vv 9-10).

This essential correlation between God and the poor also appears in several ways in the New Testament. The kingdom of God is for the poor; to the little ones it has been given to understand the mysteries of the kingdom; and in the end everything depends on how the poor are treated, because "the Lord is in them." Jesus proclaims God's salvation as the liberation of the oppressed against the oppressor. And the condition for that salvation is not in the personal stance of the oppressed (their moral quality), but in God's stance.

---

[17]"Instruction on Certain Aspects of the 'Theology of Liberation,'" IV, 3. Reprinted in Alfred T. Hennelly, ed., *Liberation Theology: A Documentary History* (Maryknoll, NY: Orbis Books, 1990).

[18]Juan Luis Segundo emphasizes that God acts out of the compassion he feels over the inhuman situation of the people in Egypt: "In the oldest traditions there is no hint of 'establishing the people of God' as the supposed purpose of the Exodus" (*Teología de la liberación. Respuesta al cardenal Ratzinger* [Cristiandad, Madrid, 1985], pp. 62 ff.; ET, *Theology and the Church: A Response to Cardinal Ratzinger and a Warning to the Whole Church* [New York: Harper Collins, 1987]).

[19]"Whatever the origin of these narratives, the real order of establishment is very clear: it is not worship—the covenant itself is a different problem—that gives meaning to the liberation of Egypt; rather, the liberation gives meaning to worship"("Historicidad de la salvación cristiana," in I. Ellacuría and J. Sobrino [eds.], *Mysterium liberationis* I [Trotta, Madrid, 1994], p. 341; ET, *Mysterium Liberationes* [Maryknoll, NY: Orbis Books, 1993], pp. 251-289).

Jesus' life shows the ultimacy of mercy. Above all, his so-called miracles show his compassion and mercy. Jesus is seen to be deeply moved by the suffering of others: "He had compassion for them" (Mk 6:34; Mt 9:36); he reacts salvifically to their suffering and makes that reaction primary and ultimate, the criterion of all his practice. In the suffering of these majorities, Jesus sees something that one can only react to with ultimacy. The verb used to describe his attitude is *esplachnizomai*, which comes from the noun *esplachnon*—womb, bowels, heart, all symbolic of *what is ultimate in a human being.*

That is how Jesus is described, and it is what he himself emphasizes in Luke's gospel when he defines full humanity in terms of mercy, the Samaritan "moved to pity" (Lk 10:33)—here the poor man is a victim—and when he defines God as mercy, the prodigal's father "filled with compassion" (Lk 15:20). See also the other parables of compassion: God acts to defend and embrace the little people. And that is what Jesus requires of us all: "Be merciful, just as your Father is merciful" (Lk 6:36).

In this sense there is an essential relationship between God and the poor. Whether it is "only to the poor," or because Jesus was "moved to the ultimate," something about the poor puts them in an intimate relationship with God. That something is their threatened, negated life. In other words, it is the suffering that comes from being poor. In this way the poor are elevated to the *theologal* realm, the realm of the ultimate. God loves and defends the poor simply because they are poor.

This correlation of God with the poor has been miraculously rediscovered in our time, although it is always hard to maintain and is seriously threatened. Monsignor Romero was pointing to this insight when he paraphrased St. Irenaeus: "The glory of God is that the poor live."[20] "The glory of God," God's outpouring of himself, takes place when the poor live. Puebla reformulated this insight in clear, conceptual terms:

> For this reason alone, the poor merit special attention regardless of the moral or personal situation in which they are found. Made in the image and likeness of God, to be God's children, this image is overshadowed and even ridiculed. That is why God comes to their defense and loves them. (n. 1.142)

In the Puebla declaration, God's love and defense of the poor depends *only* on the fact that they are poor, not on their personal or

---

[20]In more abstruse, secular language we might say: "The glory of reality, of humanity, is that the poor live."

moral situation. This is why, in our language, we can speak of "primordial saintliness." Yet that is not society's view of the poor, nor the church's. In practice, of course, we produce crucified peoples. But even in theory it is not an accepted view.

With respect to society, the democratic tradition with all its values is *theoretically* oriented to a universal horizon. Its values of liberty, equality, and fraternity are realized on this planet only rarely, poorly, and hypocritically; in any case they are not mainly about the poor,[21] although civil rights have generally spread beyond the bourgeois world as if a reservoir had overflowed. The citizen is at the center of democratic values. *In practice and in historical reality*, especially in the current process of globalization, democracy as it is historicized today is impoverishing the middle classes and drowning the poor, excluding them, depriving them of reality.

In discourse about democracy, the rule of law, and the future of the economy—however true or false it may be—the poor may be mentioned, but they are never seen as central to the society's aspirations, let alone as an inspiration to the society. And the discourse never attempts to integrate civic democracy with "partiality to the poor." Instead of language that favors the poor it uses the language of the common good, thus diluting the reality of the poor. Western democracies have reduced some of the manifestations of poverty, but they have never made the poor central in theory or in practice. I believe this is why they have been unable to eradicate such evils as isolationist individualism, the trivialization of existence, the fragmentation of the human family. When the poor are not at the center, then neither is compassion. And without compassion, humanness also disappears.

With respect to the Church, throughout its history the poor have always been an obligatory point of reference—at least in terms of charity, well or poorly understood. But with few exceptions (such as some post-Medellín churches) the poor have never become a central ecclesial reality, nor has the Church risked its life for them as its founder did. Often it has discriminated against them and cooperated with other powers in oppressing them. In its theology, the Church has seldom

---

[21]Let us remember that two centuries ago at the beginning of human rights, the poor were not even mentioned, let alone given a central place. At the beginning those new rights were framed with the English freemen in mind, the white men of Virginia, the French bourgeois. Not everyone was included, not even the people who lived with them: the English or French peasants, nor black North American slaves, even though in theory their nature as "human beings" was not denied—which in itself was a theoretical step forward.

thought about God's essential partiality to the poor, or about the ultimacy of the poor in God's sight.[22]

Indeed, that became more difficult as a result of an early, global compression of Christianity. Specifically, I refer to the idea that Christ—and therefore God—had drawn near to this world mainly to save *sinners*, which has normally been the dominant theme in soteriology. But there is an alternative, favored by the synoptic gospels: a soteriology centered on *suffering* human beings. The poor, the victims, thus regain centrality and ultimacy. J. B. Metz explains this epochal shift and its consequences:

> From being a religion sensitive to suffering, Christianity increasingly became a religion sensitive to sin. Christianity no longer focused on creaturely suffering, but on blameworthiness. Thus it lost its sensitivity to the suffering of others, and its biblical vision of God's justice which, after Jesus, would satisfy all hunger and thirst.[23]

Metz wrote these lines with Auschwitz in mind, but they have a universal relevance. This does not diminish the importance of sin, especially the sin of oppression, which among other things causes the victims' suffering, as we emphasized in the previous chapter. Rather, Metz is insisting that God's eyes are fixed directly, above all, on the suffering, the poor, the victims. It is essential to regain this insight; without it, it makes little sense to speak of primordial saintliness.

The Poor and the Victims, Principle of Salvation

Speaking of *primordial saintliness* is another way of emphasizing the centrality of the poor and the unconditionality of God's love for them, which we call the *Jesuanic principle*: simply because they are poor, God defends them and loves them (in an analogy to the Pauline principle: God justifies the sinner by grace alone). In this way the poor are raised to a theologal level, where theology and the Church can better understand the reasons for and the necessity of taking them *seriously*. And speaking of *primordial martyrdom* is a way of emphasizing the affinity of the victims to Christ, simply because they are victims. "There cannot be a Christ without the cross; and inversely,

---

[22]This is what we have described as the theologal dimension of the poor, based on their relationship to Jesus.

[23]"Hacia una cristología después de Auschwitz," *Selecciones de Teología* 158 (2001), p. 114.

Christ cannot be absent when a cross is being carried anywhere in the world, whatever the religion of the person carrying it."[24]

The poor and the victims, primordial saintliness and primordial martyrdom, are central to a Christian discussion of any theological subject. But they are also central because of the salvific and humanizing potential that they possess according to the Christian faith—which is also confirmed by historical experience, although it is seldom analyzed and taken in seriously. In programmatic language, the poor and the victims are chosen to bring salvation. Let us see why.[25]

The Christian biblical tradition knows a lot about salvation and the dynamics that make it possible. *Salvation* implies the promise and hope of fellowship, solidarity, a shared table. But what is unique to this tradition is that salvation comes from the weak and the small: a barren old woman, the insignificant people of Israel, a marginal Jew. The weak and the small are central to the dynamic of salvation. They are not only its beneficiaries, but its bearers. Utopia does not respond to the hope of the powerful, but of the weak and the small. Not *hybris*, but smallness expresses the gratuitousness of salvation.

This tradition of smallness as salvific is found throughout Scripture, but that is not all. There is the mysterious Old Testament figure of the suffering servant of Yahweh; he is not only "poor" and "small," but also a "victim." This servant is chosen by God to take away the sin of the world and to bring salvation. Thus the scandal of smallness is further complicated by the absurdity of victimhood. Ellacuría has commented: "In a difficult act of faith, the song of the servant is able to uncover what to the eyes of history seems like just the opposite."[26]

The Church and theology generally have not historicized and put into practice this central biblical insight. It has been relegated to a theoretical model in soteriology—the model of substitutionary atonement—explaining how Christ could bring salvation; it has not been historicized as a *present* and *collective* reality. It certainly is not treated as a bearer of salvation *today, in this world.*

Yet this double historicization has occurred in the Third World, as

---

[24]Aloysius Pieris, S.J., "Cristo más allá del dogma. Hacer una cristología en el contexto de las religiones de los pobres (II)," *Revista Latinoamericana de Teología* 53 (2001), p. 8.

[25]The following paragraphs are taken in large part from my article, "Redención de la globalización. Las víctimas," *Concilium* 293 (2001).

[26]I. Ellacuría, "El pueblo crucificado. Ensayo de soteriología histórica," *Revista Latinoamericana de Teología* 18 (1989), p. 326. See Sobrino and Ellacuría, eds., *Systematic Theology*, pp. 257-278.

we have seen, and it is a new development with long-range implications. Ellacuría insisted on the reality of the suffering servant in the historical present and added that although we cannot identify precisely in whom the servant is present, "it is not happening in the First World but in the Third World; not in the rich, oppressor classes but among the oppressed."[27] That is: the servant is a collective entity.

And these "present-day victims" bring salvation, including historical salvation.[28] Later on we shall analyze two important dimensions of this salvation: solidarity and civilization. Here we want to emphasize that historicizing the servant as the focus of salvation has not been done in the affluent world but only in the Third World, because "location (concrete historical reality) causes the source of revelation (Scripture) to reveal different aspects of itself."

An example from Asia. The poor are chosen for a mission not because they are saintly but because they are powerless, rejected; "the poor are called to mediate salvation for the rich, and the weak are called to liberate the strong."[29]

This African example vigorously expresses the same insight: "The African Church, because it is African, has a special mission to the universal Church. The African Church is the wounded heart of Christ in the broken body of the universal Church. . . . Through its poverty and humility it must remind all its sister churches how essential the beatitudes are and proclaim the good news of liberation to those who have succumbed to the temptation of power, wealth, and domination."[30]

An example from El Salvador, Ignacio Ellacuría wrote in 1990:

All the blood of the martyrs, spilled in El Salvador and throughout Latin America, far from causing discouragement and despair, has brought a new spirit of struggle and a new hope to our people. In this sense, we may not be a "new world" or a "new continent," but we are clearly and verifiably (not necessarily by outsiders) a continent of hope; that is an interesting mark of a future society, in the eyes of other continents that have no hope—only fear.[31]

---

[27]*Ibid.*, p. 331.

[28]The subtitle of this article by Ellacuría means "An essay of historical soteriology." His last theological article, "Utopía y profetismo desde América Latina" (*Revista Latinoamericana de Teología* 17 [1989], pp. 141-184), is similarly subtitled, "A concrete essay of historical soteriology."

[29]Aloysius Pieris, "Cristo más allá del dogma," p. 16.

[30]Engelbert Mveng, "Iglesia y solidaridad con los pobres de Africa: empobrecimiento antropológico," in *Identidad africana y cristiana* (Estella, 1999), pp. 273 ss. Mveng was the first Cameroonian Jesuit. He was assassinated in 1995.

[31]"Quinto centenario de América Latina. ¿Descubrimiento o encubrimiento?"

There is an *a priori* of faith in all these affirmations. Mysteriously and scandalously, it is an essential affirmation of faith that the paschal lamb brings salvation. Unlike the soteriologies of the past, which made this logical and positive affirmation about the resurrection of Jesus, here it also refers to the cross despite its negativity. Today we also recognize how dangerous the affirmation is, for it has led to a soteriology in which suffering is an efficacious cause of salvation, which in turn leads to the idealization of sacrifice and suffering in theory, and to cruel and inhuman practices. There is no room for naïveté here.[32] But at some point Christians have to ask seriously what good, if any, came from the cross of Jesus; what historical salvation, if any, the cross has brought.[33] Unless we want to dehistoricize the Christian faith, and thus annul or dilute it at important points—"that's the way it was twenty centuries ago, but not now"—we have to ask that question in the present, propose an answer, and verify it. If there is a verifiable answer, then it is not only an *a priori* of faith but also a real dimension of history to affirm that the poor and the victims bring salvation.

That is what I want to do now, by briefly analyzing two pertinent points in this time of earthquakes. First and most important: the poor and the victims, primary saintliness and primary martyrdom, become the principle by which we can adequately historicize solidarity among human beings as *solidarity among unequals*; by their mutuality they form a single, shared table. This is also the principle by which we can adequately historicize a civilization that—as crazy and scandalous as it sounds—in order to be human, must become a *civilization of poverty*.

Of course we can and should also analyze solidarity and civilization in terms of universal principles, based on human nature and dignity, the common good, universal human rights, dialogue, etc. All that is good—and necessary, given the present course of history. But I would insist that this universal perspective alone is not enough and can be

---

Revista Latinoamericana de Teología 21 (1990), pp. 281 ss. Earlier in the same article he says: "From my viewpoint—and this may be at once prophetic and paradoxical— the United States is much worse off than Latin America. Because the United States has a solution, but in my opinion it is a bad solution, both for them and for the world at large. In Latin America on the other hand there are no solutions, only problems; but however painful they may be, it is better to have problems than to have a bad solution for the future of history" (p. 277).

[32]I have attempted to develop a "non-sacrificialist" interpretation of Jesus' cross in *Jesus the Liberator*, pp. 219-232.

[33]I have written that the victims of globalization may be the principle of its redemption, in paradoxical Christian terms, and that unless we put them at the center there will never be a "humane" globalization ("Redención de la globalización. Las víctimas," *Concilium* 293 [2001], pp. 129-139).

dangerous. This is why we must approach both from the concrete reality of the poor and the victims. If they are involved in the process of solidarity and civilization from the beginning, it will move in the right direction. If not, sooner or later it will go off course, may degenerate, and will be more easily manipulated. This, I believe, is shown by modern history and the history of progress in our time.

PRIMORDIAL SAINTLINESS AND SOLIDARITY: "SUPPORTING ONE ANOTHER"

An earthquake starts the aid process, and we have already said that the intrinsic dynamics of this process—besides drawing on the necessary knowledge and technical skills—can lead to deeply human attitudes: not only giving but "self-giving"; not only going to the disaster area but "being present," physically or spiritually; not just for a while but "forever." We mentioned these elements in discussing how aid can give way to solidarity. Now I want to go more deeply into solidarity: *who* calls us to solidarity, and what it means to *support one another*.

The Call to Solidarity

The very reality of an earthquake naturally produces a need for aid; there are more and more institutions, governments, churches, different types of nongovernmental organizations to ask for, receive, and coordinate this aid. But in a deeper sense, we must ask who calls human beings to provide aid, and to provide it in the right way.

Sharpening the question a bit, we must ask—without assuming that the answer is obvious—what has the power to attract, to *call* us so that we are pulled out of ourselves and can do nothing but answer. We must also ask what has the power to call, not only an individual but a group, community, church, people, enabling us to overcome selfish rivalries and sinful loyalties, promoting instead a response from "all of us." Finally, we must ask what has the power to lead those who help—with resources, organization, ideas—to be in *common-union*, communion, with the injured and homeless, and to feel "at home" in that communion. In other words, we must ask what can call us in such a way that in giving aid we begin to form a human family.

We ask these questions because to *call* is more than asking for or demanding aid, in the brutal context of a catastrophe, or in the diplomatic and bureaucratic context of pragmatism and convenience. And to *feel called* is to go beyond professional obligation, beyond the ethical feeling that something must be done, beyond the need to overcome a feeling of guilt. In this sense the awareness that we are not only needed, but called, comes from the insight that by answering the call we are doing something fundamentally human: coming close to other human beings and rejoicing in that closeness as the highest good. The material aid comes later and must be well organized, professionally and ethically. But the call comes first and must be analyzed first, because how we respond determines whether and how the problems arising from a catastrophe will be solved.

We have already answered these questions. What attracts us irresistibly, what has the power to call us, is to be found in primordial saintliness and primordial martyrdom, in the poor and crucified peoples. What comes from churches, governments, nongovernmental organizations is the *secondary* call, if you will, but they must first hear and transmit the primary call, which comes from the victims. The real call, the one that sets the process in motion and in the right direction, comes from the crucified peoples. And there is nothing obvious about that answer.

In our world we usually think differently, even quite the contrary, although the difference is not made explicit. No one denies that chronologically, the triggering event for aid is the catastrophe. But in obvious or subtle ways the powers and institutions give the impression that it is they who call for aid, who really set the dynamic of salvation in motion, who will save the victims. This is true of the UN and its agencies; governments, especially the G-8, with their official summits and declarations; the economic powers, the world banking system, and all their strategies; and the nongovernmental organizations, political parties, churches, etc. One hopes there is at least some truth in this, not only propaganda and self-deception. But in any case the primary call does not come from them, either chronologically (which is obvious) or logically (which is important to keep in mind).

This understanding of the primary call for aid—without which other, mediating calls usually fall short or go astray—is basically a theological understanding, an *a priori* one if you will: the suffering servant has been chosen to be "a light to the nations" (Is 42:6; 49:6).[34] In John's theology it is the Crucified One who will draw all people to himself (Jn 12:32; 19:37). But it is also a historical understanding, which as we have said has only been fully understood in the Third World. Here is an example from my own experience.

Years ago, the world knew nothing of El Salvador. It began to hear

---

[34]This applies to the "active" servant. Of the "suffering" servant Scripture says, on the one hand, "they shall admire him" (Is 52:15), and on the other, that "others hide their faces" from him (Is 53:3).

in 1977 with the assassination of a priest, Rutilio Grande. The Western, democratic, and Christian world was shocked, and some people were horrified to hear that fliers were circulating with slogans like "Be a patriot, kill a priest." But most importantly, the assassination made people aware that peasants, workers, students, catechists, and delegates of the word were also being massively persecuted, tortured, murdered. That led to a more fundamental and more deeply concealed truth: El Salvador, as a whole, is a crucified people.

This new attention to El Salvador triggered another little-known dynamic: many people let themselves be touched, began to offer help, and became committed. Soon aid began to take on a different meaning: it was no longer only material aid but personal commitment, not only temporary but lasting. And it was not only about giving but receiving. This was the birth of solidarity, not only in El Salvador but in other crucified peoples of the Third World.

This is our thesis: the crucified people have the power to call us. In 1977 it was the victims of repression and barbarity, a historical catastrophe. Now it is an earthquake that crucifies them and shows, as we have seen, that a people can be crucified "in times of normalcy." The *suffering* of these crucified people has the power to move our hearts, which would otherwise remain hardened, distant, numb. Their *truth* has the power to move our reason and intelligence, to give birth to compassionate reason and *intellectus amoris*, to bring about the miracle of honesty toward "real" reality. With all of this, the crucified people have the power to call us.

"Unequals Supporting One Another"

Let us take this idea a little further. As we have just said, the solidarity that arises from this call is not just humanitarian *aid*. Aid is obviously good and necessary, and it is a correct response to an ethical demand. But if solidarity were only aid, it would be nothing more than glorified charity: the donors give something from what they possess, without being drawn into a deeply personal commitment or feeling the need to continue the aid. But in solidarity, that first act of giving aid commits the givers to something more than just giving, and makes it more a continuous process than a momentary giving of aid.

Furthermore, through the initial aid relationships are established among groups (peoples, institutions, communities, sister parishes, etc.), which give to and receive from one another. Aid is not one-way, but a mutual giving and receiving among people who in reality are unequal. For this reason solidarity cannot be seen as a mere *alliance*, as might occur among substantially "equal" countries, parties, or churches in defense of common interests—which in any case would express a certain, legitimate or illegitimate, cooperation of one group against another.

So what distinguishes solidarity from simple aid or alliances? First let us give a descriptive answer. In El Salvador the process began conspicuously and massively in the churches because, as we have said, it was triggered by the assassination of priests, catechists, delegates of the word, and Christian peasants. For that reason we shall focus on the process as it occurred in the churches, although there was also solidarity among political, ideological, revolutionary, and professional groups. It happened more or less as follows:

1. The solidarity was triggered when churches from outside began to aid the Salvadoran church, not as "church," but because it had dedicated itself to the poor and oppressed among the people, and because—in defending them—it shared their reality and fate: it was persecuted.
2. This aid by its very nature led to contact among the churches, which led to the fundamental element: the outside churches began to discover the crucified people, and the Salvadoran church was strengthened in its commitment to them. The churches were united by having come together for the people.
3. Furthermore, the crucified people moved the churches inside and outside El Salvador—the poor and affluent churches—to give the best of what they had and to share it with each other. This self-giving quickly became a giving-to and receiving-from others. The churches began to give and receive the best they had. The churches outside discovered that what they were receiving was different from, and more important than, what they gave; they often described it as a new spirit of faith, and as help in discovering their human, ecclesial, Christian, and theologal identity.
4. They discovered that reaching out to other churches is essential to a local church, and that this sharing had to occur at all levels, from material aid to faith. They began to understand their relationship with other churches as "supporting one another."

We have said that "ecclesial" solidarity developed along with other solidarities: political, labor, armed resistance, ideological—all of which appear at one point or another in our previous analysis. What is important is that all these groups, in this case the churches, entered into solidarity with each other because they were committed to the crucified people; and the people have given back with interest what was given to them. The deepest solidarity is not among the churches, political parties, universities, or parishes, but between these groups that are unified for action, and the crucified people. That is the primary solidarity. This now enables us to formulate a more far-reaching understanding of solidarity.

In the world there are "unequals," both groups and individual persons. This is true in normal times, and is even more evident in times of natural disaster (earthquakes, floods, droughts, etc.) and historical disaster (wars, repressions, waves of immigrants and refugees, situations of impunity, etc.).

Why this "fundamental inequality"? There are human groups, majorities, for whom reality is terribly hard—nothing close to the lightness of being. It is they who must "bear the burden of reality," with all its weight. Now, the first step of solidarity is taken when "the others" help to carry the weight of the reality borne by the crucified peoples, which means, in some way, bearing it themselves. The second step is to understand that—surprisingly—as they begin to carry that reality, the reality is actually carrying them. The crucified people are carrying them, offering them light, strength, and encouragement. Now the relationship between them is one of giving and receiving. Secular attitudes that seemed unchangeable and untouchable, between "helped" and "helpers," begin to change. People come to the existential conclusion that no one should presume to think that they can give but not receive. And no one should be so timid as to think that they can receive but not give. This is what it means for unequals to support one another. Let us see how it works.

It often happens in *historical-social reality* that some people (the "solidary" outsiders) give what others (the crucified peoples) need: knowledge, technology, resources, time, platforms, contacts, voice. Along with these things, very importantly, they give respect and affection. And in doing so they sometimes—there are innumerable examples in El Salvador—run risks, even to their life. Now the solidary ones are no longer giving what they have, but what they are. Their martyrdom is received with indignation and despair, but also with ultimate gratitude for the love they have expressed. The solidary ones have become one with the crucified people.

The solidary ones in turn are awakened (as many have said) to the truth of their own reality, and that of their countries, cultures, and religions. They receive truth, and above all, they receive the light that will help them to go on discovering the truth. They also receive attitudes and values not necessarily present in the places they come from: a sense of community beyond or against isolationist individualism; a sense of celebration, the human joy of being with one another, beyond mere entertainment that can be mass-produced and marketed; seriousness, not as a trait of temperament but as firmness in the face of life's hardship, against the surrounding trivialization that seldom allows anything to be taken seriously; a human embrace that expresses the ideal of the human family; the "forgiveness" that the solidary ones bring back from the poor to the countries that have oppressed them for centuries, and reconciliation; hope that goes beyond resignation, disillusionment, and even scientifically calculated optimism. And they receive "faith," not necessarily in a religious (let alone confessional) sense, but rather in the sense that there is something more and deeper than realism and pragmatism: they become aware that there is something pointless about rational positivism, that indeed the "tremendous" and the "fascinating" will always stand as an offer of humanization.

A second example comes from the *personal reality of faith*, which I mention because in our countries religiosity is widely accepted and seen as essential by the majorities;[35] and many of the solidary ones—though not all—are motivated by religion or open to it. The relationship between them gives a good example of what we mean by solidarity. We begin with the "inequality"[36] between the faith of "simple" Salvadorans and the "enlightened" solidarity workers from the First World; and analyze how these unequals share their faith, since we have seen it happening with positive results. On the one hand, a person's faith is deeply personal and therefore cannot be given to others. But it is also true, on the other hand, that people are helped to make their own faith real by seeing the faith of others. This is the "solidarity" of faith. Let us look at the faith of the "simple ones" and the "enlightened" outsiders, and the differences between them.

One difference is in the way they see the relationship between God and life. The solidary outsiders are believers who "take life for granted" and therefore would not normally pay much attention to prayer for the basic necessities of survival. The people who pray for necessities are the ones who don't have them. The poor, on the other hand, are really pleading in their prayers (as they did during the earthquakes, and now during the drought), asking for life. The relationship between God and living is very clear to them.

A second difference: poor believers do not think of lowering them-

---

[35]Here I should make the following clarification. In the 1970s and '80s the solidary ones came into contact with a type of religiosity we might call "liberating." Since then a "spiritualistic" religiosity has become more widespread, although there are still important signs of the liberating kind.

[36]Some perhaps do not see it this way, but the faith of human beings is always "unequal." "My God is not like the one you are thinking of," Rahner used to tell his students. And that should not come as a surprise.

selves as part of their faith and of following Jesus, since to them it seems natural to be on the downside of history. For the solidary outsiders, in contrast, lowering themselves to Third World living conditions may well be a prime expression of their faith. A third difference: simple believers in the Third World are giving the simplicity and certainty of their faith, while the solidary outsiders are committing themselves to a faith threatened by secularization with its doubts and challenges.

There are also differences in the behaviors that stem from faith. Poor believers tend to be grateful to the solidary ones (they are not used to "others" visiting and helping them), while the visitors may feel baffled and humbled by their gratitude; the poor give of their poverty, while the solidary ones feel obliged to grow in generosity. Poor believers in conflict situations give their life quite naturally as martyrs for the cause of the kingdom, for the cause of Jesus; while the solidary ones work—sometimes from outside, and effectively—for human rights, in defense of life, although some of them have also given their lives.

These are examples of the different ways people express their faith, their understanding, and their shared Christian experience. The point I want to stress is their diversity, and that this diversity can be experienced as "solidarity" (even between the charcoal vendor and the scholar if they both have faith and commitment to God, *pace* Miguel de Unamuno), as a way of supporting one another in the faith[37] and in life. In my experience that happens sometimes, or often.

The act of faith is personal, non-repeatable, and nontransferable, but it is open to giving and receiving from the faith of others. The faith of the "enlightened" is expressed in their sincere attempts to lower themselves, and in their life-risking struggle for justice; but this faith has been brought out by the primary faith of the crucified people, for whom it is entirely natural to live in humility and to take risks in the struggle for life. The faith of the enlightened is strengthened by the real faith of the poor, and conversely, the poor are encouraged by the faith that leads the enlightened to live "freely" what they have always lived "by necessity." And sometimes the poor with their simple, unquestioning faith in the mystery of God are able to restore the challenged, tormented faith of the enlightened. A single example: an English visitor said, "I am Catholic and I teach religion. I am also attracted by atheistic humanism. But when I hear what the Salvadoran

---

[37]St. Paul wrote to the Romans: "For I am longing to see you so that I may share with you some spiritual gift to strengthen you—or rather so that we may be mutually encouraged by *each other's faith, both yours and mine*" (Rom 1:11-12).

Christians are doing and remember the witness of Monsignor Romero, although I cannot explain how or why, I feel truly Christian. My darkened faith becomes a reality again."[38]

This description of solidarity is obviously pretty utopian; and my theory of solidarity is based on real, but very concrete, situations. But this does not disqualify it as a model—unlike any other in history—for relationships among human groups, churches, peoples. And by focusing on this model we can better see the limitations of other models.

From the standpoint of solidarity, neither homogeneity nor pluralism (in the Church or civil society) offers an adequate way to live with inequality in a humanizing way. Homogeneity does not take inequality seriously; pluralism does not take seriously the fact that relationships still exist among unequals, so that they cannot ignore each other.

With respect to globalization, solidarity as a theoretical model for human organization serves above all as a critique of the inequality and injustice it causes. The goal of solidarity is not only to live "all together" on the globe, but for unequals to "support one another," each one giving and receiving the best they have, in all areas: economics, culture, knowledge, faith, etc. But in that case the "globe" is not an adequate metaphor. "The family" works better: "The world becoming a *home* for everyone," as E. Bloch said. A place of *closeness* instead of distance, although that idea is being appropriated by the tourist industry; *appreciation* instead of the disrespect usually shown to those who come without being called; *joy* instead of fear of the newcomers as invaders. A "quality" globalization is a table shared by all including unequals, like the one Jesus offered; like the one Rutilio Grande described: "A single table, large, with long tablecloths for everyone." It is the table that makes unequals equal and builds up the human family.

We end this section with three observations on the phrase "among unequals." We use this term because in Third World disaster situations there is an obvious inequality between those who help, especially from outside, and the victims. That is why we refer to "inequality" in the model of solidarity. But some clarifications are needed.

The first is obvious. "Unequals" has two different meanings. In one, the inequality involves injustice, as in the Salvadoran earthquake. Here the first thing we must do with inequality is to eradicate it. In the other meaning, inequality stems from different cultural and historical identities; this should be maintained, not as inequality but as diversity or difference. In this sense, there can be solidarity among different peoples, giving and receiving. The power of globalization to de-

---

[38]I quoted this testimony in "Bearing with One Another in Faith," *The Principle of Mercy* (Maryknoll, NY: Orbis Books, 1994), 170.

stroy diversity is the reason why some Asian and African theologians are opposed to it,[39] just when globalization seems to offer a utopian movement toward equality.

The second clarification takes us more deeply into human reality. *Grace* is an essential component of the solidarity model (as opposed to the model of globalization, homogeneity, pluralism, or alliance); grace entails becoming, not only giving but receiving. In simple and existential language, it would be an expression of grace for the peoples of the Group of Eight, and their supporters, to become peoples by receiving from the peoples of the African Great Lakes: salvation comes from outside, unmerited and unexpected, from those of whom we would expect the least, from those who are "not our equals" but completely unequal. That is what could turn our present history upside down, along with its assumptions: that the strong impose on the weak and look down on them. And it could turn our history into something different: the weak offering acceptance, forgiveness, love—salvation against all expectations. That is why we must speak of unequals: it reminds us just how unexpected salvation is. That is the experience of grace.

If readers are wondering why we mention grace in the context of social models, of globalization in particular, I fear they have not understood Jesus of Nazareth—or human beings, who do not make themselves human, but are made human by others. We have repeatedly seen outsiders confess, gratefully, that where they least expected or deserved it they have received more than they gave, and that what they received was far superior to what they came to give. They have received acceptance, affection, hope, faith, realities that are woven into the human fabric and can truly "globalize" the human family. Without putting it in these words, without knowing it, they have experienced grace.

Finally, solidarity must also be expressed as solidarity among those who are equal in their poverty. We have spoken of the solidarity of unequals as mutual support between the world of poverty and the world of affluence. But we must also speak of "solidarity among equals," among the poor of this world, which in the long term is more important than solidarity among unequals. Mutual relationships and aid among the poor, giving and receiving within their diverse realities in the continents of the Third World, can bring the best kind of change to the planet. Although the language we use is not important, I don't like to call this "an alliance of the poor," perhaps because in our time "alliances" are what the affluent world forms; they presuppose great power and are used to destroy enemies.

---

[39]See the articles by Felix Wilfred, Teresa Okure, and Michel Amaladoss in the monographic issue of *Concilium* 293 (2001), on globalization.

Solidarity among the poor should not seek to imitate an alliance, but should be based on a different set of anthropological and religious assumptions. As the song says, "When the poor believe in the poor . . ." When the poor believe that their common humanity is humanizing, where power is not, then we will be on the way to human solidarity.

PRIMARY SAINTLINESS AND
THE CIVILIZATION OF POVERTY

The poor know that the world is in a bad way. We won't say more about that, since we have already discussed it in the context of the sin of the world. John Paul II refers to it constantly, sometimes threateningly, pointing out its causes. In Canada, in September 1985, he said that on the day of judgment the poor will judge their oppressors. And we have mentioned that James Wolfensohn, president of the World Bank, describes the aid of the rich world to the poor as a "crime." Each of them is pointing out a great truth in different words: there is crime, and there must be a judgment. Furthermore it should be clear *a priori* that if this is really a crime, the rich world is not humanizing the poor. That is what I want to analyze here.

We have said that globalization has not "globalized" the good. Exclusion is increasing, not inclusion; trivialization proliferates and humanness is not emerging; the cruel division among peoples is widening, and a universal embrace is nowhere in sight. Perhaps the worst part is the denial of existence itself; thus for instance, "Africa does not exist." Africa, ironically, has been excluded from reality by an anti-globalization of silence.

If this is true, then it is clear that the planet needs a radical change rather than a quick fix or an increase in globalization. That was Ellacuría's theory: realistically, but with prophetic and utopian vision, he insisted on the need to "turn history upside down." Today he would say, to turn upside down the assumptions of the present globalization. That meant a need for something radically new. Discussing the shape of the world economy, he repeated a Marxist-sounding idea from John Paul II: "the priority of labor over capital." But he also saw a need to turn civilization upside down. The popes have spoken of a "civilization of love," but Ellacuría expressed it more radically, turning it into a truly revolutionary thesis: the need for a "civilization of poverty." Provocative as this formulation was, he never softened it, and neither shall we.

In my understanding—this is why I spoke earlier of the forgotten Ellacuría—very few people have echoed this thesis, even to debate it. Pedro Casaldáliga is the exception who proves the rule, on this and many other issues: the martyrs, Medellín, etc. We should add to the "civilization of love" the felicitous phrase that the Jesuit, Spanish, Basque, Salvadoran theologian Ellacuría used: the "civilization of poverty."[40] In programmatic terms, this is

A civilization . . . in which poverty no longer means the deprivation of basic necessities by the historical action of social groups or classes and nations or groups of nations, but a universal state of things which guarantees the satisfaction of fundamental needs, freedom of personal choices, and a sphere of personal and community creativity that permits the appearance of new forms of life and culture, new relationships with nature, with other people, with themselves, and with God.[41]

This is a beautiful description, but it seems too generic to be very useful. Moreover, it does not make clear how it relates to *poverty*, and therefore why we speak of a *civilization of poverty*. But it is reasonable and comprehensible, if we understand it *in contrast to the civilization of wealth*. We are not speaking of universal poverty as an ideal, but rather offering to a world sinfully shaped by the dynamic of capital and wealth *a different, and salvifically better, dynamic*. The civilization of poverty "rejects capital accumulation as the engine of history and the possession/enjoyment of wealth as the principle of humanization."[42]

The civilization of wealth *has failed as a way of guaranteeing the life* of the majorities because its "quality" of life cannot be universalized, given the universal correlation between resources and population; even if it could be universalized *it would not be desirable* to do so, because it has also failed as a *way of humanizing people and peoples*. Ellacuría's thesis is that another civilization besides the civilization of wealth *must be possible*. And that possibility, not only in formal contrast to wealth but on its own merits, lies in "poverty." The missing dynamic can come from the world of poverty:

It is this poverty that really opens up space for the spirit, which is no longer stifled by the desire to have more than others, by the selfish desire to have all sorts of luxuries when most of humanity lacks the necessities. Then the spirit can flourish, the immense spiritual and human wealth of the poor and the peoples of the

---

[40]"A los quinientos años: 'descolonizar y desevangelizar,' " *Revista Latinoamericana de Teología* 16 (1989), p. 118.

[41]"El reino de Dios y el paro en el Tercer Mundo," *Concilium* 180 (1982), p. 595.

[42]"Utopía y profetismo desde América Latina," *Revista Latinoamericana de Teología* 17 (1989), pp. 170 ff.

Third World, which today are suffocated by misery and by the imposition of cultural models that are more developed in some aspects, but not necessarily more fully human.[43]

Ellacuría makes this case on several grounds, but his unique argument is that the search for a "new" civilization takes us back to the Christian biblical tradition, which gives centrality to the poor, the victims, the crucified people. This tradition—and others, at their best—can generate a knowledge that does not conceal the truth, a praxis that does justice to reality, a hope that all this is possible, a mutuality and celebration of life for everyone, with the poor at its center.

These poor should not be idealized, as we have already seen, but neither should they be merely "loved" and "defended" because they are poor; they must be appreciated and "made productive" in order to turn this civilization upside down. We have analyzed the reality of the poor and the conditions for their humanization elsewhere,[44] insisting that this is done by analogy, since not all the poor fulfill the conditions of humanization in the same way. Here let us mention two of the more important ways in which the poor can humanize.

The first way is by means of a tautology, which I believe is fruitful rather than sterile: if the poor are the truest reality, we can only be "real" by entering into their reality, relating effectively to their reality (in the diverse ways that analogy allows).

But setting aside the question of injustice and focusing on what is "real," a civilization that calls itself human must at least be real. If we live in an unreal world, not the world of the poor, we simply are not real; therefore we are not human. In Christian terms we have not overcome what in christology is called *Docetism*: the denial of Christ's flesh, his *sarx*, his reality. The social Docetism that marks the affluent world is the principle of the negation of civilization, because it leads to living at the margins of reality.[45]

The same is true of ecclesial Docetism, on which I want to focus briefly. A Docetist Church is one that distances itself from "real" reality and chooses the sphere of reality in which it wants to be Church: the religious, the doctrinal, the liturgical, the canonical. This entails grave consequences. The option for the poor loses its ultimacy and is

---

[43]"Misión actual de la Compañía de Jesús," *Revista Latinoamericana de Teología* 29 (1993), pp. 119 ff.

[44]*Jesus the Liberator,* pp. 79-82.

[45]The affluent society obviously exists; it is "factual." But its reality shows more superficiality than depth; thus it is dehumanizing. For this qualitative reason, not only the more obvious quantitative factor, we do not describe it as "real."

now balanced with another, apparently more primordial and more real option: that of living in harmony with the established powers. The Church does not radically identify its being and doing in relation to the poor but to other things, which may be necessary and even good, but which have nothing to do with its essence as Church. At the moment of truth its institutional organization, combating the sects, maintaining the number of members and their religiosity (even an alienating religiosity), its obsessive faithfulness to the magisterium, and a long list of other concerns carry more weight than the reality of the poor.

In this sense, perhaps the greatest contribution of Monsignor Romero was to go beyond Docetism and build a "real" Church. He used to say: "I am glad, brethren, that the Church is persecuted because of its preferential option for the poor and for trying to incarnate itself in the interest of the poor" (September 15, 1979). And even more clearly: "It would be sad if in a country where people are being murdered so horrifically, there were not also priests among the victims. They are the witness of a Church incarnated in the problems of the people"(June 24, 1979). Monsignor Romero's Church was "real." Breaking with centuries of history, thinking about the Church, he said: "We don't want to be any different." And this new thing, which is at the root of other, more visible new things—his passion for the truth, his compassionate embrace of the poor, his strength and martyrdom—is what has made of Monsignor Romero an imperishable, immortal figure.[46]

To summarize: there can be no civilization on the basis of unreality, of what we have called Docetism. Reality offers us redemption from unreality, and the poor offer us redemption from social and ecclesial Docetism. To put it more modestly, they invite us to come close to them, to be real.

Second, the poor humanize us when they develop the power that comes from the world of poverty; when they become aware of their situation and its causes, convert that awareness into praxis, and fill it with spirit: mercy, strength, hope . . . It is the "poor with spirit"[47] who have an evangelizing potential (Puebla, 1.147). As we have seen, the poor are sinful but also full of grace, and they often have the greatest love. Thus they are able to shape a civilization of honesty toward reality, of mercy, of

---

[46]If I may be allowed a personal word, there were times when we wanted to be "perfect," "holy." Later we expressed it more modestly: we wanted to be "Christian," "authentic"; still more modestly, we wanted to be "human"—others might say "progressive," "revolutionary," "democratic," "socialist." Now we are satisfied with a minimum, which seems to us a maximum: we would like to be "real" in this world of the poor, to participate a little in their primordial saintliness.

[47]See I. Ellacuría, "Las bienaventuranzas, carta fundacional de la Iglesia de los pobres," in *Conversión de la Iglesia al reino de Dios*, Sal Terrae, Santander, 1985, p. 151.

the joy of the beatitudes, that goes beyond the present civilization full of the trivialization of existence. In this civilization of course we may see expressions of nobility, kindness, beauty, but it is always threatened by the danger of turning away from the great majorities (Docetism, injustice), or worse yet, of offensive ostentation (disdain). In any case, the present civilization does not produce a civilized society.

This process of being humanized by the poor obviously does not occur mechanically, or in ideal ways. But in the poor peoples we see many signs that the civilization of poverty can humanize, and thus civilize. Those signs come from what we have tried to show in this chapter: primordial saintliness and primordial martyrdom, utopia, and prophetic vision. The poor and the victims are a practically unparalleled—and utopian—principle by which to turn history upside down and reshape it, but the future depends on how we put the principle into practice.

APPENDIX ON "COUNTERCULTURAL GOODNESS"

We have discussed the primordial saintliness that appeared in the earthquake, and the consequences of that saintliness, as something obviously positive and good. This goodness, appropriately historicized, might well serve as a "frame of reference" and "principle" for the appreciation and defense of life "in normal times." Therefore we want to end this chapter with a brief comment on why so little has been said about that goodness—which has to do with what we said in the third chapter about honesty toward, or concealment of, reality.

Except for a few brief stories, the goodness that appeared during the earthquake has not been publicized or properly appreciated; thus the people's impressive will to live and their generous dedication have been reduced to a few inspiring anecdotes. The reason for this, now expressed as a thesis, is that *goodness is—can be—countercultural,*[48] and therefore, strange as it seems, it is concealed. That is, reality itself is concealed, hiding not only the bad but the good. This is surprising, but also understandable and consistent with the shape of the world we live in.

In effect, to show goodness is also to show evil; it can even unmask the causes of evil that people want to hide. But more importantly it is

---

[48]It may seem ridiculous even to raise the question: why do the communications media have sections on the economy and economists, politics and politicians, culture and writers, songs and singers, athletics and athletes, etc., but no sections on goodness and good people? One reason may be that good people are naturally modest, but another is the lack of popular interest in goodness.

the most effective way to deny the justification of evil, when evil is fatalistically perceived as historically inevitable. There is much truth in this, obviously, but not the whole truth. Goodness shows that evil can be overcome, although sometimes at a very high cost. The generosity, integrity, and solidarity that appear in times of earthquake show that the good is possible, but at the same time they unmask the selfishness, corruption, and arrogance of governments and agencies, and they challenge those who helplessly or cynically hide behind the perception of inevitability. Thus against all apparent logic, goodness becomes something conflictive and countercultural.

I should explain that a *good* temperament does not need to cause conflicts, but a praxis of *doing good* often does—if at the same time it unmasks and combats evil.[49] That is why, consciously or unconsciously, people tend to silence goodness, cover it up, and eventually fight against it. Jesus of Nazareth is a clear example.

Jesus' *word of truth*, his prophetic denunciation, clearly troubled people; but his adversaries were probably even more angry about his *praxis of goodness*, since it took away their strongest arguments. Jesus showed with his life that it is good to attend to a victim rather than walking around him, to "proclaim good news to the poor," to "condemn their oppressors." But above all he showed that it was possible to do those things, even at the cost of his life.

Jesus' goodness must have exasperated his adversaries, because— since he spoke the truth—it left them without justifiable arguments against him. It would have been easier for his adversaries if Jesus had spoken truth but done evil. It must have been even more exasperating that Jesus made "doing good" the ultimate criterion by which to judge all human and religious reality, and by which to interpret their traditions. At one point in Mark's gospel—strategically placed at the end of the controversies, which at bottom were about God's truth (Mk 3:1-6)—Jesus heals a man with a withered hand, and he does so in the synagogue, on a Sabbath, in front of Herodians and Pharisees who were looking for something of which they could accuse him. After the healing they were talking about how to get rid of him. Jesus disarmed and exasperated them with this question: "Is it lawful to *do good* or to

---

[49]The conflictiveness of good also depends on what kind of evil it is confronting. With all respect and affection, everyone knows that Mother Teresa's heroic goodness was directed at profound evils, and brought to public attention many of the evils of our world. But it did not cause social conflict because her goodness did not confront historical, structural evils. Her goodness was countercultural in the sense of being sacrificial and unusual, but it did not lead to negative reactions as the Third World martyrs' goodness did.

do harm on the Sabbath?" In other words he was saying, "If you're not pleased by goodness, there is no solution for you." In a way they are sinning against the Holy Spirit.

The context of this gospel is obviously different from that of an earthquake, but in any context Jesus' words shed light on what is ultimate in human life, and helps us to judge—on the Sabbath or whenever—what is to be done and not done, even at a high cost. The tragedy of human beings is that they do not want to proclaim good in a world of evil, especially historical evil, because to do so is threatening. This is what I mean by speaking of goodness as countercultural.

If I may close with a slight digression, that is what happened with Monsignor Romero. In his life, obviously, he troubled people *directly* with his word of truth and his praxis of goodness; that is why they "conspired . . . how to destroy him" as they did Jesus (Mk 3:6). But even after his death, Monsignor Romero continues to trouble them *indirectly*. As a man of truth and goodness, people want to silence and hide him as much as possible. The powerful of this country, governments, military leaders, oligarchs, are still doing so because his memory still troubles them. In some ways, some ecclesial leaders are doing the same.

Why has the Vatican tacitly discouraged Monsignor Romero's beatification process, just when it seemed to be moving forward and even John Paul II was supporting it? In my opinion, to beatify Monsignor Romero as he really was, rather than a watered-down version, would mean more than proclaiming him an intercessor (which does not usually cause problems), a man and a Christian full of goodness, a model worthy of imitation, or at least an inspiring model. It would also automatically mean proclaiming as good and desirable a Church, a hierarchy, a way of being Christian, a ministry like Monsignor's, different and more evangelical than those of today. Above all it would mean proclaiming that such a thing is possible, not merely utopian, since Monsignor Romero made it a *reality*.

Certainly we are not all asked to achieve the same level of goodness as Monsignor, but we can let him guide our steps; we can commit ourselves to following his steps, albeit more modestly. To put it simply, to beatify Monsignor Romero means holding him up as a model of goodness, and that—if we are talking about action rather than words—can be very hard to accept. At the Vatican they may talk about Monsignor's goodness, but to beatify him would mean officially recognizing that goodness—which would logically require a conversion to his way of being and acting as a bishop, or would at least require us to wonder about it. As Pedro Casaldáliga says in his poem "St. Romero of America," "the curias couldn't understand you." Monsignor's goodness is countercultural in every curia, whether ecclesiastical or civil.[50]

Thus goodness can be conflictive, "countercultural," in the Church and in society. To beatify Monsignor Romero would mean proclaiming that it is not only good and desirable but also possible to be a Christian and a Salvadoran—a servant of the people—in a very different way from the one that prevails today: selfishness, corruption, arrogance, negligence, indifference in the midst of vulnerability, poverty and injustice, although there are always some exceptions. And what we have shown with the example of the "good" Monsignor Romero is true of countless other "good" people who were ignored in their lifetime and are still ignored in death. They are ignored by the powerful, of course, but also by some ecclesial leaders,[51] because they are troublesome.

To close, let us return to the earthquake. A community of earthquake victims met last August to talk about the homes that a European institution was building for them. The peasants were very unhappy with the houses, and they were especially indignant and offended by the way the donors were treating them. They decided: "We would rather remain homeless and go back to what we had before, than be treated this way." This primary dignity, which is related to primordial saintliness, is not newsworthy; rather it is carefully concealed, because it is countercultural.

Primordial saintliness and martyrdom are countercultural. For that reason no one talks about it; people quickly forget it and do not think about what it contributes to the country. But as we have said, no plan of assistance, of reconstruction, of international cooperation will succeed unless it is based on that contribution.

---

[50]Another more circumstantial reason is that beatification would draw new attention to his assassination, and to his assassins. Even without knowing exactly who did it, it would be very troublesome to the party in power to be reminded of the criminal actions carried out by its founding members. To put it gently, it would not be surprising if some party members or sympathizers were in some way implicated in the assassination of Monsignor. Monsignor's beatification would put the hierarchy in a difficult situation vis-à-vis the civil authorities, something which the hierarchy has tried to avoid at all costs ever since the death of Archbishop Rivera Y. Damas in 1995.

[51]They like to pretend not to be troubled by their "goodness." In fact, martyrs are easily and often canonized today—those of the Spanish War, for example—whose subjective saintliness and faithfulness to Jesus are not in question. Their goodness may have been "countercultural" in its time, as giving up one's life is always countercultural. But with all respect and affection, and without attributing any fault to them, their goodness is not at all troubling to the present-day neoliberal society; today it is not, existentially, countercultural. Canonization is harder to achieve for those whose goodness troubled—and still troubles—the neoliberal society.

6

TERRORISM AND BARBARITY:
NEW YORK AND AFGHANISTAN

We explained in the introduction why this chapter is being added.[1] By the nature of the subject, these reflections overlap with our reflections on the earthquake, but some of them are more specifically about the suffering that human beings inflict directly and intentionally on others. Let us begin.

The U.S. government did not formally define the events of September 11 as an aberrant terrorist attack but as an act of war; it responded militarily against Afghanistan, one of the poorest countries on the planet, with bombing, destruction, and the death of civilians. Alarms were soon raised about the consequences of this war: hunger and cold could produce an apocalyptic tragedy, leading to thousands of deaths. A week after the bombing began, the *New York Times* reported that 7.5 million Afghans would soon be in desperate need of a piece of bread. UNICEF warned that thousands of children might die in the coming weeks. United Nations officials called for a suspension of the bombing so they could provide relief assistance to millions of people, but the United States did not grant that request. The number of refugees was estimated in the millions. There was some talk of a "silent genocide."

It is hard to predict the future of Afghanistan. But there is a more important question about the future of humanity, which looks very dark right now. Other evils were added to the ones we have mentioned, as a result of the way the war has been conducted. When the Northern Alliance began to penetrate Taliban-controlled territory, at the fort of Qala-e-Jahngi, a few kilometers from Mazar-e-Sharif, hundreds of prisoners in handcuffs were shot to death by the Alliance. Human rights

---

[1]This chapter and the next are a reworking of my article "Redención de la barbarie y el terrorismo," *Revista Latinoamericana de Teología* 54 (2001), pp. 211-234.

organizations estimated six hundred summary executions in one day, and even President Bush in Washington had to ask that human rights be respected. In mid-December, a civilian convoy was bombed on its way to Kabul for the inauguration of the new president, leaving sixty dead. Many people protested, but the United States replied that "it was a legitimate target." On December 30 another bombing raid by the U.S. Air Force left some one hundred civilians dead, according to residents in the village of Janat Gul. Major Bill Harrison, spokesman for the U.S. Central Command, said from Tampa, Florida: "We believe it was a legitimate military target."[2] The new Afghan government has asked the United States to stop the bombing, but the reply was that the bombing—against a sovereign, allied country—would stop when the United States so decided. All told, as of mid-December, 2001, the number of civilian victims was nearly four thousand.[3]

What is at stake in this situation is above all the future of "humanity," the millions of people in Afghanistan and neighboring countries in Asia, and also—whether they know it or not—in the United States and its European allies. Our reflections in this chapter are about humanity and its future. But first let me make two preliminary clarifications.

a) We speak of "barbarity" because it is a broader term than "terrorism." We use it also because, although we need to sharpen our concepts—the United Nations and the European Union are working on a definition of "terrorism"—today we are in grave danger of reducing "barbarity" to "terrorism," and reducing terrorism to "what happened to the towers." The implication is clear: if we describe what happened in New York as "terrorism" and what happened in Afghanistan as "war," without relating the latter to "barbarity," then the United States has already won the battle of definitions; that would enable it to win the ethical battle in advance, and present itself as the defender of the good. The United States seems to be saying that because "terrorism" is an abomination—and it is—it must be fought until it disappears. But "war" is different. War can be just, noble, the salvation of humanity. (The government of Israel knows this well,

---

[2]*El País*, December 31, 2001. Harrison added: "If innocent people were killed, it would certainly be a tragedy. But the direct cause of the deaths is the enemy tactic of putting civilians in danger by living near them."

[3]A documented study by Mark W. Herold, professor of economics at the University of New Hampshire, gave a total of 3,767 civilian deaths during the first 8-1/2 weeks of the war (more or less up to December 10). It analyzes several causes for the high number of civilian deaths, but considers the main one to be "the very low value placed on Afghan civilian lives by the military leaders and political elite who planned the war"(p. 2).

and describes its struggle as a "war" against Palestinian "terrorism.")

To avoid reaching this conclusion *even before* analyzing the reality of the events, we speak of "barbarity" as a basic concept for understanding what is happening. The term describes both New York and Afghanistan. Its quantitative and qualitative seriousness comes from the facts, not from the words used to describe it. But this has not been the accepted procedure. For the past three months we have seen—and suffered—the thousands of times CNN has used the term "terrorism" to describe the attack on the towers, but it has not used—even as a way of applying suspicion—such terms as "massive cruelty," "massacres" of innocent and unarmed people, or "human tragedy" to describe the U.S. allies' actions and their consequences.

b) We have discussed the earthquake from a privileged location, *in situ*. But El Salvador is also a privileged location for talking about barbarity and terrorism. I want to say three things about that.

First, in El Salvador we have direct, massive, prolonged, and exceedingly cruel experience of barbarity and terrorism, especially from the government side. This is not hearsay testimony.

Second, we know something that is important for understanding the present crisis: countless times the U.S. government has invaded or intervened in other countries diplomatically, politically, militarily, and by means of coups d'état; it has also supported dictatorial regimes, often cruel and murderous violators of human rights. We know this firsthand here in El Salvador and in nearby Nicaragua, Guatemala, and Honduras. The U.S. government is also clearly and massively responsible for practices of barbarity and terrorist policies.

The third point is about the unique and specific gift that we in El Salvador have to offer in any discussion of barbarity and terrorism. We have known many people, many of them Christians, followers of Jesus, who have sought to "overcome" and even "redeem" this barbarity, terrorism, war, violence, and injustice, by struggling against it and bearing its burden. There are many of them, and the most outstanding of them are the "martyrs," from Monsignor Romero to the peasants of El Mozote. They have much to tell us about the meaning of barbarity and terrorism, about who the victims and principal perpetrators are, and also about how to combat and redeem them. We shall say more about this in the epilogue.

Now let us reflect, by means of brief propositions, on the fundamental human realities to which we are led as we think about terrorism and barbarity. These are not purely doctrinal reflections, but the kind of thoughts that help us to wrestle with New York and Afghanistan, with what is human and inhuman.

THE ULTIMACY OF THE HUMAN:
SUFFERING AND COMPASSION

First proposition. Barbarity and terrorism raise questions about what is ultimate for human beings, and they challenge us, inescapably, to answer. That "ultimate" is the suffering of the victims. And the "ultimate" reaction is compassion for them, co-suffering with them, living and pouring out life for an end to their suffering.

This may seem at least theoretically obvious, but it is not at all. Let us begin with September 11. Faced with the hijackings, the thousands of victims, the loss of loved ones and anguish for the missing, many people in the United States and other countries were affected by the suffering of the victims—but not everyone was. Some were even happy, and others reacted with a kind of philosophical bemusement: "They deserved it," "Now they'll know how it feels," "Let them wonder why such a barbarity happened." These people are not monsters, nor are they crazy; there is a certain rationality in what they say. Precisely for that reason, seeing them leads us to the following thesis: even without being especially evil, people may find it hard to be affected by other people's suffering, even when that suffering is obvious and cruel. And if this is true of what happened in New York and Washington, it is much more true of what happened in Afghanistan—bombing, civilian deaths, starving children, fleeing women; of what happened in Iraq with its 100,000 victims of allied bombing raids; of what is happening to people with HIV/AIDS who don't have $10,000 to $15,000 per year for retroviral medicines (it is estimated that only 400,000 of the 36 million victims can get them); of what is happening to the 1.3 billion people who have to live on less than a dollar a day.

We can identify a variety of structural reasons for this indifference to suffering in New York and Afghanistan, even without considering individual limitations and malice. On the one hand there is a general, partly justified feeling of hostility and even a desire for revenge; on the other, a general ignorance and even contempt toward the fate of people we consider inferior, as if they were metaphysically handicapped. The death of poor people in Afghanistan, the destruction of their homes, and the tragedy of the refugees do not evoke widespread sorrow in the First World.

We are looking at a kind of "existential immunization against the victims' suffering," which permeates our so-called civilization. Today's world has ways of showing that suffering and letting it challenge us (television, journalism, the Internet), but it also has guilt-free ways of numbing ourselves and suppressing the challenge (the entertainment, music, and sports industries); with few exceptions, the latter win out. It is not psychologically impossible to let the overwhelming suffering of the world's people, in its many forms, affect us. It is not primarily a matter of psychology, or even of ethics, but of fundamental anthropology. It is a matter of wondering what it means to be human, and of knowing that we cannot be human without thinking about what is ultimate in reality. That ultimate is the suffering of victims.

This is how Monsignor Romero saw it. In an interview with *El Diario de Caracas*, March 19, 1980, shortly before his assassination and in the midst of the national crisis, he was asked what could be done about the suffering of the Salvadoran people. He suggested several possible actions, and ended the list with these words: "Don't forget that we are men, and that here people are dying, running away, taking refuge in the mountains."[4]

When tragedy strikes (New York, Afghanistan, unjust poverty, and the countless wars on the planet, almost all in the Third World), the first thing to do is "not to forget that these are men," that they are "human beings." That is why, as Leonardo Boff said after the attack on New York, "Don't ask for whom the bell tolls."[5] We shouldn't ask whether the victim who suffers, or the Samaritan who helps, is a friend or enemy. We cannot see suffering and compassion from the viewpoint of this or that ethnic group or religion, cause or ideology. We shouldn't even ask whether suffering will be repaired and compassion will be rewarded in another life. In New York and Afghanistan, and in the Democratic Republic of the Congo, people are dying, injured, missing, running away, helpless, desperate. This is not the suffering of Americans, Asians, or Africans; it is the suffering of human beings.

And there is compassion, although only small gestures are widely known: heroic aid to the victims in the United States; relatives who are not looking for vengeance or war; one African-American member of the U.S. Congress, Barbara Lee, casting the only vote (420-1) against the war. We also know about the heroism of the firefighters and of one chaplain, who died attending to the victims.

At this distance it is harder to know how life and dignity are being defended in Afghanistan, but we know about the primordial saintliness and solidarity that people show in situations of desperate poverty; we have seen it here in times of repression and war. There was also compassion in the appeal of Mary Robinson, the United Nations

---

[4]J. Sobrino, I. Martín-Baró, and R. Cardenal, eds., *La voz de los sin voz*, UCA, San Salvador, 1980, p. 439.

[5]"Manifiesto por la concordia y por la paz," *Carta a las Iglesias* 481-482 (September 1-30, 2001), p. 7.

High Commissioner, for an end to the bombing "to allow food and blankets to reach the millions of Afghans" in the approaching winter.

Suffering, and the need for compassion, cannot be relativized. Barbarity cannot be justified by demeaning human beings: "They are infidels" on the one hand, and on the other, "We are the best, the most powerful." Suffering and compassion relativize—put in its place—anything else that tries to claim ultimacy: churches and religions, and also—lest we forget—the socialisms of the past, the Western democracies of the present. The great question is this: Do the victims distress and challenge us, or not? Does suffering distress and challenge us, or not? Does compassion fascinate and challenge us, or not? This is the spiritual dividing line that will decide the future of the human family.

In our world there are people, groups, a few institutions that allow suffering to affect them, and react with compassion. But that is not usually true of the powers that shape our world. Compassion is tolerated, even praised, as long as it does not turn into a struggle for justice. And suffering is relegated to the far distance, especially the suffering of the Third World. This is true in practice, but it is also tacitly present in theory.

With respect to democratic societies, certainly "liberty, equality, and fraternity" are good. But the ideal of liberty has failed in modern society; it leads neither to justice nor to solidarity.[6] And it is not clear, even in theory, that liberty, equality, and fraternity can provide an adequate response to the overwhelming suffering of the world. They do not place the poor—the ones who suffer—at the center; the citizen is central.[7] We should not be surprised to find the Western democracies lacking in compassion and mercy.

With respect to the Church, it has always tried to alleviate suffering—but only through charity, well or poorly understood. The "ultimacy of suffering" was gradually lost, even in theory. It was replaced early on by the "ultimacy of guilt," as we saw in the last chapter.

At present, with some exceptions such as churches that are faithful to Medellín in the Third World and solidarity groups in the First World, the Church does not seem to be giving ultimacy to the suffering of victims, or willing to live and pour out its life for them.

Let us close with a simple Christian reflection. Suffering and com-

---

[6]Cf. M. Vidal, "Libertad," in C. Florestán and J.J. Tamayo, eds., *Conceptos fundamentales del cristianismo* (Trotta, Madrid, 1993), p. 724.

[7]Let us remember what we said [on p. 84 n. 21] about the origin of human rights. Things have changed somewhat, of course, but not enough to reverse the historical "preference" of the democratic societies in favor of the powerful, turning it into a "preference" for the weak and poor, as happened in the biblical tradition.

passion are what enable us to be real—to overcome Docetism, as theologians say—to be simply human, and thus to live as saved human beings. Unless we allow ourselves to feel suffering and react with compassion, we lose something fundamental; that, I believe, is the great crisis of our time. We see it in various ways: in terrorism and war, in the nuclear threat of a few years ago and the destruction of mother nature, in the exclusion from life of a large part of humanity, and in the spreading senselessness of belonging to a "species" that is far from living as a human "family." But behind all this is our "immunization" from the suffering of victims and our "inability" to show compassion. Without this there is only selfishness, personal and especially social, blatant or subtle.

We cannot be human without making suffering and compassion central to our life. Admiration is what moves people to know, Aristotle said, and that is true. But there is a certain kind of admiration that sets knowledge on a human course. "Suffering comes before thought," Feuerbach said. Then, as the world became disenchanted with modernity, Adorno advocated a return to suffering as central to life: "The need to let suffering speak is the condition of all truth."

Certainly compassion is central to being human. The suffering of victims can de-center human beings and place love at the center. Who fulfills all the commandments? That is, who is truly human? The Samaritan. When he saw the victim, he was moved by pity and bandaged his wounds (Lk 10:33-34). Here is the fully realized human being, not because he is "religious," or "democratic," or "the best," but because he is moved to compassion.

THE WILL TO TRUTH: THE GREATER TRUTH

Second proposition. Freedom of expression is not the same as a will to truth. The latter is not present in today's crisis in the United States, with a few exceptions; rather there has been silence, distortion, concealment, historical amnesia. All this is dehumanizing and does not help to overcome barbarity and terrorism. It is the will to truth that humanizes.

In the Western democracies there is a lot of talk about freedom of expression, but the will to truth is something different. The barbarity of the towers is the most publicized terrorist act in the history of humanity (the destruction of Afghanistan doesn't even come close), but the official discourse and the media have not communicated the whole truth, the deepest part of the truth, about the event itself—let alone its causes. Freedom of expression, which costs money, is different from a will to truth, which requires only honesty, clarity, and courage. This is important because in today's world all reality passes through communication, so we shall discuss this theme in detail.

a) The barbarity of the towers has been communicated in half-truths. The communications media reported 5,000 to 6,000 victims, but the total was 2,553 according to the U.S. Red Cross and 2,625 according to the Associated Press; that is, about half the media estimate. As we said, in mid-December, the number of civilian dead in Afghanistan had reached 4,000.

In terms of interpretation, the World Trade Center was not only a symbol of economic power, but according to *The Guardian* (November 2, 2001) it was also a center for the CIA and the Secret Service. Thus it was an attack on a military-financial target, clearly so in the case of the Pentagon. "In short, there are two sides to the acts of September 11: the human tragedy and the personal heroism that CNN showed us, and the economic-political power struggle between the United States empire and its adversaries in the Third World."[8]

This does not mean that the terrorist attack was not an abomination or should not be condemned. But it shows the difference between freedom of expression and a will to communicate the truth. The difference is clearly visible in the world of the poor: those who have the truth and want to tell it have no voice, and those who have a voice are not interested in truth, let alone making it public. In the Western world, furthermore, taking pride in freedom of expression and seeing it as a great achievement of democracy may be—sometimes it is—an excuse to cover up the absence of a will to truth. And freedom of expression simply disappears in wartime; then it is not only a matter of failing to communicate truth, but of communicating lies. "The media report what governments tell them, and that is true of both the United States and the Afghan Taliban."[9]

Even worse than this concealment and lying is the decision to deny Afghanistan its own reality. Afghanistan is a country with 22.5 million inhabitants, with 3.695 million refugees and another million internally displaced, with a per capita gross domestic product of $178 in

---

[8]These data are taken from "El 11 de septiembre más allá de la tragedia humana," *Página de Petras*, November 10, 2001.

[9]"Guerra. Para el jesuita Pungente la información de los medios es unidireccional," from the internet, November 29, 2001. John Pungente, S.J., is director of the Jesuit Communication Project in Toronto. The late Joseph Moakley, for many years a congressman from Massachusetts and great supporter of the Salvadoran victims and refugees, used to say that to find the truth about Third World countries, he did not go to the Department of State; he would talk to the religious sisters working in those countries.

1999, with a life expectancy of forty-three years in 2000-2005, and 70 percent of the population suffering malnutrition.[10]

That is not what people think about, or what they're interested in, when they hear the word "Afghanistan." What is worse, they may excuse that fact by saying that New York and Washington are greater tragedies. They may point out that the status of women has improved in Afghanistan; women are now allowed to study, work, and choose their own dress style. That is indeed good news, although it is reported in an unconcealably propagandistic tone.

b) It is true that terrorism exists, but it is a greater truth that the powers have used terror whenever it suits them: in Auschwitz, Dresden, and Hiroshima, and years ago in the Soviet Union.

The United States in particular has intervened without compunction, using terrorism as needed, in Latin America in the 1970s and '80s, in Iraq and Sudan, and now in Uganda, Rwanda, and Burundi (to gain control of their coltan), and in the Democratic Republic of the Congo.

They do this knowing that their "manifest destiny" (a phrase coined in 1845 by journalist John O'Sullivan to justify the annexation of almost half of Mexico) is to impose their will on other countries for the other countries' own good. Simón Bolívar knew this very well: "The United States seems destined by Providence to plague America with misery in the name of freedom."[11]

c) A greater truth is that another kind of terrorism exists and persists but is seldom mentioned—a more fundamental kind, more dangerous and cruel because it kills many more people: the terrorism of hunger and poverty, which causes the exclusion and displacement of millions of people and leaves them at the mercy of AIDS, ignorance, and humiliation. Millions of human beings today are "terrorized," not by concrete acts of violence but by inhuman, anti-human structures. This kind of barbarity is barely mentioned in official reports; no massive campaigns are organized to make it known, and in any case it is never called "barbarity." Nor are its underlying causes explained, al-

---

[10]Neither is there serious emphasis on the country's recent history: the Soviet occupation of 1979-1989, the covert operations to overthrow the Soviets which were approved by President Carter in 1979 and expanded by President Reagan in 1985, the recruitment and training of thousands of volunteers to fight in Afghanistan, who later turned against their U.S. and Saudi benefactors and established an oppressive and fanatical regime. Apparently none of this is important, nor is it thought-provoking that today's terrorists were allies trained and financed by the United States.

[11]Quoted in J.I. González Faus, "De talibanes y talibushes," in *La Vanguardia*, November 29, 2001.

though the causes are largely found in the countries that defend freedom of expression. Barbarity is reported in inverse proportion to its breadth and depth: loudly in the case of the 3,000 victims, only incidentally in the case of millions of victims of war, violence, and hunger.

Several knowledgeable voices have been raised against this; we shall cite only two of them. Three Nobel laureates recently wrote to the secretary general of the United Nations. They denounced the war that was being launched, and continued:

> A struggle is needed against the silent bombs of hunger, poverty, and social exclusion, which represent a political and economic situation of structural injustice affecting a majority of the world's countries.[12]

A group of twenty-five Catholic bishops and evangelical pastors in Brazil and Mexico, writing about the war on Afghanistan and pointing out the tragic situation of whole continents, condemned neoliberal policies and "international indifference." They closed by saying:

> Only by overcoming the tensions caused by the exclusion and marginalization of large majorities; only by a concerted and sincere commitment to reduce international inequalities, to eliminate hunger, racism, and discrimination against women and ethnic and religious minorities, to cancel or reduce the debt of the poor countries, and to curb environmental damage and destruction, can the conditions for a lasting peace be created.[13]

d) It is also a greater truth that the West jealously controls "the definition" of terrorism, terrorists, and what to do with them. Thus simply by describing an event as "terrorist," they decide what can and should be done with its perpetrators. This constitutes a qualitative, and thus more serious, limitation on access to the truth.

The West frequently reserves for itself the definition of everything important, for its own benefit. We have already mentioned the underlying assumption: "The West—especially the United States—and its democracies are the measure of all things." That means they are the measure of truth, not in regard to trivialities but to fundamentals.

---

[12]Letter dated October 8, 2001, signed by Mairead Corrigan Maguire, Adolfo Pérez Esquivel, and Rigoberta Menchú Tum.

[13]"Clamor de los pueblos por la justicia, la solidaridad y la paz": *Carta a las Iglesias* 484 (October 16-31, 2001).

They impose their definition of "progress," "happiness," "goodness," "evil," "political correctness and incorrectness." Clearly, they also want to impose their definition of "humanity."

Thus they are privatizing the definition of fundamental realities, as they have done with other spheres of reality. And as with most types of private property, this privatizing dynamic deprives others of a voice; millions of victims of the above-mentioned forms of terrorism cannot say what is or is not terrorism. By images and words, the West not only offers *one* vision of reality, but imposes *the* right way to understand it. They impose political correctness, and almost no one can challenge it.

Although some people are making a goodwill effort to analyze its *formal* essence,[14] the most pernicious problem is that terrorism has been *historicized* as patrimony of the *weak*. "Terrorism" and "weakness" go together in conventional usage. Noam Chomsky suggests this possibility and explains—exposes—the reason why: "Terrorism is considered a weapon of the weak because the strong control the systems of indoctrination, and their terror does not count as terror."[15] This clearly means that no matter what the strong do—which today means especially the West and its democracies—even if they use military, physical, police, or ideological violence, that *by definition* is not terrorism. It may be something else, but it cannot be terrorism. So if civilians die in the bombing—100,000 in the bombing of Iraq—that is "collateral damage"; it does not belong to the *substance* of the war, but to its *accidents*. *A priori*, it cannot be understood as terrorism.[16]

It is true that some rank-and-file terrorists fit neatly into the definition and can be paraded on television. But a greater truth is that state terrorists also exist; there were many in the twentieth century, better dressed and politically, militarily, and economically more powerful. If we lack the will to truth to understand this, dehumanization will continue and increase. And that in turn will give the rank-and-

---

[14]Although the definition still needs refining, by terrorism we understand an action intended to "terrorize," that is, to instill fear in order to elicit specific behaviors. These actions include killing or injuring persons, and/or destroying or damaging valuable property, usually with cruelty.

[15]"Infinite Injustice," an address given at the Massachusetts Institute of Technology, October 18, 2001, p. 6.

[16]A similar type of hypocrisy surrounds the methods used by military and civilian intelligence services, such as the French in Algeria and the Latin Americans trained at the School of the Americas. Whatever technical definition is applied, these inhuman methods clearly have two purposes: to obtain immediate results from the victims and to create an atmosphere of terror, not only to paralyze subversive movements but also to prevent the exercise of human rights.

file terrorists an excuse, macabre perhaps but understandable and historically inevitable.

e) Another greater truth is that major decisions regarding the fate of the planet, and the reasons for them, are kept hidden. Obviously we are not told the whole truth of the reasons for the war in Afghanistan; in any case the reasons can change. This is not only to protect security; there are other, more fundamental and far-reaching reasons that are not discussed. The so-called "right to information" often suffers the same fate as "freedom of expression." Both are subject to quantitative as well as qualitative restrictions: how much information can be given or demanded, as well as what kind.

Certainly at the beginning of the war on Afghanistan, there was a need to respond forcefully to the humiliation and to make a convincing show of power.[17] The immediate target was Bin Laden, but the underlying purpose may have been different. "The United States is not interested in proving Bin Laden's guilt; their objective is to establish their right to do what they want when they want, and to clearly establish their credibility as a global bully."[18] And let us not forget the need to control the region's oil and to facilitate the elimination of Saddam Hussein in Iraq.

f) To close these reflections on higher truth: why is it so often said that September 11 is a key date in the history of our era, marking a line between before and after? In our opinion, one reason is that it has opened a window on the global truth of this world and exposed a fundamental deception: the fragility, and often hypocrisy, of the "human" in human progress.

The coming of the "end of history" is proclaimed as eschatological, universal good news. "Globalization" has brought, or is about to bring, the kingdom of God in economic terms (neoliberalism), in political terms (the Western democracies), and in cultural terms (the homogenization of a civilization built on television, serials, music, world championships, and multi-million dollar Olympic games). September 11 brought down an eloquent silence, and someone asked, "Whatever happened to the global village?" The higher truth does not lie in globalization,[19] but in the contradiction between political democracies and an extraordi-

---

[17]Rigoberta Menchú wrote to President Bush: "We who are tired of dying in other people's wars cannot accept the arrogance of your infallibility; neither can we follow the inflexible path you want to impose by saying, 'Every nation in every region must now decide: you are with us or with the terrorists.'"

[18]"Infinite Injustice," p. 1.

[19]See J. Sobrino and F. Wilfred, eds., "La globalización y sus víctimas," *Concilium,* monograph issue, 293 (2001).

narily powerful world regime beyond democratic control. The little people simply don't count. They don't exist.

Will this contradiction be reversed? Very probably the good news will continue to be preached, and soon it will be preached again with the same enthusiasm as before September 11. People will say, "We won." But what it means to win has not yet been explained: not in detail, which is understandable, and not in fundamentals, which is more serious. Neither has it been explained how "winning" benefits humanity. Behind the words of today's winners is a greater silence that speaks much more eloquently about today's world, a silence that is not dispelled by discreetly triumphalistic reports proclaiming the latest technological exploits but carefully ignoring the bombing raids against civilian people and institutions, refugees, and the terrorism of the victors.

There is talk about a "new world order," but we are not told what that order is. Is it "a right distribution of goods in the world," or is it a geographic, economic, military, and political redistribution of the planet among the same people as always, enabling them to go on living well and, when the scare has passed, to enjoy the good life with greater security? The question being asked today, how to balance freedom with security, suggests an intention to keep things the same. There is no thought of something new, of a new axis on which the world might turn humanely at last. Instead of the world turning on any of the prevailing forms of power, we would put the victims at the center, where they can humanize this world.

The greater truth is that the so-called "forces of good," the protectors of the world's *well-being*, do not look *well* on the rest of the world (allies or adversaries); they do not think *well*, or listen *well*, even to people who may be wiser and more prudent (the elder Bush also didn't listen to John Paul II, the only one who opposed his bombing of Iraq), and they do not respond *well*. They cannot even give an honest answer to the fundamental question: What do we want? Do we want victory parades or a fraternal embrace?

Here I want to repeat the words of Ignacio Ellacuría, prophet and thinker, who was unequalled for his vigor (which no one disputes) and also his rigor (which some may question). Months before he was killed, he said at a conference on the quincentennial:

> From my point of view—and this may be both prophetic and paradoxical—the United States is worse off than Latin America. Because the United States has a solution, but in my opinion it is a bad solution, both for them and for the world in general. In Latin America, on the other hand, there are no solutions, only problems;

painful as that is, it is better for the future of history to have problems than to have a bad solution.[20]

These are bold, utopian words. They come from his will to truth, and uncover a greater truth. September 11, and what has happened since in the Middle East, Afghanistan and Iraq, show how right he was: the giant who is supposed to save us has a bad solution. And feet of clay.

What can we say about truth from a Christian standpoint? "For the wrath of God is revealed from heaven against all ungodliness and wickedness of those who by their wickedness suppress the truth" (Rom 1:18). As a result the human heart is darkened; people are given over to all kinds of aberrations, to dehumanization. But the powerful choose to oppress the truth, so that the reality will not come to light. And as Christian tradition maintains, evil always seeks concealment, represents itself as something different. The devil is a murderer and a liar, says John's gospel, in that order. He plunders, oppresses, kills, and then covers it up.

On the other hand, John's gospel proclaims Jesus the way, the truth, and the life. The truth sets human beings on the right path and gives them life. It also fights against the lie. The great Christians of our time, like Romero and Gerardi, have done the same. And now is a good time to remember Martin Luther King. A year before he was killed, he said in a protest against the Vietnam War: "The time has come when silence is treason."

To avoid committing treason, it is not enough to use our freedom of expression and boast about it; we must put the will to truth in action. Only the will to truth—not freedom of expression alone—can guarantee a greater truth, that is to say, real truth.

THE UTOPIA OF RECONCILIATION: BROTHERHOOD BETWEEN MANHATTAN AND EL SALVADOR

Third proposition. In the midst of barbarity and terrorism, might has prevailed over understanding, destruction over reconciliation, selfish pragmatism over utopia. But if utopia disappears, humanness becomes impossible. There are small signs that utopia still lives, and that keeps hope alive.

The war of the United States, acting simultaneously as plaintiff and judge, against the sovereign nation of Afghanistan, is not a "just war." In the first place it does not meet the criteria established in

---

[20]"Quinto centenario de América Latina. ¿Descubrimiento o encubrimiento?," *Revista Latinoamericana de Teología* 21 (1990), p. 277.

traditional just war theory. Moreover, recent theory suggests that a just war is no longer possible, given the evils produced by new military technology, and given the alternative possibilities of nonviolent action and international institutions for conflict resolution. In a deeper sense, war was not the only available response to the attacks. The United States could have sought relief from international tribunals as the Nicaraguan government did, charging the United States with the death of thousands of civilians. The World Court condemned the United States, but the United States did not recognize its jurisdiction.[21]

Now that humanity is beginning a new millennium, with all kinds of promises and expectations promoted by the Western world, the failure to solve the problem politically and peacefully represents a lost opportunity—and shows how ineffective and hypocritical most Western rhetoric has been.

But it is a lost opportunity in a primordial, more fundamentally human—and more utopian—sense. Without doubt it is utopian—"it doesn't have a place"—to think of the United States submitting to the verdict of an international tribunal. It is even more utopian to think of the United States returning to itself, analyzing its past, seeking truth and feeling sorrow—and peace—when it finds the truth, even though that would require conversion. And above all it is utopian to imagine the United States seeking and offering reconciliation and brotherhood.

It may seem strange to contemplate these utopias, because they really are *ou-topia* ("that which has no place"). It is harder to write about utopia than to prophetically denounce insensitivity to suffering and compassion, and the lack of will to truth, as we have done. But it is absolutely necessary, because utopia establishes two things that are essential to humanity. In the first place it establishes the content of humanness: that which human beings must reach for and by which all progress will be judged human or inhuman. And in the second, utopia establishes the hope that humanness is possible. In both cases utopia (*eu-topia*) means goodness. Let us look at the "lost opportunities" from that vantage point. It should not be surprising that we describe them as possibilities and demands that come forth in a process of "conversion"; whether we say it in these or different words, conversion is what our world needs.

What would have happened if the United States had opened its eyes to its own reality? If Congress and the White House—encouraged and

---

[21]Nicaragua had appealed earlier to the World Court and to the United Nations Security Council. "To date, the United States is the only State that has been condemned by the World Court and has vetoed the resolution of the Security Council" (which went against it in the Nicaraguan case) ("Infinite Injustice," p. 5).

supported by the Western democratic governments, by universities that believe in liberty, equality, and fraternity, by churches and religions that believe in a good God who cares for the weak and the victims, by humanistic movements that believe in the right to life for human beings—if they had asked, what caused such horror? What has this country done to elicit such hatred? This is what used to be called an "examination of conscience," praised by priests and psychiatrists as a good thing to do in situations of personal crisis. If it is good and humanizing at the personal level, why should it not also be good and humanizing—in its proper historical context—for a people?

What would have happened if the United States had opened its heart to the pain it has inflicted on this planet? We used to call this "heartache." But apparently feeling pain is an intolerable weakness for a superpower. Thus it is imprisoned in the fundamental evil we analyzed in the first point of this chapter: there can be no humanity without participation in suffering and compassion.

What would have happened if, unilaterally and precisely in those moments of suffering from aggression, the United States had offered acts of understanding to the Muslim and Third World peoples, acts of compassion and respect for their people who have lived in poverty and suffering for centuries, acts of exchanging natural and spiritual riches—rather than plundering their raw materials and imposing a pseudo-culture on them? In the past, people have suggested "reparations" for damage done. That would be humanizing. Not the arrogance of those who consider themselves physically and morally untouchable.

What would have happened if the first word spoken—without minimizing the victims' sorrow and the pursuit of justice for perpetrators—had been an invitation to reconciliation? That is what a process of conversion leads to: the peace of feeling human again, the joy of feeling human with one another, reconciliation, a shared table.

Obviously it didn't happen that way; even the possibility wouldn't occur to most of us. Power never helps people move toward reconciliation. Not arrogance and might, but simplicity and an affectionate embrace, can put an end to barbarity, to endless bombing and destruction, to the determination to win the war despite the terrible tragedy and thousands of deaths it costs.

What did happen is not exactly a "lost opportunity," since it seems impossible. But not quite impossible. There were acts of forgiveness and reconciliation by some victims' family members:

Our son Greg is one of the missing in the attack on the Twin Towers. We see our sorrow and anger reflected in everyone we meet. But we have read enough to understand that our government is choosing a course of violent vengeance. This is what will happen: sons and daughters, fathers and mothers, friends, dying and suffering in distant countries, and new attacks being provoked against us. That is not the way. It will not avenge the death of our son. Don't do this in our son's name.[22]

There have also been acts of great sharing with the peoples who suffer. In the introduction we mentioned the appreciation expressed by Margaret Swedish, for the solidarity of peasant men and women in Chalatenango. She also said something that relates to our discussion of utopia:

What can a community of faith and solidarity offer in this moment of horror and fear? First, and perhaps most important, the gift of compassion for the victims, their families, friends, and co-workers. There is sorrow in our communities, people need our attention and our time, they need us to listen to their sorrows and fears. . . . We know that well because for years we have walked with many victims of violence through their traumas. Many families of today's victims are suffering one of the greatest horrors of the repression in Central America: the disappearance of their loved ones. I pray that most of the victims' families will have the comfort of being able to bury their loved ones with dignity, according to the traditions that are meaningful to them. That is what we learned in Central America.[23]

Encouraged by these testimonies, and reluctant to believe that the opportunity for something good has been entirely lost, shortly after September 11 I wrote a piece of utopian fiction: "In El Salvador there have been many September 11s; they were more lasting, cruel and unjust, their victims equally helpless. Now the people of Manhattan are beginning to understand the people of El Salvador, the Indians of Guatemala, the Africans of Rwanda, Burundi, and the Democratic Republic of the Congo. They are beginning to understand the Arabs and Muslims of Iraq and Palestine." Then I added even more utopian words, the only ones—I believe—that can save the Empire of the North: "Without saying so, perhaps only by intuition, they are beginning to feel part of a great family of suffering and compassion: the human family. Belonging to the most powerful country in the world has lost

---

[22]Phyllis and Orlando Rodríguez, "No lo hagan en nombre de nuestro hijo," *Carta a las Iglesias* 481-482 (September 1-30, 2001), p. 12.

[23]M. Swedish, "Lecciones de solidaridad," p. 13.

its magic. They would rather be brothers and sisters."

As utopian as they are, we cannot afford to waste these—or other more modest—opportunities for humanization. We know well that it takes power to resolve conflicts, or to impose one's will on others. But seldom or never do we try using the power that comes from love. We will never know what would have happened if the United States had followed this other, utopian path. To choose membership in the human family over being the most powerful, to offer reconciliation instead of vengeance, to support rather than destroy a poor people: this is utopian, but it is humanizing, and in the long run it is what can undermine terrorism.

In any case, the worst that could happen would be not even to try to follow utopian values; to reject that path completely, in favor of the path of power. The path of utopia is possible, but it requires a "will to humanity"—a better term than "political will," which does not seem able to change things. The above-mentioned bishops' document affirms and analyzes this possibility:

What is being spent on the operation against Afghanistan would be enough to free that country and many others from the hunger, misery, and destruction they now suffer, establishing relationships of respect and cooperation, help and solidarity, instead of intensifying their suffering and planting new seeds of hatred and misunderstanding.

This is not the first time in recent history that the United States has faced a military situation that challenges it from within—that asks very simply whether or not they want to be a human nation and a human people. Similar cries were raised about Vietnam. So now we may wonder what would have happened if the words of Martin Luther King about Vietnam had been taken seriously:

I am convinced that if we want to be on the right side of the world revolution, we as a nation must undertake a radical revolution of values . . . which leads us to question the justice and balance of many of our past and present policies. . . . A true revolution of values will lead us to look with concern on the great contrast between poverty and riches. . . . We face a tremendous urgency. . . . Today we still have a choice: nonviolent coexistence or the violent annihilation of all.

WHERE IS GOD AND WHAT IS GOD DOING IN THE TRAGEDIES?

Originally I planned to end this book with a reflection on God, the earthquake, and how the earthquake has affected the people's faith: their acceptance of God, their fear, their protests. But New York and Afghanistan brought in a new dimension: the way religion and faith in God can lead to fanaticism, which can lead even to suicide and the terrorism of the towers. (The way "secular religions" can lead to fanaticism and barbarity, like the bombing of Afghanistan, has not been much discussed as far as we know.)

Let us begin with a preliminary word about the earthquake and God. Because it was a natural tragedy (albeit with historical elements, as we have seen), God seems to be more directly related to the earthquake and even responsible for it. In popular piety, God may appear as the *mysterium* in its *tremens* dimension, destructive and irreversible. That is just how God is. Before the secularization of our societies, an earthquake might have brought to mind the question of theodicy: is God able and willing to prevent tragedy? Perhaps there is still some of that, but without the same anguish: because it is no longer existentially traumatic to think of God as not existing, and because in the affluent countries an earthquake is no longer as terrifying as it once was. Earthquakes don't normally happen in those countries, and if they do, people are better protected from their destructive effects. Earthquakes and other natural catastrophes are not generally a threat to the *good life* that we've been talking about.

This doesn't mean that believers—those who take seriously Jesus' cry from the cross, "My God, my God, why have you abandoned me?"[1]—

---

[1]"For many years—as long as I have been in regular contact with indigenous populations—I have felt the disappearance of whole peoples as an absurd mystery of historical inquity, which turns my faith into despondency. 'Lord, why have you abandoned them?' How can the father of life, the creative Spirit of every culture, allow

and honest agnostics who will not settle for triviality—never face the question of theodicy. They do, either in the religious sense of questioning God, or in the more general sense of questioning reality and the human beings within it. Theodicy is also present, in a way, for the simple people who timidly ask where God is—especially, in El Salvador, when they remember times of repression and war. Formulated as a thesis, *the earthquake brings us to the problem of theodicy.*

Now let us look at terrorism and barbarity. They also bring us back to theodicy: why did God make people like that, capable of such hatred, of killing one another so unjustly and cruelly? But the crisis that began on September 11 did not lead directly to a debate about God, but about the fanaticism that religion causes. Formulated as a thesis, today *terrorism brings us to the problem of religious fanaticism.* (Again, there is no discussion of the fanaticism—or whatever we want to call it—that has led to the war in Afghanistan.)

At this point we must make clear that both theodicy[2] and religious fanaticism[3] are age-old problems. But today the problem of theodicy has lost relevance in the public debate, while that of religious fanaticism has become central. We need to know *where* that change comes from, and why it is changing *now*.

As far as I can see, religious fanaticism is not being debated in the Third World, at least not as an evil that could lead society to question or reject religion. It is or can be very bad, but it is not an *evil* on the same level as death, injustice, poverty, ethnocide and the destruction of cultures.

The situation is different in the affluent world. Their enlightened and emancipated heritage makes them more sensitive to the evils caused by religion, and specifically to religious fanaticism. But *why*, just now, should the discussion of fanaticism become so virulent? The answer seems obvious: September 11. But it is not that simple. There was religious fanaticism in our world before September 11, as well as other secular fanaticisms generated by nationality, empire, and money; they have always been strong and produced bad effects. Those bad effects do not in themselves explain why religious fanaticism has now become a central topic of debate; it is because this time the effects have hit close to home. That is also why terrorism, which has been omni-present throughout the twentieth century, has become not

---

them to be annihilated?" (Pedro Casaldáliga, "Los indios crucificados. Un caso anónimo de martirio colectivo," *Concilium* 183 [1983], p. 387).

[2] J. A. Estrada, *La imposible teodicea* (Madrid), 1997.

[3] K. J. Kuschel and W. Beuken, eds., "La religión, ¿fuente de violencia?," *Concilium* 272 (1997), monographic issue.

just a bad thing but evil itself. It is not only a threat, but a threat to "what is ours."

None of this makes religious fanaticism and terrorism any less evil, but it puts them in a more appropriate historical context. This context is easily forgotten in the affluent world, which has always thought that *its* perspective—which includes taking life for granted and constantly improving its living standards—is *the only* perspective. It has always been this way, as perceptive Europeans are also aware.

If I remember right, when Freud identified the libido as the fundamental human energy, Ernst Bloch replied that Freud could say that because his stomach was full. Simone de Beauvoir tells in her memoirs about a similar observation by Simone Weil. Simone Weil told her that the historical task of their time was "a revolution that would give everyone enough to eat." De Beauvoir replied that the problem was not giving them food, but giving meaning to their existence. She reports that Weil "silenced me by saying, 'It's easy to see that you've never been hungry.' "[4]

I don't want to exaggerate, but I cite these testimonies to emphasize that even the most obvious and sacrosanct human reflection is conditioned by primary, material, cultural, and ethical realities. From my own concrete, equally limited, Salvadoran perspective, I now want to reflect on "where God is and what God is doing in the tragedies," on "religious fanaticism," and on "theodicy." European readers may or may not agree with these answers, but I invite them to consider non-European perspectives along with their own. Perhaps this will help them, just as we who are now here were once helped by the enlightened perspectives of other times.

RELIGIOUS FANATICISM AND THE GOD OF LIFE

First proposition. The gods, religious or secular, are present in barbarity and terrorism. The God of religions, who is certainly the God of Abraham, can be used in fanatical ways; but God is in favor of life for all, and especially for the weak. Christian tradition adds that this same God was crucified for defending the weak from every kind of barbarity.

It is undeniable that God has often been thought up by human be-

---

[4]In J. I. González Faus, "Simone Weil (1909-1943). Un paradigma para la izquierda," *Sal Terrae* (July-August 1993), p. 568. Simone Weil, an outstanding intellectual, died in London in 1934 at age thirty-four because she refused to eat more than a working woman of her day in France. Cf. S. Pétrement, *Simone Weil: A Life* (New York: Pantheon, 1976).

ings in order to take their side against other gods in the religious sphere, and against their enemies in the historical sphere. In early times there were no states without God, and no God without a state.[5] God was the protector of human groups; this required power, and the destruction of enemies was an essential art of God's protection. Religion generates objective violence, often with incredible cruelty, and to this end it generates subjective fanaticism. Speaking with sharp irony about September 11, José Saramago has repeated his thesis about the historical essence of religion:

> No religion, ever, has served to bring men together in fellowship; on the contrary religion has always been and continues to be a cause of untold suffering, massacres, monstrous times of physical and spiritual violence that constitute one of the darkest chapters of our miserable human history. . . . A majority of believers in any religion not only pretend to ignore that fact, but rise up in anger and intolerance against those for whom God is only a name, nothing more than a name that we once gave him because we were afraid of dying, which since then has interfered with our progress toward real humanization. . . . Because of God and in God's name everything is permitted and justified, especially the worst, especially that which is most horrendous and cruel.[6]

These are biting words. Some people, while conceding the tendency of religion to generate fanaticism,[7] put it more gently; they see religion itself as capable of regulating illegitimate violence,[8] and they also point out the humanizing, antiviolent potential of religion,[9] all of which Saramago denies in principle.

We do not challenge the thesis that religions can generate and have generated fanaticism and violence, but we want to add three brief reflections to place it in context, especially in today's debate: *a)* religion

---

[5] Cf. J. Moltmann, *Crítica teológica de la religión política* (Salamanca, 1973), pp. 20 ff.

[6] "El factor Dios," *El País*, September 18, 2001.

[7] "The sacrificial dimension is central in most religions. . . . The struggle between Good and Evil is another source of violence, closely linked to religion. . . . Religious expansion is also linked to the use of violence. . . . Foundational texts reflect the ritualized violence of sacrifice, the use of violence for a higher good, its necessity for the defense of the faith. . . ." (F. Houtart, "El culto de la violencia en nombre de la religión: un panorama," *Concilium* 272 [1997], pp. 618 ff.)

[8] *Ibid.*, p. 619.

[9] For example, R. Schwager, "La religión como fundamentación de una ética para la superación de la violencia," *Concilium* 272 (1997), pp. 175-187.

contains self-correcting elements to overcome fanaticism and violence; *b)* violence is a consequence of all idolatry, not only the religious form; *c)* religion is capable of generating compassion and love. We shall do this by a simple method: recalling and interpreting the commandments of God's law in the Christian biblical tradition. In the epilogue we shall add a word about the redemption of violence in some religious traditions.

"You shall not use God's name in vain" (the second commandment). Using God's name in vain is an inveterate custom. In peaceful times we do so "peacefully," almost unnoticeably; in wartime we do it in shrill voices. The custom appears early in the Old Testament: the priests of Baal were murdered in the name of Yahweh. Early Christianity was the object of violence and responded nonviolently, but the Constantinian shift soon changed the relationship between Christian religion and the use of violence. Christianity, which had maintained Jesus' values in some ways, despite its inevitable and gradual institutionalization— at least it had not grossly contradicted Jesus' values—changed its self-understanding when it became a state religion.

"By an extraordinary but almost fatal reversal of the situation, [Christianity] was changed overnight from proscribed religion to state religion. . . . It became official when the persecution once directed against it was redirected against paganism, eliminating it from the scene."[10] From then on religion, Christ, and God were used to generate and justify fanaticism. During the time of Christendom the crusaders carried a cross and earned indulgences that assured them eternal salvation. The cross and the sword came to Latin America together. We have conducted religious wars and holy wars for millennia. So let us not be naive. Throughout history religions have violated the second commandment, with grave intentions: to murder human beings.

Now this violent potential has reappeared in public, in a barbarous and incredibly threatening form, explicitly and scandalously using religious language: "God sent these planes to destroy the towers." "This terrorism is blessed." Such words are terrifying, for they speak of cruelly murdering other human beings, and they terrify believers[11] by

---

[10]J. L. Segundo, *The Liberation of Dogma* (Maryknoll, NY: Orbis Books, 1972), p. 143. R. Aguirre also comments that "a Church that was marginalized and persecuted, soon after becoming the supporter of the dominant ideology, marginalized and persecuted others" ("La persecución en el cristianismo primitivo," *Revista Latinoamericana de Teología* 37 (1986), p. 39.

[11]Tom Michel, secretary for Interreligious Dialogue of the Jesuit Curia, affirms that "among Muslims there is universal condemnation of the terrorist attacks as violations of the teachings of Islam. Muslims clearly and completely share the indignation and solidarity with the victims that is being expressed around the world."

making God ultimately responsible for those deaths. So aberrations have been committed through religion. What we need to analyze is whether this is a unique, in-depth response to its essence as religion, or whether it responds to human structures that are expressed in religion, but also in other spheres of reality. In this sense we can understand why someone has said that we need "less faith in God and more faith in man"—one of many quotes circulating on the Internet. But that may not be very helpful, since in "man's" eyes if not in "God's," it is "man" who decides how to treat others. And many things are involved in that decision.

I mention this possibility not as a kind of facile apologetic, but out of a will to truth. In the first place, unfortunately, we do not violate the second commandment only in religious contexts. In secular Europe, God's name is not invoked in matters of war (although secular gods may be), but in the United States, Bush Senior prayed to God on the eve of the bombing of Iraq (which left over 100,000 dead). "God bless you" is the obligatory ending of many presidential speeches, which often involve lying about serious matters: human rights, war, life, and death. Members of the ecclesiastical hierarchy have also blessed troops, airplanes, and helicopters in the United States and here in El Salvador—and we have never understood the purpose of that.

My purpose in mentioning examples from the United States and El Salvador is to emphasize that by using God's name and religious ritual in the context of a war, we do not necessarily make it a religious war. I don't believe God mattered much in Bush Senior and Junior's decisions about going to war, nor in the Salvadoran presidents' decisions about repression and war, even if they did mention God's name. Something else was happening there: a crass manipulation of God and of religious sentiment.

We have taken, and are still taking, God's name in vain. Just as we take in vain the name of a country, a race, the West, the revolution, democracy, freedom—and the victims of Hitler, Stalin, and the presidents who ordered the bombing of Hiroshima, Sudan, or Afghanistan are just like the victims of today's religious fanaticism. This is no comfort, let alone justification, for religious people who also manipulate God. But it helps us understand that "taking in vain" that which we hold ultimate is a part of the human condition, not only its religious dimension. We might say that "taking in vain," when it happens in the religious sphere, is especially dangerous because religion expresses, more radically than other realities, the "most absolutely absolute"—divinity—and it falsely claims to offer "definitive salvation." But as we shall see, that also happens in nonreligious spheres. Was World

War II, with its 50 million victims,[12] a war of religion? Were the wars in Central America religious wars?[13]

We humans can always invoke realities, both to motivate good actions and to justify bad ones. Since many religious traditions were present in the origins of the western world and have shaped it, it is still possible to invoke God phonetically—rightly or wrongly, to "let God be God" or to "manipulate God"—and with changing times, it will always be possible to invoke "gods."

Among many recent writings, I will cite these insightful words of Juan Barreto:

> I, a man, curse god. I curse him. One and a thousand times. God with a small "g". Many have died in his name, murdered for his sake. . . . I curse the multiform god who also hides behind so many enlightened names, of laymen and even agnostics. They all claim to establish the supreme truth, but their very disdain for the pain of mortals betrays them.[14]

It is very dangerous to invoke God, or gods. Religions, and every human being, should remember that. But we must not forget that in principle at least, religions also contain self-correcting mechanisms. Religions can offer solutions for their own dangers. It is not easy, it is like a miracle, but it happens. Medellín, the Church of the poor, the Jesus of the victims: these are not ingenious inventions or products of a sophisticated apologetic; they are at the heart of Christian tradition. They are the most profound "thesis" of the Christian religion at its very origin. And throughout history, when religion is corrupted, they have been its fundamental corrective. As modest as the corrective has sometimes been—and it was not so modest in Latin America in the 1970s and '80s—we must take it into serious consideration in order to analyze religions properly.

In terms of our current theme, the second commandment is the great intrinsic corrective of the religion that proclaims it: "You shall not take the name of God in vain."

---

[12]The suicidal kamikazes were fanatics serving the divine emperor, but the war and its barbarity involved more than religious gods. Perhaps the gods were sometimes invoked in propaganda, but they were not fundamental to the real motivation of the war.

[13]It is true that some Christians from the base communities enlisted in popular armies, also motivated by their religious faith. But defending some divinity or other was not at the center of their motivation; they were moved by love for the oppressed in their country, although they did see that love as central to the God of Jesus.

[14]"Maldición por Navidad" (Tacoronte, Christmas 2001).

Idols. "No one can serve two masters" (Jesus of Nazareth). Not only were the gods' names used in vain in New York and Afghanistan; they have been very present, on one side and the other, as *idols*. I believe—although it is theoretically debatable—that none of us can free ourselves from one god or another. The "God factor" permeates us all in some way. We all come back to something ultimate, albeit in different ways. Jesus said so with his usual wisdom: "There are many masters, and you must choose which one you will serve."[15] He gave an example that hits home in the West, with our emphasis on materialism and the good life: "No one can serve God and money."[16] There are many gods, and they are usually present in wars, precisely because in wars there are many "ultimate" things at stake.

a) Secular gods. José Luis Sicre has shown, to his great credit, that the Old Testament prophets moved idolatry out of the religious into the historical sphere.[17] In the case of Israel, idolatry consisted of placing trust in foreign powers (international politics was a sphere of idolatry!) and in the accumulation and monopolization of goods, which were used to oppress others and reduce them to misery. (In my opinion, this historical and theological thesis has not been accorded the importance it deserves, in theory and in practice.) These days we seldom see wars launched in the name of "religious" gods, but many cruel wars are made in the name of "secular" gods: gold, oil, uranium, coltan, strategic territory. The United States made a god—something ultimate—of El Salvador because of its geostrategic value: their "backyard." But we should not be deceived: these gods make the same demands as the others. The external forms of worship may change: some are more openly *fanatical* (even suicide); others are more subtle, but equally *determined* to use whatever cruelty is needed to defend the West, and especially to defend their own well-being and freedom, so that no one can threaten "what is ours."

The religious and secular gods have much in common. Let us observe it first in the secular gods, pointing out the faults that are usu-

---

[15]Some may say, against this thesis, that there is a *tertium quid*: to do without an ultimate. Now is not the time for that debate. In my opinion there always is (seems to be) something ultimate, if only the peace and serenity that may come from not having to face the ultimate.

[16]In secularized societies the alternative to the true God does not have to be something intrinsically bad, *mammon*; it can be something good such as "humanity," the "establishment of justice," etc. In such cases God does not have to be exclusive of these "divinities," at least theoretically; the two may sometimes converge.

[17]*Los dioses olvidados*, Madrid, 1979; his argument follows G. von Rad. See by the same author, *"Con los pobres de la tierra." La justicia social en los profetas de Israel* (Cristiandad, Madrid, 1985).

ally found with religious gods. They are *untouchable*. Monsignor Romero said, "I especially denounce the absolutization of wealth . . . as an untouchable absolute. Woe to anyone who touches that high-voltage wire! They will get burned" (homily of August 12, 1979). They present themselves as something that, being ultimate, *needs no justi-fication*. For example, *business is business* is a highly theologal formu-lation. And above all, *they produce victims*. As Monsignor Romero said, historical gods, like the mythological Moloch, must have victims to survive (Fourth pastoral letter, August 6, 1979). In our time, idols have produced victims directly at the Twin Towers and in Afghanistan, and indirectly in places like Africa, Pakistan, India, Haiti. It happened massively in Central and South America in recent years; there the "idols" were capital accumulation and the doctrine of national secu-rity.

In this context, both religious and secular idolatries are identified by whether or not they cause violations of the commandments that protect human life; that is, the ultimate verification of idolatry, even religious idolatry, is by a secular standard. "You shall not steal" (the seventh commandment) has always been the great problem of empires and powers: to take what belongs to others, gold, oil, uranium, coltan, territory rich in raw materials or strategic value. The fifth command-ment, "You shall not kill," is also violated—to facilitate stealing, or to protect what one has stolen, or to scare off real or potential rivals. Finally, "You shall not bear false witness" (the eighth commandment) is violated to conceal, justify, or cover up previous robberies and mur-ders.

b) Religious gods. In today's crisis the secular gods are ignored, which leads to a faulty analysis of what is happening: the potential for fa-naticism is attributed to the religious gods. There is special mention of the three Abrahamic religions that in one way or another converge in the conflict. Let us ask first, in what way they are sources of fanati-cism.

All three are *monotheistic* religions, with *one* God: Yahweh, the Father of Jesus, Allah. They are religions of the *book*: Old Testament, New Testament, Qur'an, with *one* truth. And they are religions of *elec-tion,* with a chosen people. These three characteristics can cause seri-ous problems. *Monotheism* can lead on the one hand to exclusivism and intolerance, and on the other to proselytism, which leads people to take away others' freedom. A religion of the *book*, fixed and un-touchable, may justify fundamentalism with respect to truth, although the book can legitimately be held up to the light of reason, as in the case of Christianity. *Election* may cause feelings of superiority, of hav-ing rights over others even to the point of subjugating them, although both Judaism and Christianity have self-correcting mechanisms against this danger: both denounce any mechanical understanding of salvation as derived from being a chosen people.[18]

These are real dangers, but we insist that they are not peculiar to a "religious" understanding of life. Monotheism, as an expression of exclusiveness and bellicosity, is present in the words of Bush: "You are either with us or with the terrorists." The idea of *election*—being chosen specifically to save others—is present almost from the beginning of the United States' self-awareness, and it is a decisive aspect of their foreign and military policy. I will dwell a moment on that, because of its importance today and because it is so publicly and proudly invoked.

We have already mentioned the "manifest destiny" that the United States has claimed for the past century and a half. In 1900 the Senator from Indiana, Albert Beveridge, put it in explicitly religious language. He said, referring to God:

He has given us the gift of governing, that we may give government to the savage and senile peoples. Without this power of ours, the world would fall into barbarity and night. . . . God has designated the North American people as his chosen nation to begin the regeneration of the world.[19]

This awareness of "election" has not disappeared. It is still present in the U.S. right, although not in religious words. In 1997 Madeleine Albright had this to say about manifest destiny:

We Americans have an advantage over other nations: we know who we are and what we believe. We are builders. Our responsibility is not to act as prisoners of history, but to make history. . . . We have a reason for being, and we have faith that, if we are faithful to our principles, we shall triumph.[20]

"You shall love the God of life with all your heart" (the first com-

---

[18]In the real meaning of election, Israel was chosen for a mission, that is, for the good of others rather than its own advantage. And the prophets insisted that election was not exclusive to Israel. Amos relativized election, stressing the universality of God's saving act in Egypt, which was the foundation of Israel's faith: "Did I not bring Israel up from the land of Egypt, and the Philistines from Caphtor and the Arameans from Kir?" (Amos 9:7). John the Baptist denounces the complacency of the Jews: "I tell you, God is able from these stones to raise up children to Abraham"(Lk 3:8). The New Testament breaks with the idea of election based on race or culture. Everyone can be chosen.

[19]Quoted by J. I. González Faus, "Simone Weil."

[20]*Ibid.*

mandment, freely translated). According to Christian biblical tradition, at least from the height of the prophetic period and in Jesus of Nazareth, the name of God could only be invoked to give life. Furthermore God favors the life of those most deprived of life and defends the poor and weak. The underlying thesis is that God decides not to be God-in-Godself and for-Godself, but rather God-in-others and for-others. He wants to be God-with-others, and more surprisingly, a God-at-the-mercy-of-others who will never take vengeance on them. This is the symbol of a God on the cross who does not turn against the assassins.

This decentering of God in favor of human beings, poor, weak, and victimized, is the fundamental thesis of the Christian religion. To know God is to do justice for the oppressed, as Jeremiah says (22:15-16). To respond to God's love means to love the neighbor: "Those who do not love a brother or sister whom they have seen, cannot love God whom they have not seen" (Jn 4:7-21). To find God means finding the poor, and to serve God means serving the poor, as Jesus says at the end of his life, in Matthew 25. The correlation between God and life is central. Irenaeus formulated it in the second century: "The glory of God is the man who lives." And in our time, Monsignor Romero paraphrased it in terms of God's essential characteristic of tenderness toward the weak: "The glory of God is that the poor may live."

This is the central thesis about God from God's own viewpoint, apart from human distortion. But it is best seen in contrast with the human viewpoint, as Scripture shows in several ways. God rejects "the divine" whenever it violates "the human." He says in Isaiah: "Your hands are full of blood. When you stretch out your hands [to offer sacrifices] I will hide my eyes from you. . . . Rescue the oppressed, defend the orphan" (Is 1:15-17). Says Jesus: "So when you are offering your gift at the altar, if you remember that your brother or sister has something against you, leave your gift there before the altar and go; first be reconciled to your brother or sister" (Mt 5:23-24).

These foundational texts alone support the conclusion: one can only do good for human beings in God's name. One can only defend God's rights, honor, and glory by defending the rights, honor, and glory of human beings. God does not have, or want, rights. If that seems surprising, let us say that God's right is simply the fulfillment of the rights of human beings.

These texts offer a vision of God that rules out making God-in-Godself an object of fanaticism. God does not cause *fanaticism*, but rather *passion* toward human beings. Elsewhere Jesus condemns fanaticism in greater detail, responding to attitudes of his followers. When they wanted to stop others from casting out demons, as if doing good could come only from one source, Jesus corrected them: "Whoever is not against us, is for us" (Mk 9:40). In other words the important thing is to do good, to cast out demons; this reality pertains to orthopraxis, not orthodoxy, regardless of which group is doing it. Luke also tells of another episode reflecting "terroristic fanaticism." As he passed through Samaria, the Samaritans would not offer hospitality to Jesus and his disciples. The disciples wanted to bring down fire from heaven to consume the city, "but he turned and rebuked them" (Lk 9:55). Again, Jesus is not jealous of human beings. He will not let them be hurt, not even for the sake of God's honor.

Human beings sometimes see God as the mysterious creator of all, who can arbitrarily and absolutely demand whatever he wants because all things are subject to God. This is not so, at least with the Christian God. Religious fanaticism is made possible only by perverting God's reality, and that sometimes happens. "The creator who comes into conflict with the creature is a false god, and false gods make even pious people inhuman."[21] But it goes against God's deepest reality: "God's will is no mystery, at least when it affects a brother and relates to love."[22]

So there is a difference between the way human beings see God and the way God sees human beings. We can sometimes box God in, create him in our own image, and make him serve our interests. We can pervert God, and tragically, we may be willing to give our life for a perverted God. But God does not box us in. God does not see us as "religious people," members of one religion or another, or as agnostics or atheists; God sees us first of all as "human beings," suffering and hopeful, often oppressed, sometimes acting as liberators. And God wants us to give life to this life-starved world. In Bergson's words, God "created us to be creators." From the prophets' and Jesus' viewpoint we might rephrase that: "God gave us life to give life to the poor."

This is the great "theoretical corrective" for religious fanaticism, and for many other evils caused by religion. But it raises an obvious question: whether the religions have practical as well as theoretical correctives against these evils. Such practical correctives are miracles, but we have seen them in our time: at Vatican II and Medellín, in lay popular communities, in committed religious sisters, priests, bishops, and intellectuals, and above all in the constellation of martyrs. The Council opened the way for religious men and women to relate to each other primarily as human beings. Medellín took another step, which in my opinion was more definitive: what is central before God is not

---

[21] E. Käsemann, *La llamada de la libertad,* Sígueme, Salamanca, 1974, p. 35.
[22] *Ibid.*

just the human being, the citizen, the baptized Christian, but the poor. This was an ecclesial shift as surprising as the Constantinian shift, albeit in the other direction.

The Medellín shift is the great corrective for religious fanaticism, and many other evils, because it turned Christianity toward Jesus. Incidentally, I see a great danger for the Church and for theology that Medellín may be forgotten, even when we invoke the Council. Without Medellín we fall into unreality, in today's world of poor people and victims. And we lose our main safeguard against a creeping Neochristendom, which many people yearn for today. But it is not easy to keep the focus on Medellín. For that reason we need to listen with humility to the words of Saramago, even as we invite him to reconsider these correctives. In any case, criticism did not begin with the Enlightenment.[23] Scripture warns us again and again: "Because of you the name of God is blasphemed among the nations."

Returning to the beginning of this section: historians of the Abrahamic religions will always debate differences in wording, and compare texts from the Old Testament, the New Testament, the Qur'an. They will discover some things they have in common, sometimes in the texts themselves. But beyond the texts, they may find—we hope they will—the reality of a God who is "the Father of orphans and widows," Yahweh; "good news for the poor," the Father of Jesus; the "compassionate and merciful" Allah.

If God is that way, so should the human beings be who describe their identity in religious, in Abrahamic terms. In my opinion, more than affirming specific beliefs, we need to search the human heart to see if there are echoes of those words of compassion and mercy to the weak, and if by responding to those echoes we can all find the way to be human. I see this as the true dividing line in the world: not between different religions, but between mercy to the weak (which to believers is the essence of God) and indifference to, oppression of the weak (selfishness).

That is not all. While the Abrahamic religions pose specific dangers, they also have specific contributions to make to the modern Western world. Ellacuría said that these religions, properly energized by a theology of liberation, could overcome two great evils of Western culture—individualism and positivism—by building on the central notion of "people" and "reign of God."[24]

---

[23]See J. I. González Faus, *Where the Spirit Breathes: Prophetic Dissent in the Church* (Maryknoll, NY: Orbis Books, 1989); it has a collection of texts by prominent Christians protesting the degeneration of the Church.

[24]"Aporte de la teología de la liberación a las religiones abrahámicas en la superación del individualismo y del positivismo," *Revista Latinoamericana de Teología* 10 (1987), pp. 3-28.

I have said little about Islam, because I don't know it well enough. Here I will only repeat these recent words from Pedro Casaldáliga on religious fanaticism:

The fall of the towers should also bring down some misconceptions of western Christians about the Arab and Muslim world. Since September 11—now invoked as if it were the greatest terrorism in history—the West, Christian or not, has been forced to recognize the existence of the Arab world and Islam, and to learn that Islam brings together more than a billion faithful from different peoples and cultures. For many years western society and the Church— which was always too western—have treated the Muslim East with prejudice, hostility, and war.[25]

THEODICY AND THE CRUCIFIED GOD

Let us change scenes, from terrorism and barbarity to the earthquake in El Salvador. The earthquake poses two problems with respect to God. One is the role that religion plays in times of earthquake; this is the opposite of the problem of fanaticism, since here the Church usually plays a numbing, resignation-inducing role. It is the "opiate of the people" again, although presently religion is being criticized as a potential inducement to fanaticism. So religion can be accused of causing both fanaticism (see terrorism) and resignation (see earthquake). It is the latter that sometimes occurs in El Salvador.

But the earthquake also brings us back to another ancient question: whether a good and powerful God can exist along with God's own creation, which is suffused with evil. This is the problem of theodicy. Christian biblical tradition adds yet a third reflection on God and evil, which we might formulate as follows:

Second proposition. God is hidden in the earthquake and "suffers" in silence with the victims. But hope does not die, and in hope God remains mysteriously present.

God in the Culture of Popular Religiosity

There are many different kinds of religiosity in El Salvador, but in general it is a religious country, more so in times of catastrophe. So there has been a lot of talk about God these days, in very different, even contradictory ways.

---

[25]"El mundo vuelve a empezar," *Carta a las Iglesias* 489 (January 1-15, 2002), p. 9.

An Aberration: "It Was a Punishment from God." There are Christians from different groups and confessions, fanatics and extremists, who threaten us with prophecies of catastrophe and proclamations of the end of the world; this also happens during an eclipse or at the turn of a century. Now they make God responsible for the earthquake and give God credit for sending one to this country. The earthquake was God's punishment for human sin; this was also said in the 1976 earthquake in Guatemala, which the archbishop said was caused by the sins of the priests.

This message is an insult to God and is unjustly harmful to human beings, because it intensifies the "spiritual" anguish of those who were already in "physical" anguish from the destruction, and in "psychic" anguish from uncertainty. But the message spreads and is repeated; for that reason we must say a word about it from the Christian biblical tradition.

In early biblical legends there are floods and cities razed by fire. The explanation is given: "The Lord saw that the wickedness of humankind was great in the earth, and that every inclination of the thoughts of their hearts was only evil continually. And the Lord was sorry that he had made humankind on the earth, and it grieved him to his heart. So the Lord said, 'I will blot out from the earth the human beings I have created'" (Gen 6:5-7).

I think we cannot simply ignore these words as pure myth, because apart from the language, they express historical reality very well; I have quoted them to describe our present world. And it is not an unjustified anthropomorphism to imagine God as irritated by a cruel world that generates poverty, injustice, contempt, and death for many millions of human beings. But surely this has nothing to do with the earthquake, let alone with the suffering victims.

Yahweh is said to have sent the flood as a punishment, but also to have saved Noah—and most importantly, after the flood God swore never again to destroy creation; instead God made a covenant with human beings forever. The rainbow is the sign of that covenant. Since then, and throughout scripture, God has remained faithful to human beings. He does not engineer their destruction, but wants them to have life. In Jeremiah God speaks of the new and definitive covenant (Jer 31:31-34). And Jesus summarizes his ministry by saying, "I came that they may have life, and have it abundantly" (Jn 10:10). It is absolutely false to say that God would destroy God's creation on account of sin. What God wants is conversion, especially the conversion of oppressors and the powerful, to change their hearts of stone into hearts of flesh and blood. For that purpose he sent the prophets, and then Jesus. But God does not want destruction.

The earthquake victims are not only "sinful human beings"; most of them are poor. And if the Bible is absolutely clear on anything, it is that God loves and defends the poor whom the powerful would "sell for a pair of sandals" (Amos 8:6); who lie beside the rich man's table, hoping for crumbs to fall (Lk 16:20-21). God has made a primordial, fundamental choice in their favor. Thus the Psalmist says that God is "Father of orphans and protector of widows" (Ps 68:6), and that "the hope of the poor will not perish" (Ps 9:18). Israel's confession of faith is summarized in these words: "In you the poor find compassion." God is a God of the poor, not against the poor.

Finally, Jesus announces the coming of the reign of God to the poor of this world: those bent under the weight of life, the despised and marginalized, those who have no voice and are not taken into consideration. Jesus says that the reign of God is theirs, and he died on the cross for defending them from their oppressors.

This love of God for the poor, merely because they are poor, has produced the best and deepest of the Christian tradition. "God remembers the smallest," Gustavo Gutiérrez always liked to say, remembering the Christians of colonial times. The bishops said at Puebla that "merely because they are poor, regardless of their personal and human condition, God defends and loves them" (Puebla 1.142). And Monsignor Romero cast his lot with them: "I do not want to be safe while my people are not" (homily, January 14, 1979). Yahweh, the God of Jesus, is implacable with the oppressor. But he is the God of the poor, their defender, their avenger. God does not send them earthquakes.

All this is well known, and we should not need to recall it. I only want to reaffirm it because of the cruel extremism that is unleashed at such moments against the simple people.

Submissiveness: "It Is God's Will." Most Christians do not react as extremist fanatics do, although many of them have to listen to their preaching. They turn to God in thanksgiving, "Thank God we are alive"; in hope, "God first [if God wills], we will move forward"; in submissiveness, looking for some meaning in catastrophe, "God's will be done." These are close to other, typically Salvadoran sayings: "God first," that is, "Only God can help, we cannot expect much from men." Or a less religious phrase, which suggests how the poor understand the meaning of life: when asked about the future, they often reply, "Who knows?" They don't see much logic in reality that would make the future predictable, certainly not a logic that favors them.

This reaction is understandable in the traditional religious culture, and with the present need to find meaning in the midst of sorrow and absurdity. For that reason it goes deeper than what happened in the earthquake. It is the poor majorities' way of "dominating life." It is not so much about alienation, about thinking of this life as a passing stage on the way to a future, truly livable life. It is about living *this* life with at least some meaning.

From this wider perspective of "dominating life," they are not bothered by the problem that others immediately see: "If we thank God because we are alive and in our homes, what can the dead and homeless say to the same God?"

Doubt: "What's Wrong with God?" Although traditional religiosity maintains the reality of God as something absolute, sometimes God seems to falter. It is not so easy to just hold God above the tragedy. Traditionally that has led to the question of theodicy: "Is God good, is God powerful?" The simple people sometimes speak these words, but not often. One did not hear these voices very much during the January and February earthquakes, but they were heard during the "earthquake" of the war.

A European priest who was in Morazán, an area hard hit by the repression and war, wondered how a people who had gone through bombings, disappearances, tortures, assassinations, massacres never seemed to complain to God. On the contrary: "Yesterday we had a bombing and God saved us. . . . God is acting, father. . . . God is with us, father, because if not it would have been even worse."[26] This is how they express their faith in a saving, powerful God.

But sometimes things are different, and there are second thoughts. The above-mentioned priest, born and bred in an Enlightenment culture, said after the massacre at El Mozote:

> More than a thousand peasants murdered. I'm not exaggerating. I saw many of the bodies mutilated, falling apart. For days afterward there was an unbearable smell. The houses destroyed, everyone dead. . . . When I looked at the piles of bodies, the destruction, I couldn't bear it. How could it be that here of all places, where I have come so many times to say that God is close to us and loves us, that God is not indifferent to sorrow, how could such a dreadful massacre happen precisely here?[27]

But it wasn't just the priest. The peasants were asking themselves the same question. "How many times have we said that God acts in

---

[26]María López Vigil, *Muerte y vida en Morazán* (San Salvador, 1989), p. 119.
[27]*Ibid.*, pp. 94 f.

our history? But father, if he does act, when will this end? Why so many years of war and so many thousands dead? What's wrong with God?"[28]

Theodicy

These questions were not very common at the time of the earthquake, but sooner or later they are inevitable. For that reason we want to say a few words, first about theodicy and then about how God feels suffering.

Suffering and moral evil stalk our world unhindered, whether in an earthquake, the events of New York and Afghanistan, AIDS, or hunger. That much is clear and expresses the painful reality without sugarcoating it. But if this world and this humanity are God's creation, then that God becomes a problem, or at least a puzzle.

Epicurus in Greece described it clearly, once natural—that is, rational—theology had begun to develop beyond mythical theology and politics. Given the idea of God as a good and powerful reality, reason cannot help but ask:

> Either God does not want to eliminate evil, or he cannot; either he can but does not want to; or he cannot and does not want to; or he wants to and can. If he can and does not want to, then he is evil, which must be against God's nature. If he does not want to and cannot, then he is evil and weak, and therefore he is no God. If he can and wants to, which can only be true of God, then where does evil come from and why does he not eliminate it?[29]

These ideas have survived in different forms throughout history. Voltaire updated them in the context of modernity, marked by optimism and progress, after the Lisbon earthquake of 1775. His question was: "Why do we suffer if God is fair?" Then, picking up the dilemma of Epicurus, he affirmed: "If the only way we can excuse God is by confessing that God's power could not prevail over physical and moral evil, I would rather worship a limited God than an evil one."[30]

An infinite variety of answers have been offered for these questions. For those who seek a positive answer, the key is that God can bring "good" out of evil and suffering. But this satisfies neither the mind nor

---

[28]*Ibid.*, p. 119.

[29]Text cited by Lactantius, *De ira Dei* 13, pp. 20-21.

[30]These quotes are from J. A. Estrada, *La imposible teodicea* (Madrid, 1997), pp. 243 ff.

the heart. It comes up against the most indisputable fact in human history: there is something in innocent suffering that reason cannot grasp. It is a scandal, pure and simple. Dostoyevsky's Ivan Karamazov said it beautifully: "If they tell me that the suffering of innocent children is resolved in heaven, don't invite me. I'll return my ticket right now." Camus expressed the same sentiment.

Theodicy, the attempt to justify God rationally in the presence of evil and suffering, has failed. J. A. Estrada, in the title to his excellent and exhaustive book, calls it "impossible theodicy." Our only choice, I believe, is to live with a theodicy unresolved in theory, and with a practice that goes on opening a pathway—with God walking it beside us—through the history of suffering. Perhaps we can offer these suggestions in the context of this book.[31]

The first suggestion is not to trivialize the problem God represents, not to approach it abstractly but in the presence of the poor and the victims, out of love for them. We can question and protest, not mainly out of a (Promethean) desire to shake off God in order to be free and autonomous, but rather out of ultimate respect and unconditional love for the poor and the victims. The poor present an ultimate problem, with or without God. And the success or failure of God is at stake in the poor. That is the view of the more provocative theologians (to give them another name besides progressive). "The problem of the poor is the problem of God," I. Ellacuría used to say.[32] "According to a very real, but carefully forgotten Christian tradition, the main argument against the existence of God is the existence of the poor,"[33] says González Faus. Commenting on J. B. Metz, Reyes Mate says: "Even God cannot escape that event [the holocaust]. . . . The suffering of the creature is mainly a question that must be addressed to God, if God is truly good and all-powerful."[34] And inversely, the triumph of the poor is the triumph of God.

The second suggestion is not to trivialize the answer to the problem, by saying: "God brings good out of evil," or "It would be worse if God took away human freedom," or "Who are you to hold God accountable?" or "How can we blame God, if it is human beings that cause suffering?" Something in human nature remains unsatisfied with that

---

[31]We have said this in greater detail in *Christ the Liberator* (Maryknoll, NY: Orbis Books, 1993), pp. 268-270.

[32]"Pobres," in C. Floristán and J. J. Tamayo, eds., *Conceptos fundamentales del cristianismo* (Trotta, Madrid, 1993), p. 1047.

[33]"Veinticinco años de teología de la liberación: Teología y opción por los pobres," *Revista Latinoamericana de Teología* 42 (1997), p. 224.

[34]In the prologue to J. B. Metz, *Hope Against Hope: Johann Baptist Metz and Elie Wiesel Speak Out on the Holocaust* (New York: Paulist Press, 1999).

kind of answer, because they only trivialize the suffering of the creature. Rather, the problem must be faced humbly and soberly. Triumphalism is also out of place for the Christian believer. First, because the final enemy has not yet been vanquished, and God is not yet all in all (1 Cor 15:28); also because the "not-yet" is too gentle an expression compared to the "certainly-not" of real, present suffering. For this reason Metz has proposed a Christology of the Great Sabbath (Holy Saturday), on the road between cross and resurrection, so that even with the resurrection, the cross does not entirely disappear.

The third suggestion is to propose, with all appropriate modesty, a "praxic theodicy," which might include the following elements. The first element is *indignation* in response to human suffering (indignation against what human beings have done or what God has failed to do), acknowledging that there is something irremediable about suffering. The second element is a utopian moment of *hope*, that God— whether or not God has the power to overcome suffering—does have the power to nurture human hope (Metz and Wiesel's "in spite of everything") and praxis (Ellacuría's "turning history upside down"). The third and last element is the *honesty* needed to "take charge of a horrible reality," to "take responsibility for it and bear its burden." In simple words, the decision to *practice* justice and kindness, and to *walk* humbly with God through history, in the darkness, protesting as we go, but always going.[35]

Theodicy in this sense may help us understand some things that are important to believers, and I think also to nonbelievers. It is human suffering above all that leads us to wonder and question God, and this raises a fundamental question: whether another's suffering causes us to suffer. In other words, the engine of theodicy might be resentment against God, but for us it is love. Justification comes later; believers will always seek a better understanding of who God is, and seek to "justify" God against the rejection of others ("Always be ready to make your defense to anyone who demands from you an accounting for the hope that is in you" [1 Pet 3:15]). There is an important difference in tone here: what is important is not to "make God look good," but to let ourselves be affected by human suffering. We have that vision, I believe, because that is how God is. It is God who made us that way, who makes us wonder more about the suffering of others than about anything else.

This also means that *theo*-dicy goes hand in hand with *anthropo*-dicy, the problem of justifying human beings in view of the world's suffering. The situation is different, obviously, because unlike God,

---

[35]*Christ the Liberator,* p. 270.

human beings are not all-good and all-powerful. But sometimes they pretend to be so; then by way of analogy, we have to hold them accountable as we do God. When someone says, "We are the best and the most powerful," then the obvious question is why there is so much suffering wherever they go. *Anthropo*-dicy, especially in secular societies, is what we might call an overdue assignment. Or maybe a canceled, failed assignment. So of course we should protest, hold someone accountable, refuse to be duped, keep our guard up. But the protest should not be addressed only to God.

Finally, like any other human reality, theodicy is at bottom a question about love. That helps us understand the yearning for resurrection, not as an easy answer to the problem of God (which we have already rejected), not as an equally easy, theoretical way of imagining a happy ending, but as an expression of love for the victims. To stop protesting would mean burying the victims forever—and allowing more to come after them. This, I believe, is the most appropriate context for faith in the resurrection. We close with these words of J. Moltmann:

> No human future can repair the crimes of the past. But in order to live with that past of ruins and victims, without having to repress them or relive them, we need this transcendent hope for the resurrection of the dead and the rebuilding of the ruins. Because of the resurrection of the destroyed Christ, Christians have hope for the future, in the nucleus of hope for resurrection. Without hope for the past there is no hope for the future.[36]

The Crucified God

Let us close with a reflection that seems strange in our world, foreseen by Hegel and more recently pondered by J. Moltmann: "the crucified God."[37] I am not presenting it as a sophisticated answer to the problem of theodicy, but because the question—whether God feels suffering, helplessness, inaction, silence—comes from the very heart of the gospel.

Jesus' prayer in the garden and his death on the cross show God as silent, inactive. The tradition unhesitatingly attributes to Jesus the cry, "My God, my God, why have you abandoned me?" (Mk 15:34). If God was on the cross of Jesus, it certainly isn't the God we usually

---

[36]"Progreso y precipicio," pp. 246 f. On resurrection and victims, see our book *La fe en Jesucristo. Ensayo desde las víctimas*, pp. 61-85.

[37]See *Christ the Liberator*, pp. 297-320.

think of. Apparently we must not only think of God as powerful in creation, in the exodus, and in the resurrection, but also as silent, inactive, helpless on the cross. This usually comes as a surprise, perhaps the greatest surprise a religious person can experience. But it is an important help in exploring the mystery of God, not trivializing God, not considering him merely as one—the most powerful—of the heavenly saints who can save us by doing miracles. That's not who God is.

The New Testament—making a virtue of necessity, perhaps, but also pronouncing the last word about God—says that God was on the cross of Jesus, reconciling the world (2 Cor 5:18). Precisely there on the cross, in silence, God shows his love: "God so loved the world that he gave his only Son" (Jn 3:16); "While we were still sinners Christ died for us" (Rom 5:8). It is not easy to understand, but there can be no doubt that this is what the New Testament means: God shows his love by being close to the victims, being in solidarity with them, completely and forever.

To relate God to suffering, helplessness, and vulnerability can bring on metaphysical dizziness. At the very least it forces us to look beyond what is rational and verifiable. Some theologians are reluctant to speak of God as suffering;[38] others are not. In my opinion, the different theoretical views of such a serious problem are less important than how the world's poor and victims think about it.[39] Certainly they want a God who is different from them, who has the power to save them. In technical terms, the poor of this world want God to have *alterity*, otherness. The same was true of Monsignor Romero or Ignacio Ellacuría: the poor wanted them to be different, with the power of the word and the institutional Church, the power of reason and the institutional university, that they had and the poor did not. But that is not all. When Monsignor Romero refused to accept personal protection he made himself poor, made himself vulnerable to the same risks that the people were running. When Ignacio Ellacuría returned from Spain on November 13, 1989, to be present during the offensive, the poor felt his nearness and found salvation in it. In technical language they feel *affinity*, closeness.

Let us come back to God. The poor turn to God to save them with his

---

[38]*Ibid.*, p. 307. Metz is also against softening the problem of theodicy by suggesting that God suffers; cf. *La fe en Jesucristo,* pp. 380 f.

[39]I have often wondered which God the poor would prefer: the God of Arius who did not suffer, or the God of Nicea, who did suffer. Cf. *La fe en Jesucristo*, pp. 382-387. Se also "La fe en el Dios crucificado. Reflexiones desde El Salvador," *Revista Latinoamericana de Teología* 31 (1994), pp. 49-75.

power, and in that they see effective love. But they also turn to God when they find him close to their own suffering, and in that they see credible love. In the midst of the tragedy of World War II, Dietrich Bonhoeffer said:

> God lets himself be pushed out of the world on to the cross. He is weak and powerless in the world, and that is precisely the way, the only way, in which he is with us and helps us. . . . Only the suffering God can help.[40]

The question still echoes today: "Where is God?" Jesus asked it, too, and Paul had the audacity to answer: "On the cross." They say that after the horrors of Auschwitz someone asked with understandable indignation, "Where was God?" Someone else answered with unguarded serenity: "God was in Auschwitz." We also heard after the earthquake: "God is in the Cafetalón" with the homeless.

We can never quite grasp the problem of God in everyday life, in the tragedies of terrorism, cruel wars, injustice, human evil, fanaticism, indifference. We can solve it by suspending judgment, as agnostics do, or by denying that God exists! "The only possible justification for God in view of the world's suffering, would be that he doesn't exist."

Those who do not declare God dead must bear the burden of his mystery. In my opinion, the mystery is that human salvation presupposes a God with alterity (a different, omnipotent, and therefore distant God) and a God with affinity (like us, crucified, close by).

---

[40]Dietrich Bonhoeffer, *Letters and Papers from Prison* (New York: Macmillan, 1972), pp. 360-361.

EPILOGUE

REDEMPTION AND UTOPIA

I would like to end this book with two very brief reflections, which we have already mentioned, but which I consider essential in today's world. Both are out of style today, and people are often surprised or scandalized when we mention them. They are redemption and utopia.

REDEMPTION: "WHAT IS NOT ASSUMED, IS NOT SAVED"

It is clear that we have to struggle against terrorism and barbarity. It should be equally clear that we have to struggle against the destruction caused by natural disasters, a task humanity is inclined to shirk. And most urgently of all, we need to struggle against a world system that produces injustice, death, humiliation, and exclusion; only a few people are seriously concerned with that need. Yet everyone agrees in principle on the need to combat evil in this world—although as we have seen they may disagree about what is the "worst" evil, depending on what part of the planet one lives in and whether or not one is able to take life for granted.

The next question is how to combat evil. We can start by saying how not to combat it. We cannot overcome the terrorism of the towers by means of the barbarity of war, which produces the death of innocents, hunger and cold, refugees. Let us remember that.

Putting it positively, a legitimate and effective struggle against evil requires us to look for its causes. If religion produces fanaticism, let us preach, practice, and spread a religion like that of Monsignor Romero; this is not an easy task. Some say a more radical—and easier—solution would be simply to get rid of religion. I find that a simplistic answer, because as we have already said, religion can survive not only "religiously" but also "secularly." If economics, politics, the military world, the communications media produce death, lies, and corruption, then let us work and struggle to build structures of justice and truth.

So far we have been speaking in tautologies. But we can take a less tautological step forward: in order to overcome evil we need to generate an adequate "spiritual ecology." That is, the human spirit needs to breathe pure and humanizing air, rather than contaminated and dehumanizing, in order to do what needs to be done. A will to truth is pure air, more effective than freedom of expression for combating the lie. The solidarity to bear one another's burdens is more effective than assistance, in combating selfishness and ethnocentrism. Giving ultimacy to suffering and compassion is more effective than laments and condolences, in combating a heart of stone. Looking directly at the crucified peoples in order to bring them down from the cross is more effective than indifference, in combating ignorance and culpable negligence. The list could go on. There are no solutions to offer, let alone prescriptions. We can offer the "spirit" that brings to fruition whatever solutions we seek honestly, no matter how modest they are. And as a believer let me add what Pedro Casaldáliga has said, in beautiful pages, about today's evils: we need confident contemplation, coherent witness, brotherly-sisterly community, an embrace of love and service, prophetic commitment, and paschal hope.

But we have not yet said it all. In the introduction we mentioned the need to combat evil by all legitimate and effective means, like those listed here. But that struggle against evil is carried out, we might say, from "outside" the evil itself. Here we must add something central in the Christian biblical tradition: evil must not only be removed from our midst, but eradicated—pulled out at its roots; it must not only be overcome, but redeemed. To that end it is not enough to struggle against it "from outside"; we have to combat it "from within."

In the traditional religious language, this has been associated with Jesus' cross and his shedding of blood. Obviously that is not a very popular idea today. It is absolutely countercultural, with an element of the macabre. And it is not what Christian faith tells us: it is the love of Jesus (and of God) that saves, not bloodshed. The love of Jesus saves human beings, especially victims; love that stays through to the end, even if it leads to a cross. That is what we call redemption. I think everyone can understand that, with no need for a sacrificial interpretation.

We do not even need refined religious language to understand the meaning of "redemption." The roots of evil can only be eradicated by "bearing the burden of reality," by "bearing the weight of evil." Thus evil is combatted "from within." This is the accumulated historical experience and an important insight of the biblical tradition: there is no redemption without "bearing the burden" of sin, barbarity, and injustice. This is confirmed by history, from Jesus of Nazareth to

Gandhi, Martin Luther King, and Monsignor Romero.

This is at the heart of the Christian biblical tradition. Sin must be taken away from the world, but it must also be redeemed, which means one must bear it, allow it to discharge its power on oneself. That is what the servant of Yahweh says. His life and mission is to inaugurate righteousness and justice, to be a light to the peoples—to work and struggle against evil from outside—but he ends up as the suffering servant, destroyed by sin—bearing the burden of evil from within. And when everything is taken together, it is said that the servant brings salvation.

The same is said of Christ in the New Testament: an evangelizer and prophet in life, he ends up dying on the cross. On the cross he bore the weight of sin; sin unleashed its power on him and had no power left to do more harm, as Paul's theology seems to suggest. In this sense too, we can say that the cross brings salvation.

Ellacuría, who dedicated his life to combatting sin (injustice, lies, violence, terrorism) "from outside," with all his power and all the institutional resources of the university, also believed that was not enough. One must not only "take charge of reality" through a salvific praxis, he said; one must "bear the burden of reality," with all its crushing weight. As he used it this was not spiritualistic or purely religious language, and it certainly was not masochism, but a deep conviction. Injustice and violence must be "redeemed," conquered from within, even if this means one's own suffering and death.

On September 19, 1989, in a highly political speech in the presence of Costa Rican president Oscar Arias and Salvadoran president Alfredo Cristiani, Ellacuría said that working for peace demanded immense sacrifice, and he unexpectedly added:

> There has been much pain, and much bloodshed, but now the classic *theologoumenon* of *nulla redemptio sine efussione sanguinis* reminds us that salvation and the liberation of peoples must come through very painful sacrifices.

The same is true of the struggle against injustice, barbarity, and terrorism. To eradicate it, to "redeem" it, we must take on the reality of the injustice that is its ultimate cause; we must let ourselves feel it, struggle against it, allow it to unleash its full force on those who are trying to eliminate it. We must denounce the inhumanity of all terrorism and be open to reconciliation and forgiveness even if it entails high personal and professional costs. We must enter into the pain that all terrorism produces. We must be real, faithful to the incarnation to the very end. Redemption comes from struggling against sin, and at the same time entering into the reality of sin—an idea we seldom, or never, consider.

For Christians, this understanding of redemption is ultimately justified by God. God the Creator, the shaper of this world, is present in Jesus' life and ministry; but God is also present, suffering, on the cross. This God was present in a victim, the crucified Jesus, redeeming and eradicating sin from the world.

UTOPIA: "TO MAKE LIFE POSSIBLE"

The most important question about God is not where God is in the midst of the tragedy, but how he is present. We may answer philosophically or poetically, with resignation or in protest. The answer of Christian faith is that in tragedies, God is on the cross, giving hope. Throughout history this faith has created great, active hope, great commitment, great justice and love; but we cannot ignore the fact that it has also led to cruelty, resignation, and withdrawal on the part of the victims.

As a Christian I believe in the paschal mystery: the cross and resurrection of Jesus as the culmination of a life lived for the poor and for victims. This paschal mystery still gives hope to many people. But I wonder—knowing that this type of question is unanswerable—which gives more hope, the moment of resurrection or the moment of the cross. Some will see the answer as obvious, and my reflection as absurd. But there is something in the cross that gives hope.

The main reason is that in the cross there is great love, and love always creates hope. (I also see horror in the cross, as I hope this book has already made clear.) But beyond this conceptual reason lies an existential reason: my hope is kept alive by Monsignor Romero, Martin Luther King, Gandhi, and Monsignor Munzihirwa (bishop of Bukavu, assassinated in 1996), and many others like them. From what I can see, they are also keeping hope alive for many other people, especially the poor.

That hope gives life. And because of that resurgent hope, no matter how hard it is to live through catastrophes, terrorism, and barbarity, we cannot rule out the possibility of resurgent life in the midst of everything. In this book we have recalled small and large acts of solidarity, but we have spoken especially of "primordial saintliness": that is, love and life amid all the negativity of our world. Its agents may be individuals or groups, known to us or famous for their deeds, and they include the great anonymous majorities who are threatened with death and who want to live.

Does it make sense to describe all this with the word "utopia"? On the face of it, no. It would be reasonable to claim that this has more to do with masochism and the cult of sacrifice than with goodness and life. But in the last analysis, I believe, there are signs of life in the midst of the barbarity. We have to struggle with all our power against barbarity, and in truth that doesn't happen very often. But I would insist that we must cultivate the signs of life, no matter how small, and in the First World that happens even less often.

Finally, there is an even more powerful utopia: "Where sin increased, grace abounded all the more," said Paul. "Where Auschwitz increased, Kolbe and Romero were superabundant," says Carlos Díaz.[1] He explains:

> In Auschwitz one prisoner refuses another, but Father Kolbe breaks that pattern: *one prisoner gives his life for another, unknown to him.* . . . Moved to amazement and respect, one of the fierce Nazi vigilantes exclaimed: "This priest is truly a decent man." Just like the Roman centurion who witnessed the Lord's passion on the cross at Golgotha: "When the centurion saw what had taken place, he praised God and said, 'Certainly this man was just'" (*díkaios*). *Díkaios* and *anständig* are similar words, almost literally equivalent, in Greek and German.
>
> Although the Enlightenment would never understand—being so rationalistic and parsimonious—people can live in loving grace, in dialogue with light, even at Auschwitz. A humble Franciscan friar, Father Maximilian Kolbe, understood it when he stepped forward to ask the *Lagerführer* at Auschwitz to let him take the place of a father condemned to death, thus nurturing hope and averting despair among the other doomed prisoners in that cell.[2]

It is a powerful example, cruel and heart-rending. But it is the conclusion that matters: utopia is not easy, but it is possible. Even without going as far as Father Kolbe, one can live as a "decent person" in today's world. To do so means struggling against evil, with a willingness not only to overcome it but to redeem it.

The countless victims in this world understand that very well. Against all appearances, they see that life—their life—is possible. Neither earthquakes nor barbarity can take away their love of life and their hope that life is possible. As long as this is true, even if the affluent world doesn't know how to take it, the world's poor will still have utopia.

These words feel inadequate to end a discussion of utopia. They are

---

[1]*Monseñor Óscar Romero* (Fundación Enmanuel Mounier, Madrid, 1999), p. 93.
[2]*Ibid.*, pp. 93, 95-96.

not the only possible words; God willing, the primordial saintliness of the poor will continue to flourish and humanize us all. This utopian hope is not whimsical or selfish; it is grace. And grace is born of love.

Many years ago I read these words by Moltmann: "Not every life is an occasion for hope, but there is hope in the life of Jesus who accepted the cross out of love." Through all these years I have seen a lot of the cross and also of hope, because the cross has not brought death; it has given life to love. "If they kill me I will rise again in the Salvadoran people," said Monsignor Romero. And it was so, not only in El Salvador but in many other places. He goes on living because he loved, and that love goes on giving hope for life. Certainly this language of redemption and utopia is strong language. Now let us add a final word about utopia "with nothing added." The martyrs redeem evil, but what is left when it is redeemed? What is left is humanness, beauty, justice, and brotherhood. What is left is love for one another. What is left is a shared table.

In the words of Rutilio Grande: "A table with long tablecloths, stools for everyone to sit on, and an endless supply of tortillas and things to fill them with."

The prophet Isaiah, Jesus of Nazareth, and the first Christians were not at all naive about the evil we humans do. But for the sake of the whole truth they put these words in God's mouth:

For I am about to create new heavens and a new earth; the former things shall not be remembered or come to mind. But be glad and rejoice forever in what I am creating; for I am about to create Jerusalem as a joy, and its people as a delight. I will rejoice in Jerusalem, and delight in my people; no more shall the sound of weeping be heard in it, or the cry of distress. No more shall there be in it an infant that lives but a few days, or an old person who does not live out a lifetime; for one who dies at a hundred years will be considered a youth, and one who falls short of a hundred will be considered accursed. They shall build houses and inhabit them, they shall plant vineyards and eat their fruit. They shall not build and another inhabit; they shall not plant and another eat; for like the days of a tree shall the days of my people be, and my chosen shall long enjoy the work of their hands. They shall not labor in vain, or bear children for calamity; for they shall be offspring blessed by the Lord—and their descendants as well. Before they call I will answer, while they are yet speaking I will hear. The wolf and the lamb shall feed together, the lion shall eat straw like the ox; but the serpent—its food shall be dust! They shall not hurt or destroy on all my holy mountain, says the Lord. (Is 65:17-25)

Index